Big Island of Hawaii

THE ROUGH GUIDE

KU-589-017

There are more than sixty Rough Guide titles covering
destinations from Amsterdam to Zimbabwe

Forthcoming titles include
Bali • Costa Rica • Majorca • Rhodes • Vietnam

Rough Guide Reference Series
Classical Music • World Music • Jazz

Rough Guide Phrasebooks
Czech • French • German • Greek • Italian • Spanish

Rough Guide Credits

Text Editor:	Amanda Tomlin
Series Editor:	Mark Ellingham
Editorial:	Martin Dunford, Jonathan Buckley, Samantha Cook, Jo Mead, Alison Cowan, Annie Shaw, Catherine McHale and Lemisse al-Hafidh
Production:	Susanne Hillen, Andy Hilliard, Alan Spicer, Judy Pang, Link Hall and Nicola Williamson
Cartography:	Melissa Flack
Marketing and Publicity:	Richard Trillo (UK), Jean-Marie Kelly and Jeff Kaye (US)
Finance:	John Fisher, Celia Crowley and Simon Carloss
Administration:	Tania Hummel

Acknowledgements

Thanks above all to Samantha Cook, for her much-valued moral support and encouragement during the writing of this book, and to my parents. I'd like also to thank George Applegate, Barbara and Charlie Campbell, Michael Gibson of *Ka'ū Landing*, Nicki Dugan, Elizabeth DeMotte, Sandy Yokomizo and Uncle Billy, Charlie and Judy Peladeau, Albert Solomon, John Clark, Michael Tuttle, Shari Nakamura, Miki Booth, Helene Odomi, Pru Sillito, Kirk Aeder, Charlene Goo, and Lloyd S Nakano.

At *Rough Guides*, I'm very grateful to Amanda Tomlin for her thorough editing, Mark Ellingham for a nice idea, Link for his fonts, and Mick Bohoslawec and Melissa Flack for their marvellous maps.

The publishers and authors have done their best to ensure the accuracy and currency of all information in *The Rough Guide to the Big Island of Hawaii*; however, they can accept no responsibility for any loss, injury or inconvenience sustained by any traveller as a result of information or advice contained in the guide.

This first edition published 1995 by Rough Guides Ltd, 1 Mercer Street, London WC2H 9QJ.

Distributed by the Penguin Group:

Penguin Books Ltd, 27 Wrights Lane, London W8 5TZ.

Penguin Books USA Inc., 375 Hudson Street, New York 10014, USA.

Penguin Books Australia Ltd, 487 Maroondah Highway, PO Box 257, Ringwood, Victoria 3134, Australia.

Penguin Books Canada Ltd, 10 Alcorn Avenue, Toronto, Ontario, Canada M4V 1E4.

Penguin Books (NZ) Ltd, 182–190 Wairau Road, Auckland 10, New Zealand.

Rough Guides were formerly published as *Real Guides* in the United States and Canada

Printed in the United Kingdom by Cox and Wyman Ltd (Reading).

Typography and original design by Jonathan Dear and The Crowd Roars.
Illustrations throughout by Edward Briant.

© Greg Ward 1995.

No part of this book may be reproduced in any form without permission from the publisher except for the quotation of brief passages in reviews.

224pp. Includes index.

A catalogue record for this book is available from the British Library.

ISBN 1-85828-158-X

Big Island
of Hawaii

THE ROUGH GUIDE

Written and researched by
Greg Ward

THE ROUGH GUIDES

Contents

Introducing the Big Island

The Hawaiian islands are the weatherbeaten summits of a chain of submarine volcanoes, poking up from the Pacific more than two thousand miles off the west coast of America. Only on the **Big Island of Hawaii**, where they continue to shape one of the most unique places on earth, are those volcanoes still active. The sheer rawness of its new-born landscapes may make it seem like an unlikely tourist destination, but the island also offers everything you might want from a tropical vacation – dependable sunshine, superb sandy beaches, warm turquoise fish-filled waters, swaying coconut palms and pristine rainforest.

Though tourism is crucial to the local economy, the Big Island lags well behind Oahu and Maui in terms of annual visitors. It has nothing to match the Waikīkī skyscrapers, and neither is there the large-scale strip development of the west Maui shoreline. In the 1960s it was confidently expected that the Big Island would emerge as the first serious rival to Oahu. Large sums were spent on building a highway system to cope with the anticipated influx, and luxury resorts were built on what was once bare lava, while a wide range of more reasonably priced hotels began to spring up in the Kailua area. As things turned out, however, it was Maui that mushroomed, to become plagued by traffic problems and overcrowding, while the Big Island remains remarkably stress-free.

The Big Island is not the cheapest destination in Hawaii – though it does have a few budget inns and hostels – and it can't compete

---

As explained in the *Hawaiian Glossary* on p.192, the Hawaiian alphabet consists of just twelve letters, together with two punctuation marks, the macron and the glottal stop. Strictly speaking, the word Hawaii should be written **Hawai'i**, with the glottal stop to show that the two "i"s are pronounced separately. Convention has it, however, that words in common English usage are written without their Hawaiian punctuation. Although we've done our utmost to use correct Hawaiian spellings in this book, therefore, all the island names – Hawaii, Oahu, Kauai and so on – appear in their familiar English form.

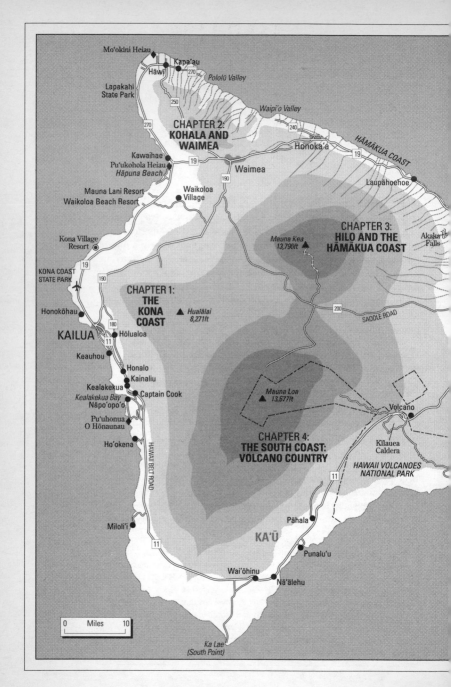

Mo'okini Heiau
Kapa'au
Hāwī
270
Pololū Valley
Lapakahi
State Park
250
Waipi'o Valley
270
240
CHAPTER 2:
KOHALA AND
WAIMEA
Honoka'a
HĀMĀKUA COAST
19
Kawaihae
Pu'ukoholā Heiau
19
Waimea
Hāpuna Beach
190
Laupāhoehoe
Mauna Lani Resort
Waikoloa Beach Resort
Waikoloa
Village
Mauna Kea
13,796ft
CHAPTER 3:
HILO AND THE
HĀMĀKUA COAST
Akaka
Falls
Kona Village
Resort
KONA COAST
STATE PARK
19
190
CHAPTER 1:
THE
KONA
COAST
Hualālai
8,271ft
200
SADDLE ROAD
Honokōhau
180
KAILUA
Hōlualoa
11
Keauhou
Honalo
Kainaliu
Kealakekua
Mauna Loa
13,677ft
Kealakekua Bay
Captain Cook
Nāpo'opo'o
Pu'uhonua
O Hōnaunau
Volcano
Ho'okena
Kīlauea
Caldera
CHAPTER 4:
THE SOUTH COAST:
VOLCANO COUNTRY
HAWAII VOLCANOES
NATIONAL PARK
HAWAII BELT ROAD
11
Miloli'i
Pāhala
KA'Ū
11
Punalu'u
Wai'ōhinu
Nā'ālehu

0   Miles   10

Ka Lae
(South Point)

MAP LIST

MAP SYMBOLS

GENERAL SYMBOLS

- ═50═ Highway
- ─── Road
- ===== Track
- - - - - Trail

TOWN MAP SYMBOLS

- ■ Building
- ⊞ Church
- ▦ Park
- ⓘ Tourist Office
- ⊠ Post Office

REGIONAL MAP SYMBOLS

- ✈ Airport
- ◉ Hotel/Restaurant
- △ Campsite
- ⸸ Church
- ♦ Ancient site
- ⚘ Public Gardens
- ▦ National Park
- ▨ Lava flow
- ▲ Peak
- ⛊ Lighthouse
- ── Waterway
- ⇟ Waterfall

HILO
11
Kea'au
130
Cape
Kumukahi
Pāhoa 132 132
PUNA
130 137
Kalapana

THE HAWAIIAN ISLANDS

KAUAI
NIIHAU
OAHU Honolulu MOLOKAI
MAUI
LANAI
PACIFIC OCEAN KAHOOLAWE

HAWAII
(BIG ISLAND)

0 Miles 50

with Honolulu for frenzied shopping or wild nightlife. The entire island has the population of a medium-sized town, with 130,000 people spread across its four thousand square miles; it has its fair share of restaurants, bars and so on, but basically it's a rural community. This is the place to come if you're looking for the elusive "real" Hawaii; it's also unbeatable if you just want to relax. "Hanging loose" is the island's watchword, and no one ever seems too busy to "talk story". There's plenty of opportunity to be active – hiking in the state and national parks, deep-sea fishing off the Kona Coast, golfing in the Kohala resorts or snorkelling in Kealakekua Bay – but most visitors are content to while away their days meandering between beach and brunch.

Thanks to massive immigration, the population of modern Hawaii is among the most ethnically diverse in the world. The Big Island divides into roughly 27 percent Hawaiian or part-Hawaiian, 25 percent Caucasian, 22 percent Japanese, 10 percent Filipino, and 16 percent others, though as more than half of all marriages are classified as inter-racial such statistics grow ever more meaningless. As befits the birthplace of King Kamehameha, the first man to rule all the Hawaiian islands, however, the Big Island has maintained strong links with its Polynesian past. Only just over two centuries have passed since the isolation of its original inhabitants came to an end, and their *heiaus* (temples), petroglyphs (rock carvings) and abandoned villages are scattered throughout the island. Otherwise, though many of its smaller towns have an appealing air of the nineteenth-century West about them, with their false-front stores and wooden boardwalks, few of the island's historical attractions are likely to lure you away from the beaches. Any time you can spare to go sightseeing is better spent exploring the waterfalls, valleys and especially the volcanoes, that were so entwined with the lives of the ancient Hawaiians.

Around The Island

All the Hawaiian islands share a similar topography, having been formed in the same way and exposed to the same winds and rains. Because the tradewinds blow consistently from the northeast, each island is much wetter on its north and east coasts, which are characterized by steep sea cliffs, inaccessible stream-cut valleys and dense tropical vegetation, and each has a drier and less fertile aspect on its west and south sides.

Only for the last fifty years or so has the title "Big Island" been widely used, to spare outsiders the confusion between the name of the state and the name of the island. It's an appropriate nickname; not only is this the biggest Hawaiian island – it would comfortably hold all the others put together – but thanks to **Mauna Loa** and **Kīlauea** volcanoes it's getting bigger by the day. Mauna Loa may be the largest object on earth, if you include its huge bulk underwater, but it's not the highest mountain on the island. That honour goes to the extinct **Mauna Kea**, slightly to the north and around 100 feet taller at 13,796 feet. Despite its gentle, gradual slope in most places, Mauna Kea is high enough to be capped with snow for a few months each year, which makes for an incongruous sight when viewed from the Kohala beaches.

It's the Kona coast, and **Kailua** in particular, where the great bulk of the tourist activity is concentrated. Although the five-mile stretch of Ali'i Drive that connects the town to Keauhou has in the last thirty years acquired a quick-fire succession of hotels and condos, Kailua itself remains recognizable as the sleepy little town where Kamehameha the Great had his royal palace. To the south lies the prime coffee-growing country of **South Kona**, and Kealakekua Bay where Captain Cook met his end, while northwards are the island's main airport and a handful of secluded beaches.

The safest and sandiest of the Big Island's beaches are located at the foot of the island's oldest volcano, **Kohala Mountain**, further north. The fact that this region also consists of barren lava flats did not prevent the creation of the lavish resorts now tucked into inlets all along the coastline. These include the Disney-like *Hilton Waikoloa Village* and a new addition on the loveliest beach of all, the *Hapuna Beach Prince*.

Continuing around the island, beyond the upland cattle ranches of **Waimea** and the broad, green **Waipi'o Valley**, you come to the lush **Hāmākua Coast**. After a century of hard work growing sugar, the small towns here are reeling from the recent closure of the plantations, as is the Big Island's only city, its capital **Hilo**. Attempts to attract tourists to Hilo in any quantity have always been thwarted by the rainfall, but it's an attractively low-key community, renowned for spectacular flowers and orchids.

Finally, the south of the island is dominated by **Hawaii Volcanoes National Park**, a compelling wilderness where you can explore steaming craters and cinder cones, venture into the rainforest, and at times approach within feet of the eruption itself. This is one of the world's most exciting hiking destinations, with scores of trails running through the still-active craters. Here and there along the southern shore the volcanoes have deposited beaches of jet-black sand, while near South Point – the southernmost point of the United States – you can hike to a remote beach composed of green(ish) sand.

Climate

Despite the power of the tropical sun, the Hawaiian climate is not prone to extremes. Of all major US cities, Honolulu has the *lowest* average annual maximum temperature and the highest average minimum, which shows just how small the seasonal variations are.

Throughout the year, sea-level thermometers on the Big Island rarely drop below the low seventies Fahrenheit (around 22°C) in the daytime, or reach beyond the low eighties (around 28°C); at night the temperature seldom falls below the low sixties. Average daily temperatures in Hilo range from 71°F in February to 76°F in August, while Kailua fluctuates between 72°F and 77°F. Waimea has similar daily maximums, but drops to the low fifties (around 11°C) at night. The highest temperature ever recorded in the whole state was 100°F (38°C), at Pāhala on the Big Island, while the summit of Mauna Kea ranges from 31°F up to 43°F.

In principle the rainiest months are from December to February, but where you are on the island makes far more difference than what time of year it is. Hilo is the wettest city in the US, with an annual rainfall of 128 inches, while the Kona Coast, and especially the Kohala resort area, receive very little rain at any time. Kawaihae in Kohala gets a mere 10 inches each year.

The only seasonal variation of any great significance for tourists is the state of the **ocean**. Along protected stretches of the shoreline, you can swim all year round in beautiful seas where the water temperature varies from 75°F to 82°F (24–28°C). Between October and April, however, high surf can make unsheltered beaches extremely dangerous, and some even lose their sand altogether. Conditions on specific beaches are indicated throughout this book; see also the section on *Ocean Safety* on p.29.

For most of the year, the tradewinds blow in from the northeast, though they're occasionally replaced by humid "Kona winds" from the south; the promontories at both the northern and the southern tips of the island are notoriously dangerous for their swirling winds. Despite the much-publicized onslaught of Hurricane Iniki on Kauai in September 1992, hurricanes are rare. However *tsunamis* (often inaccurately described as tidal waves) hit from time to time, generally due to earthquakes or landslides caused by volcanic eruptions.

Mention should also be made of a unique Big Island phenomenon. While the summits of Mauna Loa and Mauna Kea are renowned for having the clearest air on earth – and astronomical observatories to take advantage of it – down below, when the tradewinds drop, the island is prone to a choking haze of sulphurous volcanic emissions known as "**vog**". The pollution on such days hits levels worse than those in Los Angeles or London; the only spot on the island that is consistently downwind of Kīlauea, the Ka'ū Desert, is a lifeless wasteland.

The Basics

Getting There from the US and Canada

The Big Island has two main airports. Keāhole Airport is on the west coast, seven miles north of Kailua, and is universally referred to as **Kona Airport**, while General Lyman Field is on the outskirts of **Hilo**, on the east coast. The majority of tourists arrive at Kona, but Hilo is kept busy with local travellers, and the two airports receive similar numbers of flights each day. Most of them come from the state capital, Hawaii's major transport hub, **Honolulu** on the island of Oahu.

Only one daily **non-stop flight** comes straight to the Big Island from the US mainland – United's morning service from San Francisco to Kona. All other journeys from the mainland involve touching down elsewhere in Hawaii, usually Honolulu though you can also travel via Maui.

Your onward flight to the Big Island may be on the same carrier, or even the same aircraft, but in most cases it will be with one of the two main inter-island carriers – *Aloha Airlines* and *Hawaiian Airlines*. There are around 66 flights daily between Honolulu and the Big Island – for more details, see *Inter-Island Travel*, on p.11. However, the last flight each day is around 8pm, so if you arrive in Honolulu much after 7pm you may have to spend the night in the city. A basic survival guide to Honolulu appears on p.12, with a list of hotels.

Virtually every large US airline flies to Honolulu, with *United* being the major player; *Hawaiian Airlines* also runs its own services to and from the western states. *United*, *American* and *Delta* can book passengers all the way through from the mainland to the Big Island, connecting with one of the inter-island carriers. If you're buying your ticket direct (as opposed to using a travel agent or taking a package deal) from *TWA*, *Northwest* or *Continental*, you will have to book the inter-island portion yourself. That can be an advantage, however, as it gives you the opportunity to shop around for the best fares – flying with the third Hawaiian carrier, *Mahalo* (see p.11), can cut your costs by half.

As for the **journey time**, crossing the Pacific from Los Angeles or San Francisco to Honolulu takes roughly five and a half hours, while flying from Honolulu to the Big Island takes forty minutes. Add at least an hour on the ground in Honolulu, and that's well over seven hours. For a note on time differences, see p.36.

Fares and Cutting Costs

The cheapest option is usually to buy an **Apex** ticket, which has to be booked and paid for at least 21 days before departure, but can be almost impossible to change once you've bought it. Unless otherwise stated, the prices quoted below are all for Apex fares – you should only have to pay the full, published prices if you're trying to arrange things at the last minute during a peak period.

The simplest way to save money on a trip to Hawaii is to buy a **package** deal including both your flight and your accommodation (and possibly car rental as well). Even if you normally prefer to travel independently, you'll get a much better deal on room rates if you book ahead as part of a package. Most of the operators listed on p.5 & p.6 can tailor an itinerary to meet your specific needs and are able to reserve accommodation in more than one hotel or on more than one island. The airlines themselves offer some of the best deals –

Seasons

Because Hawaii is a domestic destination, there is no high and low season for flights to the islands. However, while fares remain relatively consistent year-round, there are very definitely **peak periods** – June to August and around Xmas, New Year and Thanksgiving – when services tend to be fully booked for months in advance, and you might find yourself paying a slight premium. What always makes a difference is flying on weekends; weekday flights work out anything from $50 to $200 cheaper for a round trip.

American's round trip to the Big Island from New York, for example, costs around $1140, the same price as the flight *plus* a five-night package at the luxurious *Hilton Waikoloa Village*.

If you're not booking a full package but want to reserve a hotel in advance, check with the management to see if they offer any discounts on inter-island flights; it's normal for even the most basic hostel to have an arrangement with one or other of the local carriers.

If all you want to buy is the flight itself, you can normally cut costs by going through a **specialist flight agent**, such as those listed in the box below. At a very rough estimate, given plenty of notice, you should be able to save around forty percent on the regular fares, bringing a round trip from New York to Honolulu down from $1000 to $600, or from the West Coast down to more like $300 instead of $500. Always check how much extra is added to cover the round trip to the Big Island from Honolulu; if it seems to be the $150 standard

fare on either *Aloha* or *Hawaiian*, consider calling *Mahalo* direct (☎1-800/462-4256; see p.11) and buying it yourself for just $70.

If you travel a lot, **discount travel clubs** are another option – the annual membership fee may be worth it for benefits such as cut-price air tickets and car rental.

Be advised also that the pool of travel companies is swimming with sharks – exercise caution and *never* deal with a company that demands cash up front or refuses to accept payment by credit card.

Flights from the West Coast

All the airlines quote round-trip fares of $400–600 from the West Coast to the Big Island. **Los Angeles** is generally the cheapest departure point, and is served by six carriers (*Hawaiian, United, American, Continental, Northwest* and *Delta*); all of those except *Delta* fly from **San Francisco** as well.

Other than the one daily non-stop flight to Kona **from San Francisco** (which departs at 9.05am), *United* connects three times daily in Honolulu with *Aloha* flights to the Big Island. Departure times from San Francisco to Kona or Hilo are at 8.55am, 11.40am and 1.30pm. **From Los Angeles** there are two daily flights to Kona or Hilo (at 8.30pm and 11.50am) on *United* and *Aloha*, changing in Honolulu, and an extra one to Hilo only at 1.20pm.

Hawaiian Airlines flies from five mainland US cities to Kona and Hilo, via Honolulu. **From Las Vegas**, there are four flights a week (Tues & Sat at 9.50am, Thurs & Sun at 8.15am). The airline flies daily **from Los Angeles** at 9.11am, with an extra flight on Mon, Tues, Fri & Sat at 12.15pm. Flights **from Portland** leave Fri–Mon at 9am. **San Francisco** is linked daily with Kona and Hilo at 9.15am and flights **from Seattle** leave daily at 9.35am.

Of the **other operators** who fly to Honolulu from the West Coast, *Delta* offers three daily flights from LA; both *American* and *Continental* have two daily flights from LA and one from San Francisco; and *Northwest* has two services from LA and one

Airlines & Flight Agents in North America

Airlines

American Airlines	☎1-800/433-7300
Canadian	☎1-800/426-7000
Continental	☎1-800/525-0280
Delta	☎1-800/221-1212
Northwest	☎1-800/225-2525
TWA	☎1-800/221-2000
United	☎1-800/242-6522

For the numbers of *Aloha*, *Hawaiian* and *Mahalo*, see p.11.

Flight Agents

American Travel Association	☎1-800/243-2724
Cheap Tickets Inc	☎1-800/377-1000
Council Travel	☎1-800/743-1823
STA Travel	☎1-800/777-0112.
Travel Information Center of Hawaii	☎1-800/266-3646

each from San Francisco and Seattle. *Delta* also has a daily service from LA to Kahului on Maui.

From the rest of the US

There are no non-stop flights from the **East Coast** of the US to Hawaii, so if you're flying from **New York** or from a smaller city in the US, the most obvious approach is to go to San Francisco or Los Angeles and pick up an onward connection from there.

American, Continental, Delta and *United*, however, fly direct to Honolulu **from Chicago**; probably the quickest through service to Kona or Hilo is on *United* and *Aloha*, leaving Chicago at 12.30pm and arriving on the Big Island at 7.40pm. There are flights to Honolulu **from Dallas** on *American* and *Delta*, **from Detroit** and **Minneapolis** on *Northwest*, **from St Louis** on *TWA* and **from Atlanta** on *Delta*; all these flights take 8–10 hours. *Delta, United* and *American* can give you details of onwards connections to the Big Island, or contact *Mahalo* direct (see p.11).

Fares from Midwestern cities range around $900 round-trip; from the East Coast you can expect to pay about $1000, so it's worth shopping around for the best deal.

Note that Canadians flying to Hawaii on vacation should carry valid passports, but do not need visas.

From Canada

Getting to the Big Island from any **Canadian** city apart from Vancouver is no easy matter. The journey will almost certainly require you to change planes at least twice, once on the US mainland and then again in Honolulu.

The basic choice is whether to fly on an American or Canadian airline, with the major difference being that some of the American carriers can book you all the way through to the Big Island, and the Canadian ones can't.

United offers routings via San Francisco and Honolulu to Kona **from Toronto** for CDN$1156, or from **Vancouver** for CDN$754–900. Flying from either **Toronto** or **Montréal**, you can go via Chicago or Dallas with *American* (CDN$1400); via Detroit on *Northwest* (CDN$1174 upwards); or via Atlanta on *Delta* (CDN$1333).

Canadian flies non-stop to Honolulu from **Vancouver** (CDN$575); the through trip from **Montréal** costs CDN$1020, or from **Toronto**

North American Tour Operators

Above The Clouds Trekking, PO Box 398, Worcester MA 01602; ☎508/799-4499 or 1-800/233-4499. Specializes in hiking trips, including two in Hawaii; the 8-day *Earth, Fire & Sea* to Big Island costs $975 and the 12-day *Hawaii Walking Odyssey* to Big Island, Maui and Kauai starts at $1590. Prices include hiking, sailing, accommodation and any inter-island travel, but not the air fare.

American Airlines FlyAAway Vacations, 4200 Amon Carter Blvd, PO Box 2215, Fort Worth TX 76155; ☎1-800/321-2121. Independent tours to Hawaii; five nights from New York to Big Island, including flights, accommodation and car rental, costs $1141 at the *Hilton Waikoloa* and $1135 at the *Aston Kona By The Sea*.

Backroads, 1516 Fifth St, #L101, Berkeley CA 94710; ☎510/527-1555 or 1-800/462-2848. Tours of Big Island; biking $1698 for 7 nights, hiking $1395 for 5 nights, not including air fare.

Canadian Holidays, 191 West Mall, 6th Floor, Etoeicoke, Ontario M9C 5K8; ☎416/620-8050.

Customized, independent packages to all islands; prices including flight and accommodation start around CDN$1300.

Cartan Tours, 2809 Butterfield Rd, Oakbrook IL 60521; ☎1-800/422-7826. Packages to two or more islands, not including flight, from $1300 for independent travel or $1779 for guided tours.

Continental Grand Destinations, 10832 Prospect Ave, Albuquerque NM 87112; ☎1-800/634-5555. Individually tailored Hawaiian vacations, with flights, accommodation and car rental.

Delta's Dream Vacations, PO Box 1525, Fort Lauderdale FL 33302; ☎1-800/872-7786. Good-value Hawaiian package vacations with all combinations of flights, accommodation and car rental.

Fun Sun Vacations, 439 Wellington St, 2nd Floor, Toronto, Ontario M5V 1E7; ☎416/979-2359. Custom-designed Hawaii trips to all specifications.

Continued overleaf

North American Tour Operators continued

Globus/Cosmos, 5301 S Federal Circle, Littleton CO 80123; ☎303/797-2800 or 1-800/221-0090. Independent tours in multi-island permutations; 13 days on Oahu, Maui, Kauai and Big Island, or 14 days focusing on national parks of Maui and the Big Island. Land-only rates from $738.

Hot Spot Tours, 160 E 56th St, New York NY 10022; ☎212/421-9090 or 1-800/433-0075. One- or two-island packages to Oahu, Maui and Kauai from $579 excluding air fare.

Kona Coast Divers, 75-5614 Palani Rd, Kailua-Kona HI 96740; ☎808/329-8802 or 1-800/KOA-DIVE. Diving-plus-hotel packages from $275 for 3 nights/4 dives to $425 for 5 nights/6 dives.

Maupintour, PO Box 807, Lawrence KS 66044; ☎913/843-1211 or 1-800/255-4266. Assorted packages on two or more islands; 13 days on Oahu, Maui and the Big Island from $1585, excluding air fare.

New England Hiking Holidays, PO Box 1648, North Conway NH 03860; ☎603/356-9696 or 1-800/869-0949. Two seven-day spring-time hiking tours of the Big Island, for $1369, excluding air fare.

Pacific Quest, 59-603 Kawoa Place, Haleiwa HI 96712; 1-800/776-2518. Adventurous eco-tourism: guided hiking, swimming, camping vacations, with a multi-island tour for under $2000 excluding air fare.

Palm Hawaiian Adventures, PO Box 811, Makawao HI 96768; ☎808/243-0110, or 1-800/654-0021. New Age vacations, with *kahuna* teachings, *lomi-lomi* massage and the like. Seven nights from $818 including air fare from LA.

Perillo Tours, Perillo Plaza, Woodcliff Lake NJ 07675; ☎201/307-1234, 1-800/431-1515 or 1-800/341-2222. Ten-night tour of Oahu, Kauai and Maui for $2699 including air fare from New York.

Pleasant Hawaiian Holidays, 2404 Townsgate Rd, Westlake Village CA 91361; ☎1-800/242-9244. The leading supplier of independent packages, combining flights, car rental, accommodation, etc.

Questers Worldwide Nature Tours, 257 Park Ave S, New York NY 10010; ☎212/473-0178 or 1-800/468-8668. Two-week nature tours; Volcanoes National Park and Kona coast for $3685 excluding air fare.

Rocky Mountain Worldwide Cycle Tours, PO Box 1978, Canmore, Alberta T0L 0M0; ☎1-800/661-2453. Eight-day cycling tours of the Big Island, with some hiking, for $1495 excluding air fare.

Sierra Club, 730 Polk St, San Francisco CA 94109; ☎415/923-5630. Guided wilderness travel trips to all the islands; the Big Island tour concentrates on hiking and backpacking, from around $1000 per week excluding air fare.

Tauck Tours, PO Box 502,7 Westport CT 06881; ☎203/226-6911 or 1-800/468-2825. Fully-escorted tours; 9 days on Oahu, Maui and the Big Island for $2065, 13 days including Kauai as well for $2780 excluding air fare.

TWA Getaway Vacations, 10 E Stow Rd, Marlton NJ 08053; ☎1-800/GETAWAY. All permutations of islands and accommodation.

United's Vacation Planning Center, PO Box 245890, Milwaukee WI 53224; ☎1-800/328-6877. Custom-made individual vacations, combining islands and hotels to your specification.

Voyagers International, PO Box 915, Ithaca NY 14851; ☎607/257-3091 or 1-800/633-0299. Bird-watching and natural history tours, including the Big Island, from $2995 land-only.

Wilderness Hawaii, PO Box 61692, Honolulu HI 96839. Outward-bound-style wilderness backpacking trips in Volcanoes National Park, from $425 for four days up to $900 for fourteen days, air fare excluded.

CDN$898–986. *Air Canada* only offers a weekly charter flight to Honolulu, on Saturdays, from **Toronto** (CDN$989) via **Vancouver** (CDN$625). It can arrange an onward flight to the Big Island, but you'd probably have to overnight in Honolulu.

Finally, during the winter of 1994–95, *Fiesta West* (☎1-800/663-9757) ran a weekly **charter flight** non-stop to Kona from Vancouver. It sold flights starting at CDN$578 and one-week all-inclusive packages in Kona-side hotels from CDN$899. At the time of going to press, the company was still considering whether to operate the service in future years; call for the latest details.

Cruises

No scheduled American **ships** travel between the US mainland and Hawaii – the Jones Act of 1896 prohibits the carrying of passengers between US ports unless the ships stop at a foreign port en route. That means it's only possible to sail to Honolulu on a luxury **cruise**, most of which start in Canada or Mexico. If you have the time and a minimum of $20,000 to spare, call *Holland America* to see if there's one coming up (☎1-800/426-0327).

Other than local ferries between Maui, Molokai and Lanai, the only scheduled sea services **between the islands** are the weekly luxury cruises on board the *Independence* and the *Constitution*, operated by *American Hawaii Cruises* (2 North Riverside Plaza, Chicago IL 60606; ☎312/466-6000 or 1-800/765-7000; fax 312/466-6001). Each ship does one round trip from Honolulu each week (departures Sat and Tues evenings), calling at Kailua and Hilo as well as Maui and Kauai. Add-on stays on any island can be arranged before or after your cruise, at rates similar to any other agent, but you can't interrupt the cruise itself to stay at any of the ports en route. Quoted fares per person range from $995–1795 for an inside cabin, to $1195–3000 for an ocean view, and do not include any off-ship excursions; you may be able to secure better prices through *Cruiseworld* (☎1-800/994-7447) or *National Discount Cruise Co* (☎1-800/788-8108).

Insurance

You may already be covered by your existing insurance – some homeowners' policies are valid on vacation and credit cards, such as *American Express*, often include some medical or other insurance, while most Canadians are covered for medical mishaps overseas by their provincial health plans. If not, however, you should consider taking out specialist **travel insurance**. Reasonably priced policies include those offered by *Access America* (☎1-800/284-8300); *International Student Insurance Service (ISIS)*, as sold by *STA Travel* (☎1-800/777-0112); *Travel Assistance International* (☎1-800/821-2828); *Travel Guard* (☎1800/826 1300) and *Travel Insurance Services* (☎1-800/937-1387). You'll have to make sure that your policy covers you for water sports, if you plan to do any snorkelling, water-skiing or diving.

Getting There From Australia and New Zealand

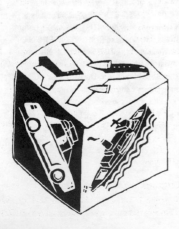

Seasonal variations in air fares from Australia and New Zealand depend on the specific airline and routing, but broadly speaking **low** season runs from February to April and September to October; **shoulder** is May to August and November; and **high** season is December and January.

There are no **charter flights** to Hawaii from Australasia, and neither are there any scheduled **boat** services or cruises, though you might find the odd luxury cruise in December or January.

Only *Qantas* (Sydney ☎02/957 0111; Auckland ☎09/303 2506) and *Air New Zealand* (Sydney ☎02/223 4666; Auckland ☎09/366 2424) offer direct services to Hawaii. **From Sydney**, *Qantas* flies daily direct to Honolulu

(AUS$1119–1345), but all flights from the other southeastern state capitals are routed via Auckland, on both *Qantas* (same fares) and *Air New Zealand* (daily; AUS$1019–1245). If you're flying from **New Zealand**, fares for the direct daily flights to Honolulu are the same on both airlines (NZ$1369–1516).

Both *Aloha* and *Hawaiian* airlines will sell you as many coupons as you want for inter-island flights at AUS$78/NZ$81 each, so long as you buy them at the same time as your main ticket and book accommodation through the airline (without accommodation there's a surcharge of around $20 per coupon). *Hawaiian* also offers 5- to 14-day air passes for unlimited inter-island travel, which again must be purchased along with your main fare (AUS$162–259/NZ$169–269).

Round The World fares from Australasia including Hawaii start at roughly AUS$2000 or NZ$2500; the *Qantas-British Airways Global Explorer Pass* allows six stopovers worldwide in any city served by either airline (except South America), from AUS$2270/NZ$2840.

Entry Requirements

All **Australian** travellers to the United States require visas, but they're easy to obtain and they're free. Pick up an application form from a travel agent, and either bring it or post it (with an SAE), along with your passport and one signed passport photo, to the American Embassy, 21 Moonah Place, Canberra (☎06/270 5000) or the consulate at 39 Castlereagh St, Sydney (freephone ☎1-800/805924).

Most **New Zealand** travellers staying for less than ninety days do not require visas, providing they arrive on a commercial flight and have an onward ticket. Check first with the US Embassy, 29 Fitzherbert Terrace, Thorndon, Wellington or the consulate at the corner of Shortland and O'Connell streets, Auckland (☎09/303-2724), or by mail to Non-immigrant Visas, Private Bag 92022, Auckland 1.

Tour operators in Australia and New Zealand

Budget Travel, PO Box 505, Auckland; ☎09/309 4313. As its name suggests, budget flights and holidays.

Creative Tours, Level 3, 55 Grafton St, Woolahra, Sydney; ☎02/386-2111. Car rental, accommodation and inter-island travel packages.

Hawaiian Island Golf Tours, 12 Bullecourt Ave, Mosman, Sydney; ☎02/968-1778. The name says it all; tailor-made itineraries on Big Island, Maui or Kauai.

Hawaiian Islands Tourist Centre, 39 York St, Sydney (☎02/299-7401); 180 Russell St, Melbourne (☎03/663-3649); 217 George St, Brisbane (☎07/229-9844). Accommodation and tours from overnighting to multi-week stopovers. Specializes in fly/cruise packages, combining return air fares with inter-island cruises on the *Constitution*.

Hawaii Reservation Service Centre, Shop 3, 4–14 Walpole St, Kew, Melbourne; ☎03/853-5096. All levels of accommodation, plus car rental, tours, inter-island flights and cruises.

Hawaii Unlimited, 232 Flinders St, Melbourne; ☎03/650-5333. Knowledgable advice and help in putting together personalized Hawaiian tours.

Pro Dive Travel, Shop 620 Royal Arcade, 225 Pitt St, Sydney; ☎02/264-9499. Tailor-made dive packages to the Big Island (through *Kona Coast Divers*; see p.30) and Maui, primarily for qualified divers.

STA Travel, 732 Harris St, Ultimo, Sydney (☎02/212 1255 or 281 9866); 256 Flinders St, Melbourne (☎03/347 4711); Traveller's Centre, 10 High St, Auckland (☎09/309 9995); 233 Cuba St, Wellington (☎04/385 0561); 223 High St, Christchurch (☎03/379 9098). Also has Australian branches in Townsville, Cairns and state capitals and New Zealand branches in Dunedin, Palmerston North and Hamilton.

USA Travel, 169 Unley Rd, Unley, Adelaide; ☎08/272-2010. Air fares, accommodation and tours to all islands.

Getting There From Britain and Ireland

Much the quickest and cheapest route from the UK to Hawaii is to **fly via the United States**, which means that your options are more or less the same as they are for north Americans. Fly to one of the mainland US cities mentioned on pages 4 or 5 and change there for your onward trip.

With a ten-hour flight across the Atlantic to the West Coast, a five-hour flight over the Pacific and another short hop between the islands, that makes for a very long journey. If you fly straight to the West Coast, it's just possible to get to Honolulu on the same day you set off (thanks to the 10–11 hour time difference; see p.36). However, no flights currently leave London early enough to get you through to the Big Island in one day. The ideal choice is probably to spend a night in San Francisco and catch *United*'s direct flight to Kona at 9.05am the next day, though you may prefer to stay a few days in both California and Honolulu en route. In any case, it's the journey back from the Big Island that's the really exhausting leg – if you fly direct, you're likely to arrive home on the second morning after you leave, having "lost" two entire nights' sleep.

Only two airlines fly non-stop **from London** to the West Coast and on to Honolulu – *United* flies

via Los Angeles and San Francisco and *American* flies via Los Angeles only. *Delta Airlines* now has a code-share agreement with *Virgin Atlantic*, which means you could fly to Los Angeles with *Virgin* and then pick up a flight to Honolulu on *Delta*.

Delta is also the only American airline to fly **from Ireland** direct to the US, with daily services to Atlanta from Dublin and Shannon; surprisingly there's a daily non-stop flight on to Honolulu from Atlanta, though you couldn't connect with it the same day as you fly from Ireland.

As for fares, a typical return ticket to Honolulu through the operators and specialists listed below would cost you just under £400 from January to March (which happens to be peak season in Hawaii), up to more like £600 in July and August. To get to Kona or Hilo on the same ticket, add another £100 or so for the inter-island flight on *Hawaiian* (which has its own sales office in the UK; see box overleaf) or *Aloha*. If however you make your own booking for that flight with *Mahalo*, you can cut the cost in half (see p.11).

Also listed overleaf are a number of specialists who can tailor **package deals** to suit your needs; if you know you want to stay in one of the larger hotels, they should be able to get you considerable savings on the hotels' quoted rates.

Finally, many Europeans visit Hawaii as part of a **round the world** trip. Tickets through companies such as *Trailfinders* and *STA* (see below) start at around £800.

Entry Requirements

Citizens of **Britain**, **Ireland** and most European countries in possession of full passports do not require visas for trips to the United States of less than ninety days. Instead you are simply asked to fill in the **visa waiver form** handed out on incoming planes. Immigration control takes place at your initial point of arrival on US soil, which if you're flying from Britain will not be in Hawaii.

For further details, contact the **American embassies** in Britain (24/31 Grosvenor Square, London W1A 1AE; ☎0171/499 9000) or Ireland (42 Elgin Rd, Ballsbridge, Dublin; ☎1/668 7122).

Insurance

Travel insurance including medical cover is essential in view of the high costs of health care in the US; plenty of specialist policies are available from any travel agency or bank. Alternatively, both *STA* and *Campus Travel* (see below) offer reasonably priced policies as do specialists *Columbus Travel Insurance* (☎0171/375 0011) and *Endsleigh Insurance* (☎0171/436 4451). From any of these companies, you can expect to pay around £60 for a three-week policy.

Flight Agents

Campus Travel	☎0171/730 3402
Council Travel	☎0171/437 7767
Direct Line Flights	☎0181/401 6000
Flightbookers	☎0171/757-2000
Quest Worldwide	☎0181/546 6000
STA Travel	☎0171/581 4132
The American Dream	☎0181/471 5545
Trailfinders	☎0171/937 5400
Travel Bug	☎0161/721 4000
USIT (Dublin)	☎01/679 8833

Airlines

American Airlines	☎0345/789789
Continental	☎0800/776464
Delta	☎0800/414767
	(Dublin) ☎01/768080
Hawaiian Airlines	☎01753/664406
Northwest Airlines	☎01293/561000
United Airlines	☎0181/990 9900
Virgin Atlantic	☎01293/562345

Tour Operators

Bon Voyage, 118 Bellevue Rd, Southampton, Hants SO1 2AV; ☎01703/330332. One of the best-informed and most helpful operators in the business. Flights only or complete packages; a week at the *Royal Waikoloan*, including flight, costs $839–1039, at the *King Kamehameha* it's $762–962.

Destination Pacific, Strauss House, 41–45 Goswell Rd, London EC1V 7EH; ☎0171/336 7788. Full itineraries that can take in the mainland US or the South Pacific as well as Hawaii; a week at the *Hilton Waikoloa*, with car, including air fare from London, starts at $1070.

Hawaiian Travel Centre, 42 Upper Berkeley St, London W1H 8AB; ☎0171/706 4142. Tailor-made Hawaiian holidays – anything from flights only (Kona from $494 in winter to $740 in summer) to all-inclusive packages, such as the *Hilton Waikoloa* including flights from $1067 for one week or $1608 for two, or the *Keauhou Beach* from $788 for a week. Also car rental from $104 per week, West Coast stop overs and Hawaiian weddings.

United Vacations, United House, Perimeter Rd, Heathrow Airport, Middx TW6 3LP; ☎0181/750 9648. Personalized packages arranged with *United*. A week at the *Hilton Waikoloa* costs around $1000, including air fares and car rental; the *Royal Waikoloan* and the *King Kamehameha* are a little cheaper.

USIT, Aston Quay, O'Connell Bridge, Dublin 2 (☎01/679 8833); 10–11 Market Parade, Cork (☎021/270 900) and Fountain Centre, College St, Belfast (☎01232/324073). Youth specialist which can organize student discount flights from Ireland to Hawaii, via London.

Inter-island Travel

In the absence of any scheduled boat services (see p.6), the only way to travel to the Big Island from any other Hawaiian island is to **fly**, on one of three inter-island carriers. Except for a few non-stop services from Maui, almost all flights are either from or via Honolulu.

Hawaiian Airlines flies to **KONA** from **Honolulu** (10 daily), from Kahului on **Maui** (2 daily), from **Molokai** (1 daily) and from Lihue on **Kauai** (5 daily). The last flight of the day back to Honolulu is at 8.20pm.

Hawaiian also has regular flights to **HILO** from **Honolulu** (11 daily), from **Maui** (2 daily), from **Lanai** (1 daily) and from **Kauai** (5 daily). The last flight of the day back to Honolulu is at 8pm.

Aloha Airlines flies to **KONA** from **Honolulu** (19 daily), from Kahului on **Maui** (4 daily) and from Lihue on **Kauai** (12 daily). *Aloha* also has 17 daily flights to **HILO** from **Honolulu,** 3 daily from **Maui** and 12 daily from **Kauai**. The last flight of the day back to Honolulu is at 8.05pm, from both Kona and Hilo. Note that *Aloha's* affiliate, *Island Air*, does not serve the Big Island; it connects Honolulu with Maui, Molokai, Lanai and Kauai only.

As for **fares**, both *Hawaiian* and *Aloha* have a standard one-way fare of $74 though, subject to availability, *Hawaiian* sells seats on its first and last flights of each day, to and from Honolulu and Maui, for just $39. Both airlines offer all sorts of **discount packages**, which seem to vary week by week. Thus *Hawaiian* sells a "book" of six tickets valid for any inter-island flight for $234, while *Aloha* sells five for $179; in addition *Hawaiian* offers the *Hawaiian Inter-Island Pass*, which allows unlimited travel for anything from five days ($169) up to two weeks ($269).

Finally, there's a new kid on the block, the latest in a long line of would-be budget alternatives. **Mahalo Air** concentrates on the most popular routes, connecting each of the Hawaiian islands with Honolulu. It currently has eight daily flights each way between **Honolulu** and **Kona** (6.20am–6.15pm; last flight back at 7.30pm) and has a flat fare of $35 one-way for all its services – less than half the standard fare on either *Hawaiian* or *Aloha*. It too issues discounted "books" of tickets, charging $183 for six flights.

Remember that virtually all the resorts, hotels, B&B agencies and even hostels on the Big Island can arrange discounts on inter-island flights and rental cars.

Inter-island Carriers

	Aloha	*Hawaiian*	*Mahalo*
US/Canada	☎ 1-800/367-5250	☎ 1-800/367-5320	☎ 1-800/462-4256
Hawaii			☎ 1-800/277-8333
Oahu	☎ 484-1111	☎ 838-1555	☎ 833-5555
Big Island	☎ 935-5771	☎ 326-5615	
Kauai	☎ 245-3691	☎ 245-1813	
Lanai		☎ 565-7281	
Maui	☎ 244-9071	☎ 871-6132	
Molokai		☎ 535-3644	

Honolulu Survival Guide

Most visitors to the Big Island spend at least a day or two en route in the state capital **Honolulu**, on the island of **Oahu**. The city boasts a beautiful setting, right on the Pacific and backed by dramatic eroded mountains as well as the extinct volcanoes, Punchbowl (used as a military cemetery) and Diamond Head. Virtually all the accommodation on the island is crammed into the high-rise district of **Waikīkī**, a couple of miles east of downtown, where millions of visitors each year come to enjoy the sheer hedonism of shopping, eating and generally hanging out in the sun. Hawaii's broad ethnic mix and Honolulu's status as a major world crossroads mean that Waikīkī is a cosmopolitan place where something is always happening (and everything is for sale).

The major tourist attractions in and around Honolulu are **Pearl Harbor**, scene of the surprise Japanese attack of December 7 1941; the **Hawaii Maritime Center**, home of the sailing canoe *Hōkūle'a* (see p.184); the **Bishop Museum**, one of the world's finest museums of Polynesian culture; the **National Memorial Cemetery of the Pacific** in Punchbowl Crater; **Hanauma Bay**, a superb beach and snorkelling spot; and of course **Waikīkī Beach** itself.

Getting to and around the City

The runways of Honolulu's **International Airport**, just west of downtown, extend out to sea on a coral reef. Car rental outlets abound, but a car is not especially desirable in Honolulu, what with city traffic and hefty parking fees in Waikīkī. The nine-mile – not at all scenic – drive to Waikīkī takes anything from 25 to 75 minutes. The *Airport Waikīkī Express* **shuttle** (☎566-7333; one-way $7, round trip $12) picks up regularly outside all the terminals. It will drop you at any Waikīkī hotel and pick you up again, by appointment, to get you back to the airport any time from 7.15am to 11.45pm daily. A **taxi** costs around $20.

A network of more than sixty **bus** routes, officially named *TheBus*, covers the whole island of Oahu. All journeys, however long, cost $1, with free transfers onto any connecting route if you ask as you board (enquiries ☎848-5555).

Routes #19 and #20 connect Waikīkī with the airport, but *TheBus* doesn't allow large bags, cases or backpacks (there are left-luggage lockers at the airport). The most popular routes with Waikīkī-based tourists are #8 to the huge Ala Moana mall, #2 to downtown, #20 to Pearl Harbor, #22 to Hanauma Bay and the bargain "Circle Island" buses #52 (clockwise) and #55 (anticlockwise), which take four hours to tour the island, still for just $1.

Waikīkī Accommodation

Accommodation possibilities in Waikīkī cover a wide range; the highest rates will buy absolute luxury, but it's possible to pay much less. It's also such a tiny place that there's little point paying the extra $50 that it takes to get an oceanfront room. All the prices below are coded with the same symbols used for accommodation on the Big Island: see p.20.

Aston Island Colony, 445 Seaside Ave; ☎923-2345. Good rooms with and without kitchenettes. ④.

Hale Aloha AYH Hostel, 2417 Prince Edward St; ☎926-8313. This hostel in the heart of Waikīkī accepts AYH/IYHA members only. It has $15 dorm beds, plus a few doubles, with a seven-day maximum stay. ①/②.

Honolulu International AYH Hostel, 2323-A Seaview Ave; ☎946-0591. Smaller, quieter hostel, with no curfew, a couple of miles back from Waikīkī, near the University in Manoa Valley. Only has dorm beds at $12 for AYH/IYHA members, $15 for non-members. ①.

InterClub Hostel Waikīkī, 2413 Kuhio Ave; ☎924-2636. Mixed and women-only dorms plus private en-suite rooms, in an incongruous light blue motel-style place tucked in a block from the ocean. ①/②.

New Otani Kaimana Beach Hotel, 2863 Kalakaua Ave; ☎923-1555 or 1-800/356-8264. Intimate beachfront hotel a half-mile east of central Waikīkī. ⑤.

The phone code for Honolulu is the same as for the Big Island; ☎808.

Outrigger, numerous locations around Waikīkī; reservations ☎1-800/688-7444. A chain of mostly high-rise hotels, whose least expensive options include the *Maile Sky Court*, 2058 Kuhio Ave (④) or, for a little more luxury, the *Waikīkī Surf*, 2200 Kuhio Ave (④). On request, a free *Dollar* rental car is provided for every day of your stay. Most of the others hotels in the chain are also ④.

The Royal Hawaiian, 2490 Kalakaua Ave; ☎922-7311 or 1-800/782-9488. One of Waikīkī's best-loved landmarks, this 1920s pink palace commands a large stretch of the beach. ⑧.

Waikīkī Gateway Hotel, 2070 Kalakaua Ave; ☎955-3741 or 1-800/633-8799. Relatively budget-oriented high-rise hotel at the western end of central Waikīkī, with excellent restaurant, *Nick's Fishmarket*. ③.

Waikīkī Joy, 320 Lewers St; ☎923-2300. Small-scale "boutique hotel", offering friendly and personalized top-of-the-range accommodation. ⑤.

Waikīkī Prince, 2432 Prince Edward St; ☎922-1544. Small, basic but perfectly adequate budget hotel near the beach. ②.

Information and Maps

Vast quantities of written information are available about Hawaii. Tourism is big business on all the islands, and plenty of people and organizations are eager to tell you all about what's on offer.

Foremost among these is the **Hawaii Visitors Bureau**, which has offices ("chapters") on every island – two on the Big Island, in fact, in Hilo and Kailua – as well as dotted across the US mainland and all around the world. Contact your nearest office – listed in the box overleaf – or simply call in when you arrive in Hawaii, and you'll be deluged with all sorts of hand-outs and brochures. The most useful of all are three free annually updated booklets – *Accommodations and Car Rentals*; *Entertainment and Dining*, which covers activities and tour operators, too; and *Calendar of Events*. You can also buy copies of the glossy *Islands of Aloha* travel guide ($5.95), and even the *Visit Hawaii* CD-ROM, for $19.95, both of which will whet your appetite with colour photos, and are packed with listings, but are not surprisingly devoid of anything approaching critical reviews. In fact the one drawback with the **HVB** (as it's usually abbreviated) is that it's a member-driven organization, which means that hotels, restaurants, and other operators pay to join and to have their activities publicized. If you can't find something in an HVB publication, that doesn't mean that it doesn't exist; the chances are the relevant business is not an HVB member.

In all the major hotels and malls and in the two airports, you'll find racks of leaflets including free listings magazines such as *This Week*, *Guide to the Big Island* and *Big Island Gold*, which are very advertising-led. Kailua in particular is full of **activities desks**, kiosks that act as information booths but are primarily concerned with persuading you to buy tickets for some specific activity such as a cruise, horse-ride, island tour, or whatever. Details on the various operators can be found on p.17, 19 and 30.

Hawaii Visitors Bureau Offices

Hawaii Offices

Waikiki Business Plaza, 2270 Kalakaua Ave,
Honolulu HI 96815
Admin (8th floor) ☎923-1811; fax 922-8991
Information (7th floor) ☎924-0266

Oahu Chapter
Waikiki/Oahu Visitors Association,
1001 Bishop St, #477 Pauahi Tower,
Honolulu, HI 96813
☎524-0722; fax 538-0314

Big Island Chapter
250 Keawe St, Hilo HI 96720
☎961-5797; fax 961-2126
and
75-5719 W Ali'i Drive,
Kailua-Kona HI 96740
☎329-7787; fax 326-7563
also affiliated:
Hawaii (Big Island)-Hilo
Destination Hilo, PO Box 1391,
Hilo, HI 96721
☎935-5294; fax 969-1984

Maui Chapter
1727 Wili Pa Loop, Wailuku HI 96793
☎244-3530; fax 244-1337

Kauai Chapter
Lihue Plaza Building, Lihue HI 96766
☎245-3971; fax 246-9235

Lanai
Destination Lanai, PO Box 700,
Lanai City HI 96763
☎565-7600; fax 565-9316

Molokai
Molokai Visitors Association,
PO Box 960, Kaunakakai HI 96748
☎553-3876; fax 553-5288

North American Offices

180 N Michigan Ave, #2210
Chicago IL 60601
☎312/236-0632; fax 312/236-9781

Central Plaza, #610
3440 Wilshire Blvd, Los Angeles CA 90010
☎213/385-5301; fax 213/385-2513

Empire State Building, #808, 350 Fifth Ave,
New York, NY 10118
☎212/947-0717; fax 212/947-0725

Australia

c/o *Walshes World*, 92 Pitt St, 8th Floor,
Sydney NSW 2000
☎02/235-0194; fax 02/221-8297

Hong Kong

c/o *Destination Marketing & Management Ltd*,
Tung Sun Commercial Bldg #2102
194–200 Lockhart Rd, Wanchai
☎02/519-8585; fax 02/588-1810

New Zealand

c/o *Walshes World*
87 Queen St, 2nd Floor,
Auckland
☎09/303-2035; fax 09/309-0725

United Kingdom

56–60 Great Cumberland Place,
London W1H 8DD
☎0171/723-7011; fax 0171/724-2808

Maps

Much the best **map** of the Big Island is published by the *University of Hawaii* at $3.95. Plenty of free maps are available on the island itself, mostly issued as advertising ventures – you'll almost certainly get a booklet of maps from your rental car agency, for example. These can be useful for pinpointing specific hotels and restaurants, but only the *University of Hawaii* map is at all reliable for minor roads.

Costs, Money and Banks

Although it's possible to have an inexpensive vacation in Hawaii, there's no getting away from the fact that prices on the islands are consistently higher than on the mainland. With 85 percent of the state's food and 92 percent of its fuel having to be shipped in, the cost of living is reckoned to be around forty percent above the US average. Locals call it the "Paradise Tax", because they say it's the price you pay for living in paradise.

How much you spend each day is of course up to you, but it's hard to get any sort of breakfast for under $5, a cheap lunch will easily come to $8 or $9, and an evening meal in a restaurant, with drinks, is likely to be $25 or $30 even if you're trying to economize. Buying groceries and cooking for yourself can obviously cut costs, but even at the new Kmart in Kailua prices will probably be more than you're used to. If you stay in the cheapest hotel or B&B you'll probably pay over $50 for a double room, and a rental car with gas won't cost less than $25 per day. That works out at $75 per person per day before you've even done anything; pay for a snorkel cruise, let alone a helicopter ride, and you've cleared $100.

Throughout this book, you'll find detailed price information for lodging and eating on the Big Island. Unless otherwise indicated, hotel price symbols (explained on p.20) refer to the cheapest double room for most of the year, exclusive of taxes, while restaurant prices are for food only and don't include drinks or service.

A state **sales tax** of 4.17 percent is currently imposed on all transactions – it's likely to rise to five percent in the near future, in part to fund a legal settlement with native Hawaiians (see p.176) – and is almost never included in the prices displayed in stores or on menus. Hotels impose an additional six percent tax, making a total of more than ten percent on accommodation bills.

Money and Banks

US dollar **travellers' cheques** are the best way to carry ready money, for both American and foreign visitors, as they offer the security of knowing that lost or stolen cheques will be replaced. In the US, you can find the nearest bank that sells a particular brand, or buy cheques by phone, by calling American Express (☎1-800/673-3782); Citicorp (☎1-800/645-6556); MasterCard International/Thomas Cook (☎1-800/223-7373); or Visa (☎1-800/227-6811).

If you don't already have a **credit card**, think seriously about getting one before you set off. For many services, it's taken for granted that you'll be paying with plastic. Hotels routinely require an imprint of your credit card whether or not you intend to use it to pay, and you'll be asked for one when you rent a car – or even a bike. *Visa*, *Mastercard* (known elsewhere as *Access*), *Diners Club*, *Discover* and *American Express* are the most widely used.

The two major banks in Hawaii are the *Bank of Hawaii* and the *First Hawaiian Bank*. Usual opening hours are from 8.30pm until 3pm or 3.30pm on Monday to Thursday, and until 6pm on Friday. Most small towns hold branches of one

---

Lost Credit Cards and Travellers' Cheques – Emergency Numbers

American Express ☎1-800/221-7282(TCS);
☎1-800/528-4800 (credit cards)
Diners Club ☎1-800/234-6377
Mastercard ☎1-800/999-0454
Thomas Cook ☎1-800/223-7373
Visa ☎1-800/227-6811

or both, though Kailua and Hilo are very much the commercial centres of the island. The *Bank of Hawaii* belongs to the *Plus* network of **ATM machines**, and the *First Hawaiian Bank* to the *Plus* and *Cirrus* networks, so if you have a cash

withdrawal card the chances are you'll be able to use it. Call *Plus* on ☎1-800/THE-PLUS, or *Cirrus* on ☎1-800/4CI-RRUS, for more details. Kailua's **Lanihau Center** mall holds the island's widest range of ATM machines.

Transport and Tours

There's no avoiding the fact that if you want to travel around the Big Island you're going to have to **drive**; public transport is all but non-existent. It's possible to get from either of the airports to your hotel by cab, there's a limited network of local buses and there are even three once-daily long-distance bus routes; however, without a car your movements will be extremely restricted. You may be happy to stay in your hotel and take some sight-seeing tours, but if you want to explore the island in any depth, you'll need your own vehicle.

Renting a Car

Fortunately, the demand for **rental cars** in Hawaii is so great – as well as the millions of tourists, there are all the locals who can't take their cars with them when they travel from island to island – that prices are among the lowest in the US.

All the major rental chains are represented at both the Big Island's main airports; their phone numbers and national toll-free numbers (which are the ones to call for all reservations) are listed in the box below. In addition, *Avis* also has

outlets at the *King Kamehameha* and *Hilton Waikoloa* hotels, *Dollar* has an office at 75-5799 Ali'i Drive, Kailua (☎329-2699) and *Hertz* is at the *Ritz-Carlton Mauna Lani*. With so much competition between the various outlets, and special offers often being advertised, it's hard to quote specific prices, but a target rate for the cheapest economy car with unlimited mileage should be something around $33 per day or $170 per week. *Alamo* can usually be relied upon for budget deals. At present, no companies will rent cars to anyone under 21, and drivers aged 21 to 24 often have to supply additional guarantees or simply pay extra.

Before you commit yourself to a rate, check whether the **airline** that flies you to the Big Island or your **hotel, B&B** or **hostel**, can offer a discount on car rental. Some hotels even supply free cars for guests who stay for a week or longer.

The national chains forbid drivers to take their vehicles off the main roads and refuse to provide insurance cover or emergency help if you drive the high-altitude cross-island **Saddle**

National Automobile Rental Chains

	Kona Airport	Hilo Airport	US/Canada	Britain
Alamo	☎329-8896	☎961-3343	☎1-800/327-9633	☎0800/272300
Avis	☎327-3000	☎935-1290	☎1-800/321-3712	☎0181/848 8733
Budget	☎329-8511	☎935-6878	☎1-800/527-0700	☎0800/181181
			☎1-800/935-7293*	
Dollar	☎329-3161	☎961-6059	☎1-800/367-7006	
			☎1-800/342-7398*	
Hertz	☎329-3566	☎935-2896	☎1-800/654-3011	☎0181/679 1799
National	☎329-1674	☎935-0891	☎1-800/227-7368	
* Inter-island only				

THE BASICS

Road (see p.127) or **South Point Road** down to the southernmost tip of the island (see p.165). Both roads are in fact perfectly passable; the ban has more to do with the difficulty of providing assistance should you happen to break down. The only legal way to explore those areas is in a **four-wheel-drive vehicle**, which can be rented from *Harper Car & Truck Rentals*, 1690 Kamehameha Ave, Hilo (☎969-1478). This also enables you to drive to the summit of Mauna Kea, but prohibits all off-road driving, such as along the dirt track to Green Sand Beach (see p.166) and along the surfaced but incredibly steep road into Waipi'o Valley (see p.124).

Driving the Big Island

The Big Island does not have a lot of roads; in a sense it has just one, the **Hawaii Belt Road** circling the entire island. However, thanks to a programme of highway improvements carried out in the Sixties and Seventies – at a time when it was assumed that the Big Island and not Maui would be Hawaii's next major tourist destination – traffic problems are all but non-existent.

If you have to, you can get from anywhere on the island to anywhere else pretty quickly; you can sleep in Kailua and catch a plane out from Hilo the next day, and every night there's an after-dark exodus from the Kīlauea eruption at Volcanoes National Park to drive the hundred-plus miles home to the resorts of Kona. Unlike all the other Hawaiian islands, however, the Big Island is just too big for it to be a good idea to attempt a complete island circuit in a single day, while visiting the volcanoes as a day trip from Kona won't give you enough time at the park.

Bear in mind that night never falls much later than 7pm and **driving at night** isn't fun; street lighting is deliberately subdued on the island to help the astronomers on Mauna Kea, and long stretches of road between towns are not lit at all.

You should also keep a closer eye on your fuel gauge than usual; **gas stations** are common around Kailua and Hilo, but in several parts of the island it's possible to drive fifty miles without seeing one. The two most obvious problem areas are in the national park, especially Chain of Craters Road – the nearest gas station is back in Volcano Village, off the main highway – and on Queen Ka'ahumanu Highway between Kailua and the Kohala resorts, where the only station is again off the main road, in Waikoloa Village. Typical gas prices are around \$1.50 per gallon.

Renting Bikes and Motorbikes

The Big Island makes an ideal choice for a **cycling** vacation. Unless you really know what you're doing, you shouldn't attempt to cycle up to the summit of Mauna Kea (Mauna Loa is out of the question) and should probably avoid the

---

Bike Rental and Tours

Chris' Bike Adventures, Box 657, Kula HI 96790; ☎326-4600. A wide programme of customized bike tours, including Waipio, Mauna Kea, down Mauna Loa and across the flanks of Kohala Mountain.

DJ's Rentals, 75-5663A Palani Rd, Kailua-Kona (☎329-1700) and King's Shops, Waikoloa Resort (☎885-7368). *Harley-Davidson* motorbikes for rent, as well as lesser makes.

Hawaiian Pedals, Kona Inn Shopping Village, Kailua; ☎329-2294. Mountain bike rental at daily rates of \$20 for a single day or weekly rates of \$9 per day; performance bikes go for \$25 a day, dropping to \$15 on a weekly rate, and even tandems are available at \$35 per day.

Island Riders, 75-5819 Ali'i Drive, Kailua; ☎326-7220. Tours of the island for groups or individuals on *Harley-Davidsons* – you ride pillion with one of their "captains" – as well as rentals for fully licensed drivers over 21.

Mauna Kea Mountain Bikes, PO Box 44672, Kamuela; base in *C&S Cycle & Surf*, Waimea; ☎885-2091 or 925-0530. Rental from \$20 for five hours to \$125 per week. Mostly two- to three-hour customized tours, with exact rates depending on the number in your party. *Kohala Downhill* \$75 per person or less, *Mauna Kea Kamikaze* \$80–110, *Old Māmalahoa Hwy* \$40–55 and Volcano trips of varying lengths.

Teo's Mountain Bike Safari, HCR 2 Box 110151, Kea'au; ☎982-5221. Two-hour rainforest tours for \$30 per person, plus bike rentals for \$5 per hour, \$65 per week, including helmet.

Saddle Road altogether. On the rest of the island the gradients don't pose too many problems and regions such as North Kohala, South Kona, and the Hāmākua Coast offer superb scenic rides. The only major problem in attempting an island tour is that there are several very exposed twenty- or thirty-mile stretches across baking lava desert: be sure to carry vast quantities of water. An easier option is to rent a **motorbike** from one of Big Island's two outlets. Note that neither motorbikes nor bicycles are allowed on hiking trails in national or state parks.

By Air

If you're really in a hurry, both *Hawaiian* and *Aloha* airlines run one 25-minute **flight** each way daily between Hilo and Kona. *Hawaiian* leaves Hilo at 9.30am and Kona at 3.55pm; *Aloha* leaves Hilo at 9.40am and Kona at 5.25pm. Standard inter-island rates apply (see p.11 for further details).

Local buses

Hilo's *Mass Transportation Agency* (☎935-8241) is responsible for the Big Island's only **long-distance** buses, the *Hele-On* network. One bus daily, except on Sundays, runs all the way around the north of the island between **Hilo** and **Kailua** and also through South Kona as well; a full timetable appears below. Fares range from 75¢ for a short hop up to $6 for the whole journey. In addition, on weekdays only, there's one service around the south of the island from

Hilo as far as Ocean View, which you could use to get to and from **Hawaii Volcanoes National Park** (see p.135), and another to **Pāhoa** (see p.142).

Minimal **local buses** operate in the immediate vicinity of both Kailua and Hilo. The *Ali'i Shuttle* in Kailua runs back and forth between the oceanfront hotels and the centre of town (see p.43), while the commuter services in Hilo are of little use to tourists.

Bus tours

Straightforward one-day circle-island **minibus tours** with *Roberts Hawaii* (☎329-1688) cost between $52.50 and $60 (under-12s $46–53), depending on whether you start from Kona or the Kohala resorts. The price does not include lunch, which you are expected to eat at Hilo's Nani Mau Gardens.

A couple of specialist operators can take you up to the **summit of Mauna Kea** – a road only four-wheel-drive vehicles should attempt. *Waipio Valley Shuttle* (☎775-7121) does a six-hour tour for a minimum of four people, at $75 per person, leaving from the Parker Ranch Shopping Center in Waimea, while *Paradise Safaris* (☎322-2366) operates similar-priced sunset and stargazing trips. It picks up in west Hawaii and provides parkas, hot beverages and a telescope.

Both the island's hostels, *Patey's Place* in Kailua (see p.45) and *Arnott's Lodge* in Hilo (see p.104), run informal mini-van trips for their guests, depending on demand.

Hilo–Kona Bus Timetable

	16 KAILUA/KONA	7 DOWNTOWN HILO
HILO Prince Kuhio Plaza	1.10pm	10.05am
HILO Mooheau Bus Terminal	1.30pm	9.45am
Peepe'ekeo	1.45pm	9.30am
Honomū	1.50pm	9.25am
Laupāhoehoe	2.20pm	8.55am
Honoka'a *Dairy Queen*	2.50pm	8.25am
Waimea Police Station	3.30pm	7.45am
Waikoloa	3.50pm	7.25am
KAILUA *Waldenbooks* Lanihau Center	4.30pm	6.45am
Keauhou *Kona Surf*	4.50pm	6.25am
Kainaliu	5.05pm	6.10am
Captain Cook	5.15pm	6.00am
Hōnaunau	5.20pm	5.55am
Keālia	5.30pm	5.45am

Note that this service operates Mon–Sat only. Call ☎935-8241 for more details.

Alternative Excursions

Possible **horseback** excursions include the ride down to Kealakekua Bay with *King's Trail Rides O Kona* (☎323-2388), described on p.63, and tours of North Kohala with *Kohala Na'alapa Trail Rides* (☎775-0330) or *Paniolo Riding Adventures* (☎889-5354); see p.92. Operators of **snorkelling**, **diving** and **fishing** cruises as well as other ocean excursions are listed on p.30.

Flight-seeing tours

Over the last couple of decades, helicopter **flight-seeing tours** have been one of the few booming sectors of the Hawaiian economy. On most of the islands, you can circle the entire island in a relatively short flight and feel that you've glimpsed wonders you would otherwise never have seen. The Big Island is too large to see on one trip – and the summits of Mauna Kea and Mauna Loa are too high and inaccessible – but it has the incomparable attraction of the unpredictable Kīlauea eruption, which is liable to break out in different places on different days.

However, the industry has recently run into difficulty, after the deaths of fifteen people in accidents over the last three years. Most of those involved plunges over the enormous Na Pali cliffs of Kauai, but on the Big Island there was a much-publicized incident in which a camera crew crash-landed as they filmed Kīlauea and were trapped for two days in the erupting crater. As a result, hasty regulations have been introduced, requiring all single-engined aircraft, including helicopters, to fly at an altitude of at least 3000 feet, and imposing other restrictions as well. Helicopter rides are now more sedate affairs, not the roller-coaster rides they used to be, and they no longer swoop down to hover over single spots. As a result demand has dropped, so you may see special offers advertised. However, fixed-wing, twin-engined aircraft can still fly low; as they're cheaper than helicopters, they make a good-value alternative to a chopper flight.

Operators are listed in the box below. If it's the volcano you want to see, opt for a flight from Hilo; many of the cheaper ones on the Kona side go up the Kohala coast and miss out Kīlauea.

	Number	Departs	Prices
HELICOPTERS			
Blue Hawaiian	☎961-5600	Hilo	from $120
	☎1-800/786-BLUE		
Hawaii	☎1-800/994-9099 (Big Island)	Hilo, Kona	$114–159
	☎1-800/346-2403 (US)		
'Io Aviation	☎935-3031	Hilo, Kona	$79–245
	or 1-800/942-3031		
Kenai	☎969-3131,	Hilo, Waikoloa	$145–297
	1-800/622-3144 (US) or 1-800/824-9560 (HI)		
Mauna Kea	☎885-6400	Hilo, Waimea	$95–145
	☎1-800/400-4354		
Papillon	☎329-0551	Hilo, Waikoloa	$89–295
Safari	☎969-1259	Hilo	$89–139
	or 1-800/326-3359		
FIXED-WING			
Big Island Air	☎329-4868	Kona	$99–169
Classic Aviation	☎329-8687	Hilo, Kona	$65–250
Island Hoppers	☎969-2000	Hilo, Kona	from $49

To shop around for **discounts** on flights, call the *Chopper Shop* (☎969-4900 or 1-800/829-5999), the *Activity Connection* (☎329-1038) or the *Activity Information Center* (☎329-7700).

Accommodation

Where you stay on the Big Island, and in what kind of accommodation, depends very much on the sort of vacation you're planning. If you want to spend most of your time on the beach, the prime areas are the **Kona** and **Kohala coasts**, which are filled with upscale **hotels**, **condos** and exclusive self-contained **resorts**. If you want to explore the rest of the island, **Hilo**, the largest city, is a better bet with its big hotels, as well as a handful of smaller, more characterful **inns**. Elsewhere, however – including, surprisingly, the **national park** area – your choice is likely to be restricted to **B&Bs** in private homes.

Prospective visitors who think of Hawaii as an **expensive** destination won't be reassured by the official statistics that show the average cost of a single night's accommodation on the Big Island to be **$129**. That alarming figure, however, is boosted by the rate for the mega-resorts of

Kohala; the Kailua area is a more reasonable $83 and Hilo's average is just $63. Overall occupancy rates are currently just over seventy percent, so at most times of the year it's possible to book a room at short notice.

All these prices, along with the prices indicated throughout this book, are based on the hotel's own **rack rates** – the rate you'll be offered if you simply walk through the door and ask for a room for the night. There's little scope for bargaining in the smaller inns or B&Bs, but if you know you want to stay in one of the larger hotels it's very possible to cut costs. Most obviously, buy a **package deal** through one of the operators or airlines listed in the *Getting There* sections of this book. Ask your local travel agent or even inquire directly from the hotel, which should be able to offer you an all-inclusive deal. If you're happy to stay in local inns and hostels, then you can of course budget for much lower room rates – and it's worth considering also the possibility of **camping** (see p.32 for further details).

The one thing you need to be aware of before you book is that it's barely possible to see all the Big Island from a single base. While most of your time is likely to be spent on the Kona or Kohala coasts, at the very least you should reckon on spending a night or two in the national park area or possibly in Hilo. It may even be worth simply not using your pre-paid Kona-side room for one night, to give yourself time at the volcanoes. As the oceanfront hotels tend to charge the highest rates, there's no point

---

Accommodation Price Codes

Throughout this book, accommodation prices have been graded with the symbols below, according to the quoted rate for the least expensive double room for most of the year, not including state taxes of 10.17 percent.

Rates in categories ③ and upwards tend to rise by an average of $10–20 in peak seasons – from Christmas to Easter and June to August. However, as explained above, it's possible to obtain much better rates for top-range accommodation by booking your room as part of an all-inclusive package. Detailed lists of tour operators appear on p.5–6 (US/Can), p.8 (Aus) and p.10 (UK).

①	up to $30	④	$75–100	⑦	$170–225
②	$30–50	⑤	$100–130	⑧	$225–300
③	$50–75	⑥	$130–170	⑨	over $300

staying in them if you're going to be sight-seeing in other parts of the island for most of the time. Instead book yourself an itinerary of small inns or B&Bs, ideally with a couple of nights in each of the areas covered by the four chapters in this book.

Resorts

If you haven't visited a major tropical vacation destination before, you may not be familiar with the concept of a **resort**. These gigantic, sprawling enclaves, each holding hundreds or even thousands of rooms, are more than just hotels; located far from any town, they are equipped with their own restaurants, stores, swimming pools, beaches, golf courses, tennis courts, walking trails and anything else you can think of, all designed to ensure that guests can spend their entire vacations without ever feeling the need to leave the property.

The Big Island was one of the pioneers of this kind of development, and offers some of the most extreme examples of the genre. On face value, the Kohala coast is a bleak and inhospitable desert, but in the 1960s entrepreneurs such as Laurance Rockefeller saw that conditions were dependably dry and hot enough to make it worth constructing brand-new oases from scratch. Where beaches didn't exist they were sculpted into the coastline, coconut palms were flown in and re-planted and sand poured on top of the lava. Once landscaped and kept well watered, lava is capable of supporting the lush greens and fairways of championship-quality golf courses. The three main resort areas of **Waikoloa**, **Mauna Lani** and **Mauna Kea** now have at least two hotels each, all catering for a slightly different market. However, unless you book as part of a package, only at the *Royal Waikoloan* (see p.75) will you get away with paying less than $150 per room per night.

Hotels, Motels and Condos

In terms of the guest rooms, standards in the resort hotels are of course high, but not significantly higher than those in the upmarket conventional **hotels** found in towns such as Kailua and Hilo. En-suite bathrooms can be taken for granted and most rooms have balconies of some description (known as *lanais*). The distinction between a hotel room and a **condominum** apartment is not always clear, as the same building can hold some private condo apartments and others let by the night to casual guests. The balance basically lies according to what facilities you require. An individual condo apartment is likely to be more comfortable and better equipped than a typical hotel room, often with a kitchenette, but conversely the building as a whole may well not have a lobby area, daily housekeeping service, restaurants or other amenities. The vast majority of the Big Island's condos are found along Ali'i Drive, stretching south from Kailua to Keauhou on the Kona Coast; like the nearby hotels, they tend to charge around $100 per night for a double room.

Motels on the usual American model are rare; there's one tucked away in Wai'ohinu in the far south and Waimea has something very like one. Certain older towns – often those that have declined rather than grown in the last century – do however retain basic hotels that were originally built to accommodate migrant agricultural labourers. In most cases these are

---

Big Island Accommodation Agencies

When you contact any of the agencies below, be sure to ask about discounts on inter-island flights and rental cars.

All Islands Bed & Breakfast, 823 Kainui Drive, Kailua-Kona HI 96734; ☎263-2342 or 1-800/542-0344; fax 263-0308. B&Bs of all standards, throughout Hawaii.

Hawaii's Best Bed & Breakfast, PO Box 563, Kamuela HI 96743; ☎885-4550 or 1-800/262-9912; fax 885-0559. Top-quality B&Bs on all the islands, with an especially wide range on the Big Island.

Kona Vacation Resorts & Travel, 77-6435 Kuakini Hwy, Kailua-Kona HI 96740; ☎329-6488, 1-800/367-5168 (US), 1-800/KONA CAN (Canada) or 1-800/321-2558 (HI); fax 329-5480. A wide selection of Kona-coast condos.

Volcano Accommodations, PO Box 998, Volcano HI 96785; ☎967-7244 or 1-800/736-7140; fax 967-8660. Specialist in B&Bs near the national park.

---

minimally-equipped flophouses, which can charge as little as $20 per night, though as the years go by those that don't shut down altogether have tended to upgrade. Examples include *Inaba's Kona Hotel* in Hōlualoa and the recently modernized *Hotel Honoka'a Club* in Honoka'a.

Finally, a special mention should be made of the Big Island's two best **hotel bargains**. At both the *Manago Hotel* in Captain Cook on the Kona side (see p.61), and Hilo's *Wild Ginger Inn* (see p.105), it's still possible to get an attractive en-suite double room for under $40, so long as you book well in advance.

Bed and Breakfasts

The definition of precisely what constitutes a **bed and breakfast** stretches from a simple room or two in a private home, through self-contained, self-catering cottages to luxurious fifteen-room inns. In principle, however, the standards are once again very high. The cheapest rooms, perhaps sharing a bathroom with one other guest room, start at just under $50, while for around $75 per night you can expect your own well-furnished apartment, with all facilities.

Most small-scale B&Bs tend to be located in areas that otherwise offer little choice of accommodation. You won't find many in either Kailua or Hilo, but each of the smaller towns on the island tends to have one or two, with the greatest concentrations in the village of Volcano, just outside Hawaii Volcanoes National Park, and in upcountry Waimea. The owners are often friendly and full of advice on making the most of your vacation, but it's unusual to find a B&B run by anyone other than recent immigrants from the mainland.

Recommended properties include *Hale Kukui* at Kukuihaele, near Waipi'o Valley (see p.127), and *Waimea Gardens Cottage* in Waimea (see p.86). The best options among the larger inns are the *Holualoa Inn B&B* in Hōlualoa just above Kailua and *Kilauea Lodge* in Volcano, which is unusual in having its own, very good restaurant.

Hostels

The Big Island has two budget **hostels**, one on each side of the island, where you can get a bed in a dormitory for under $20 per night. Both *Patey's Place* in **Kailua** (see p.45) and *Arnott's Lodge* in **Hilo** (see p.104) are strongly geared towards young surfers, but neither offers any reduction for members of national or international youth hostel organizations.

Food and Drink

If you imagine that eating in Hawaii will consist of an endless feast of fresh fruits and fishes, you'll be disappointed to find that the islands are not bountiful Gardens of Eden: the state produces less than twenty percent of the food it consumes. Year by year less of its land is devoted to agriculture, with the main crops in any case being sugar and pineapples. Polynesian cuisine can sometimes mean little more than putting a pineapple ring on top of a burger and, amazingly, more than half of all the Spam eaten in the United States is consumed in Hawaii.

However, there are two strong factors working in your favour. First of all, there's the state's **ethnic** diversity. Immigrants from all over the world have brought their own national dishes and recipes, which you can sample in restaurants around the Big Island and, in some cases, traditions have mingled to create intriguing new cuisines. Secondly, the presence of many thousands of **tourists**, prepared to pay top rates for good food, means that the island has some truly superb restaurants, run by renowned international chefs.

The Hawaiian Tradition

Cooking in ancient Hawaii was the exclusive responsibility of the menfolk, who had to prepare food for themselves and their wives in separate calabash gourds and ovens. Women were forbidden to eat pork, bananas or coconuts, as well as several kinds of fish, or to eat at the same table as the men – this great *kapu* was broken in 1819 (see p.173), signalling the end of the old religion.

The staple food was *poi*, a purple-grey paste produced by pounding the root of the *taro* plant (cultivated in wetlands such as Waipi'o Valley – see p.122). *Poi* is eaten with the bare hands and comes in three basic grades, one-finger, two-finger or three-finger, according to how many fingers it takes to scoop a satisfactory portion out of the pot – one-finger is the thickest and best. One of Captain Cook's crew described it as "a disagreeable mess", and it remains the butt of a million jokes by tour guides for its supposed resemblance to wallpaper paste.

These days, there's no such thing as an authentic "Hawaiian" restaurant; the closest you can come to eating traditional foods is at a *lū'au* or "banquet". Primarily tourist money-spinners, and always accompanied by some form of Polynesian entertainment and *hula* performance, these provide an opportunity to sample such dishes as *kālua* **pork**, an entire pig wrapped in *ti* leaves and baked all day in an underground oven known as an *imu*; *poke*, which is raw fish, shellfish or octopus, marinated with soy and oriental seasonings; and *lomi-lomi*, a sort of marinated raw salmon. As *lū'aus* always involve mass catering and canteen-style self-service, the food itself rarely provides sufficient incentive to go. Furthermore, you're unlikely to be served such historically authentic dishes as boiled hairless dogs (which were fattened on *poi*; that's where the expression *poi dog* comes from), while the *nēnē* goose, of which the nineteenth-century Hawaiian historian David Malo remarked

> ### Big Island *Lū'aus*
>
> There are currently four regular *lū'aus* on the Big Island, all based at major hotels on the Kona side of the island. The *Kona Village Resort's lū'au* wins hands down for atmosphere, due in part to its remote location.
>
> **Drums of Polynesia**
> *Royal Kona Resort;* ☎ 329-3111
> Mon, Tues, Fri, Sat at 5.30pm; $55
>
> **Island Breeze**
> *King Kamehameha;* ☎ 326-4969
> Tues–Thurs & Sun at 5.30pm; $55
>
> **Kona Village Lū'au**
> *Kona Village Resort;* ☎ 325-5555
> Mon & Fri at 5pm; $63
>
> **Royal Lū'au**
> *Royal Waikoloan;* ☎ 885-6789
> Sun & Wed at 6pm; $45

"its body is excellent eating", is now protected as the state bird, and being nursed back from the brink of extinction.

Local Restaurants

The Big Island has its fair share of outlets of the national fast-food chains, but typical budget restaurants, diners and takeout stands throughout the island tend to serve a hybrid cuisine which draws on the traditions of the US mainland along with Japan, China, Korea and the Phillipines, giving the resultant mixture a slight but definite Hawaiian twist.

Breakfast tends to be the standard combination of eggs, meat, pancakes, muffins or toast. At midday, the usual dish is the **plate lunch**, a moulded tray holding meat and rice as well as potato or macaroni salad and costing something between $5 and $8. *Bento* is the Japanese equivalent, with mixed meats and rice; in Filipino diners, you'll be offered *adobo*, which is pork or chicken stewed with garlic and vinegar and served in a similar way. Korean barbecue, *kal bi* – prepared with sesame – is especially tasty, with the word "barbecue" indicating that the meat or fish has been marinated rather than necessarily cooked on an open grill. One simple but filling recipe – thought to be of Chinese origin – is *saimin* (pronounced *sy-min* not *say-min*). This bowl of clear soup filled with noodles and other mixed ingredients has become some-

Ten Big Island Favourites

The following ten restaurants represent a cross section of the best the Big Island has to offer; they're listed in ascending order of price, not quality.

Jolene's Kau Kau Korner, Honoka'a p.121

Bamboo Restaurant & Bar, Hāwi p.95

Su's Thai Kitchen, Kailua and Waimea p.54 & 88

Café Pesto, Hilo and Kawaihae p.112 & 84

Roussel's, Hilo p.113

Kilauea Lodge, Volcano p.161

The Gallery, Mauni Lani Bay Hotel p.77

Merriman's, Waimea p.88

The Dining Room, Ritz-Carlton Mauna Lani p.78

Hale Moana, Kona Village Resort p.58

thing of a Hawaiian national dish. Finally, the carbohydrate-packed *loco moco* is a fried egg served on a hamburger with gravy and rice.

Food in general is often referred to as *kaukau*, and it's also worth knowing that *pu pus* (pronounced *poo-poos*) is a general term for little snacks, the kind of finger food that is given away in early-evening Happy Hours.

Fine Dining

Many of the Big Island's best **restaurants** are in its most expensive hotels. The resorts of the north Kona and Kohala coasts in particular are blessed with a captive clientele who aren't going to drive forty miles in the dark for a cheap meal in Kailua, and for whom the food is in any case one of the chief pleasures of their vacations. These are the places where something approaching a distinctive Hawaiian cuisine is being created, known by some as **Pacific Rim**, others **Euro-Asian**, and still others **Hawaii Regional**. In its ideal form it consists of combining foods and techniques from all the countries and ethnic groups that have figured in Hawaiian history, using the freshest ingredients possible. The top chefs seek to preserve natural flavours by such methods as flash-frying meat and fish like the Chinese, baking it whole like the Hawaiians or even serving it raw like the Japanese. The effect is enhanced by the delicate addition of Thai herbs and spices and by the sheer inventiveness of modern Californian cooking.

The Big Island also has plenty of conventional **American** shrimp and steak specialists, as well as high-class **Italian**, **Thai** and **Chinese** places; there's even a rather unlikely **Austrian** restaurant in Waimea (see p.88). Many restaurants offer all-you-can-eat **buffets** one or more nights of the week; they all sacrifice quality to quantity, so you might as well go for the cheaper ones. Lastly, to cater for that much-prized customer, the Japanese big-spender, some of the larger hotels have authentic and very good **Japanese** restaurants, which tend to specialize in discreet *sushi* and *sashimi* dining rather than the flamboyant *teppanyaki* style, where knife-juggling chefs cook at your table.

Local ingredients

As well as the many kinds of **fish** listed in the box opposite, widely used **local ingredients** include **ginger** (the Big Island is the major producer of ginger in the US) and **macadamia nuts** (large, creamy, and somewhat bland white nuts said to contain a hundred calories per nut, even when they aren't coated with chocolate). Bright-red **'ōhelo berries**, which taste like cranberries, were once sacred to the volcano goddess Pele and to eat one was punishable by death; now they're served up in gourmet restaurants. **Avocados** are widely grown, and are even richer than you may be used to, as are fruits such as **guava**, **papaya** and **mango**. Watch out also for the small yellow **apple bananas**, with their distinct savoury tang and, of course, the ever-present **coconut**.

Drink

The usual range of **wines** (mostly Californian, though the Big Island does have its own tiny *Volcano Winery*) and **beers** (mainly imported either from the mainland or from Mexico) is sold at Big Island restaurants and bars, but at some point every visitor seems to insist on getting wiped out by a tropical **cocktail** or two. Among the most popular are the **Mai Tai**, which should contain at least two kinds of rum, together with orange curacao and lemon juice; the **Blue Hawaii**, in which vodka is coloured with blue curacao; and the **Planter's Punch**, made with light rum, grenadine, bitters and lemon juice.

As for non-alcoholic drinks, tap **water** in Hawaii is safe to drink, though it's a scarce enough resource on the Kona side that some restaurants will only bring it to your table on request. If you're hiking, however, make sure you take enough water with you – never drink untreated stream water: see p.33.

Mention should also be made of the Big Island's most famous home-grown product,

Kona coffee. It's widely available in small cafés and espresso bars throughout the island, and especially in the South Kona district where the farms are located. For more details, see p.61.

Hawaiian Fish

Although the ancient Hawaiians were expert off-shore fishermen, as well as being highly sophisticated fish farmers, with intricate networks of fish ponds laced around the coastline, the great majority of the **fish** eaten in Hawaii nowadays is imported. Local fishing is not on a large enough scale to meet the demand, and in any case many of the species that tourists expect to find on menus thrive in much cooler waters. Thus salmon and crab come from Alaska, mussels from New Zealand, and so on, although Maine lobsters are now being farmed in the cold waters of the deep ocean off Hōnokohau.

However, if you feel like being adventurous, you should get plenty of opportunity to try some of the Pacific species caught nearby; the list below translates the most common Hawaiian names. If it still leaves you in the dark, personal recommendations include *opah*, which is chewy and salty like swordfish; the chunky *'ōpakapaka*, which because of its red colour (associated with happiness) is often served on special occasions; the succulent white *ono* (which means "delicious" in Hawaiian); and the dark *ahi*, the most popular choice for *sashimi*.

To get an idea of the range of fish that lurk in Hawaiian waters, call in at Hilo's early-morning *Suisan Fish Auction* (see p.100).

'ahi	yellow-fin tuna	*moi*	thread fish
a'u	swordfish or marlin	*onaga*	red snapper
'ehu	red snapper	*ono*	mackerel or tuna-like fish
hāpu'upu'u	sea bass	*'ōpae*	shrimp
hebi	spear fish	*opah*	moonfish
kākū	barracuda	*'ōpakapaka*	pink snapper
kalekale	pink snapper	*pāpio*	pompano
kāmano	salmon	*uhu*	parrot fish
kūmū	red goat fish	*uku*	gray snapper
lehi	yellow snapper	*ulua*	jack fish
mahimahi	dorado or dolphin fish	*weke*	goat fish
mano	shark		

Communications and Media

Telephone connections on and between the Hawaiian Islands and across the Pacific to the mainland US are generally efficient and reliable. The snail-like pace of mail services to the islands means that fax is probably your best bet for written communications.

Phones and the Mail

The **telephone area code** for the entire state of Hawaii is ☎808. Calls from anywhere on the Big Island to anywhere else on the island count as local; you don't need to dial the area code and it costs a flat-rate 25¢ on payphones. Calling any of the other islands, you have to prefix ☎1-808 before the number; charges vary according to the time of day and distance involved. The cheapest long-distance rates apply between 11pm and 8am from Monday to Thursday and between 5pm Friday and 8am Monday; an intermediate rate applies between 5pm and 11pm from Monday to Thursday.

Hotels impose huge surcharges on calls made from guest rooms, so if you intend to

---

To make an **international call** to Hawaii, dial your country's international access code, then 1 for the US, then 808 for Hawaii. To place a call from Hawaii to the rest of the world, dial 011 then the relevant country code (Britain is 44, Ireland is 353, Canada is 1, Australia is 61 and New Zealand is 64).

---

make any long-distance calls it's well worth getting hold of a **phone card**. All the major US phone companies issue their own cards; other possibilities include the *People's Telephone Company* cards sold in *Global Link* stores in the US (call ☎1-800/864-3311 to find your nearest outlet) and the *Swiftcall* service in the UK (☎0171/488-2001).

There are **post offices** in all the main towns, generally open between 8.30am and 4pm on weekdays and for an hour or two on Saturday mornings. **Mail services** are extremely slow, as all the post has to go via Honolulu first, even if coming from another island. Allow a week for anywhere in the US and as much as two weeks or more for the rest of the world.

Newspapers, Radio and TV

The *Hawaii Tribune-Herald*, a broadsheet based in Hilo, and the tabloid *West Hawaii Today* are the Big Island's two home-grown **newspapers**, both published daily except Saturday, though the *Honolulu Advertiser* and *Honolulu Star-Bulletin* are also widely distributed and cover island issues. The monthly *Big Island Review Journal* is hardly hard-hitting, but *Ka'ū Landing* is an excellent monthly concentrating on environmental news and issues – especially those affecting the south of the island – whose remit extends to Hawaiian history and culture in general. In addition, you're certain to come across glossy **free magazines** aimed at tourists, such as *This Week*, *Guide to the Big Island*, and *Big Island Gold*, whose copy – predominantly advertising – barely changes from week to week. These are especially useful for the discount offers and coupons scattered throughout.

The Big Island has around half a dozen **radio** stations, both AM and FM, and the average rental-car radio will pick up perhaps another half-dozen the closer you get to Maui and Oahu. That's one of the reasons why there's generally far more choice, especially of nationally syndicated shows, on the Kona side; in the remoter southern stretches you can be reduced to one, none or, even worse, a thirty-second repeating promo loop from a local real estate agent. The music-minded *KIPA* on 620AM is the most ubiquitous; for local news steer your dial towards Hilo's *K-BIG* FM98 or *KPUA* 670AM.

There are also six Big-Island **TV** stations – all satellites of Honolulu stations and affiliated to one or other of the principal US networks – plus one **cable TV** station each in Kailua, Hilo and Kohala. In almost every hotel, at least one channel plays an endless loop of tourist information about the island, which features promotional clips on tourist activities interspersed with dramatic volcano footage to keep you watching.

Entertainment and Festivals

such activity happens in the prime tourist areas of Kona and Kohala, the biggest venue for those Hawaiian performers who command strong local followings is the *Crown Room* at Hilo's *Hawaii Naniloa Hotel*. For more about *hula* and Hawaiian music, see p.186.

Restaurants and **cafés** too use live music to attract diners, whether in the form of fully fledged bands, as at *Lehua's* in Hilo, or simple acoustic strummers, as at Kailua's *Island Lava Java* or the *Bamboo Resturant* in Hāwī.

An ideal way to get some local flavour is to visit one of the old-style **community theatres** that still

If you're hoping for wild **nightlife** during your stay in Hawaii, the Big Island is probably the wrong island to choose; it has nothing to compare with the bright lights and glitter of Waikīkī. However, there is a wide variety of **festivals** throughout the year – some genuine, traditional Hawaiian celebrations, some laid on specifically for tourists.

Nightlife and Entertainment

Most of the nightlife and entertainment is arranged by the major **hotels** – almost all of them put on some form of entertainment for their guests and many feature live musicians every night. The music as often as not consists of anodyne medleys of 1950s Hawaiian hits with a cocktail-jazz tinge, but the setting is usually romantic enough for that not to matter. In a typical week, the biggest events are the various *l'ūaus* listed on p.23, but visiting artists from the other islands or the mainland also make regular concert appearances. Although nearly all

Public holidays	
As well as observing the national **public holidays**, Hawaii also has a number of its own:	
Jan 1	New Year's Day
3rd Mon in Jan	Dr Martin Luther King Jr's Birthday
3rd Mon in Feb	President's Day
March 26	Prince Kūhiō Day
Easter Monday	
May 1	Lei Day
Last Mon in May	Memorial Day
June 11	Kamehameha Day
July 4	Independence Day
3rd Fri in Aug	Admissions Day
1st Mon in Sept	Labor Day
2nd Mon in Oct	Columbus Day
Nov 11	Veterans' Day
Last Thurs in Nov	Thanksgiving
Dec 25	Christmas Day

survive in smaller towns across the island. Most were built early this century, to provide entertainment for the plantation labourers; some still have their original Art-Deco adornments. Fine examples include the *People's Theatre* in **Honoka'a**, **Kainaliu**'s *Aloha Theater*, and the *Akebono Theater* in **Pāhoa**; there are also a couple of old picture palaces in downtown **Hilo** that seem to hover forever on the brink of reopening. These days such places tend only to open for special occasions, like

amateur dramatic society productions or one-off concerts; look out for advertisements.

Finally, if you want to see a **movie**, there's not all that much choice. The main movie theatre in Kailua is in the Kona Marketplace. Hilo has movie theatres in the Prince Kuhio and Waiakea malls, while the second floor of the Kress Building on Kalakaua Street will soon become a four-screen complex, bringing films back downtown for the first time since 1982.

Big Island Festivals And Events

By far the most important of the Big Island's annual festivals is Hilo's **Merrie Monarch Festival**, a *hula* showcase for which tickets go on sale each year on January 1 and sell out almost immediately; for more details see p.111.

Feb	Mardi Gras, Hilo
June	Hawaii State Horticultural Show, Hilo
March	Hawaii Ski Cup, Mauna Kea (snow permitting)
April	Merrie Monarch Festival, Hilo
May	Western Week, Honoka'a
Early June	Inter-Cultural Dance Festival, Kalani Huna Centre
June 11	Kamehameha Day; Floral Parade, Kailua; also ceremonies at Kapa'au
June	Hawaii State Horticultural Show, Hilo
June	Foundation Festival, Pu'uhonua O Hōnaunau
July 4	Parker Ranch Rodeo, Waimea
July	International Festival of the Pacific, Hilo
July	Kīlauea Volcano Marathon, Volcano
Aug	Hawaiian International Billfish Tournament, Kailua
Early Sept	Queen Liliuokalani Long-Distance Canoe Races, Kailua
Sept	Hawaii County Fair, Hilo
Oct	Aloha Week Festival, island-wide
Oct 15	Ironman Triathlon, Kailua
Nov	Kona Coffee Festival, South Kona
Dec	Honoka'a Music Festival, Honoka'a

Sea Sports and Safety

Because the Big Island is the youngest member of the Hawaiian / archipelago, it's the least suitable for a **beach vacation**. That's only relative, of course – it has some magnificent palm-fringed beaches and the facilities to go with them. However, it takes millions of years for a tropical island to acquire a protective reef of coral and millions more for parts of that coral to break down and produce white sandy beaches. By contrast, much of the Big Island's shoreline has

been shaped by new lava flows within the last century and some of it within the last week. Only along the north Kona and south Kohala coasts – the oldest, most sheltered parts of the island – are conditions really perfect. That's where the beaches are concentrated, and that's where the hotels are too.

According to the state's own figures, the Big Island has 19.4 miles of sandy beach, of which just 1.2 miles are considered **safe beaches**, meaning they're clean, accessible and generally suitable for swimming. So long as you observe the necessary precautions, however, there's plenty of scope for enjoyment, with some of the best snorkelling, surfing, scuba diving and plain swimming in the world.

What constitutes the "**best beach**" on the island is a matter of personal taste, but among those you should make a point of visiting are **Hāpuna Beach** (p.79), **Kona Coast State Park** (p.57), **Old Kona Airport** (p.49) and two more unusual ones, the black sand beach at **Punalu'u** (p.163), and **Green Sand Beach** near South Point (p.166).

Ocean Fun

With average water temperatures of between 75° and 82°F (24–28°C), the sea in Hawaii is all but irresistible, and most visitors are tempted to try at least one or two of the state's range of **ocean sports**.

Snorkelling

Probably the easiest activity for beginners is **snorkelling**. Equipped with mask, snorkel and fins (which are available for rent all over the island), you can while away hours and days having face-to-face encounters with the rainbow-coloured populations of the Kona-side reefs and lava pools. Among the best sites are **Kahalu'u Beach** in Keauhou, at the southern end of Kailua's Ali'i Drive; **Kauna'oa Beach** at the Mauna Kea resort; and the beach at the **Puu'honua O Hōnaunau** (the "City of Refuge") in south Kona. You might also want to join one of the many available snorkel cruises; see overleaf.

Scuba and Snuba

Scuba diving is both expensive and demanding, but with endless networks of submarine lava tubes to explore, and the chance to get that bit closer to some amazing marine life forms, the Big Island is one of the planet's greatest dive destinations. Several dive-boat operators are listed in the box on p.30; experienced divers can also enter the water direct from the shoreline, at the same beaches that are recommended for snorkellers. Note that for medical reasons you shouldn't dive within 24 hours of flying, so don't leave it until your last day.

For a taste of what it's all about, you might like to try **snuba**, which is basically snorkelling

from a boat, equipped with a longer breathing tube. Both the *Fair Wind* and the *Body Glove* (see box) offer snuba for an extra charge on their snorkel cruises.

Surfing

The nation that invented **surfing** – long before the foreigners came – remains its greatest arena. A recurring theme in ancient legends has young men frittering away endless days in the waves rather than facing up to their duties (see p.179); now young people from all over the world flock to Hawaii to do just that. The sport was popularized earlier this century by champion Olympic swimmer Duke Kahanamoku, using a sixteen-foot board; these days most are around six-foot. Nowhere on the Big Island can quite match up to Oahu's fabled North Shore, but once again the Kona and Kohala coasts offer the best prospects, at beaches such as 'Anaeho'omalu Bay at the Waikoloa resort. Unless you're a real expert, don't join the locals you'll see surfing at spots along the Hāmākua Coast; in fact avoid the east side of the island in general.

At some of the most popular beaches, such as Hāpuna Beach and Spencer Beach Park, surfing is forbidden in order to prevent collisions with ordinary bathers. Use of the smaller **boogie boards**, which you lie on, *is* allowed; these make an exhilarating initiation for beginners into the world of surfing. **Windsurfing** too is rapidly growing in popularity, from many of the favourite surfing beaches and also in Hilo Bay.

Ocean Safety

It's essential whenever you're in or near the ocean to be aware of **safety issues**. Foremost among these is the fact that Hawaii is one of the remotest islands on earth, which means that waves have two thousand miles of the misnamed Pacific Ocean to build up their strength before they come crashing into the islands. People born in Hawaii are brought up with a healthy respect for the sea and learn to watch out for all sorts of signs before they swim. You'll be told to throw sticks into the waves to see how they move, or to look for disturbances in the surf that might indicate powerful currents; unless you have local expertise, however, you're better off sticking to the official beach parks and most popular spots, especially those that are shielded by offshore

Ocean Activities

Dive Boats

All the following operators are based on the Kona and Kohala coasts. One-dive cruises tend to cost $50–70 and two-dive trips more like $80–90, with a $20–30 surcharge for unqualified divers. Most operators offer two-day courses leading to certification for around $300.

Big Island Divers	☎ 329-6068
Eco Adventures	☎ 329-7116
Hawaiian Divers	☎ 329-2243
Jack's Diving Locker	☎ 329-7585
Kona Coast Divers	☎ 329-8802
Mauna Kea Divers	☎ 880-3488
Sandwich Island Divers	☎ 329-9188
Sea Paradise	☎ 322-2500

Snorkel Cruises

Most of the companies below run snorkel cruises every morning and afternoon. Typical half-day trips cost between $40 and $60, depending on the size of the boat and whether or not you're given a full meal. Once again they all operate along the Kona and Kohala coasts, with departure points ranging from Keauhou Bay in the south via Kailua, Honokōhau and the Waikoloa resort up to Kawaihae in the north. Kealakekua Bay is the prime destination – for more details, see p.66 – but there are plenty of alternatives. *Red Sail Sports* for example run trips up to secluded inlets in north Kohala.

Body Glove	☎ 326-7122
Captain Cook VI	☎ 329-6411
Captain Zodiac	☎ 329-3119
Fair Wind	☎ 322-2788
Kamanu	☎ 329-2021
Lanakila	☎ 987-3999
Red Sail Sports	☎ 885-2876
Sea Quest	☎ 329-7238

Deep-sea Fishing

Countless vessels which congregate in Honokōhau Harbor (see p.56) can be chartered for deep-sea fishing expeditions. Typical rates are $55–75 per person for a half day or upwards of $400 for a whole boat for a day.

Cherry Pit Sportfishing	☎ 326-7781
Ihu Nui Sportfishing	☎ 885-4686

Jack's Kona Charters	☎ 325-7558
Jun Ken Po	☎ 325-7710
Kris-Tara-Jo	☎ 329-3390
Reel Action	☎ 325-6811
Sea Wife Charters	☎ 329-1806
The Charter Locker	☎ 329-5603

Sight-seeing Cruises

If you're more of a sedentary type, you may prefer a cruise that shows you ocean life from the comfort of a nice dry seat.

Atlantis Submarines, main office in the *King Kamehameha Hotel*, Kailua (☎ 329-6626; $85 for a one-hour trip). Passengers leave hourly from Kailua Pier to a small landing stage on the open sea, where they're greeted, James-Bond-style, by a surfacing submarine. Then follows a cramped but fascinating cruise of the ocean floor, to the accompaniment of the *Star Wars* theme, with foolhardy divers outside the portholes trying to entice sharks to come and have a look.

Dan McSweeney's Whale Watch (☎ 322-0028; $45 for a morning's excursion). This boat leaves daily from Honokōhau Harbor at 9am in search of marine mammals; in summer you may see no more than a school or two of dolphins, but in winter, roughly December to March, there's an excellent chance of sneaking up on some humpback whales.

Nautilus II (☎ 326-2003; $40 for a one-hour trip). This also goes out hourly from Kailua Pier. It's a semi-submersible not a submarine, meaning that passengers simply descend into a cabin below the water level, equipped with large viewing windows, and watch the fish from there.

Equipment Rental

In Kailua, most kinds of beach gear can be rented from *The Beach Connection* at 74-5563 Kaiwi St (☎ 329-1038), while snorkelling equipment is available at daily and weekly rates from *Snorkel Bob's*, based near the *Royal Kona Resort* (☎ 329-0770), or *Captain Jack's*, at the *Casa de Emdeko*, 75-6082 Ali'i Drive (☎ 329-3733). Most hotels, including all the Kohala resorts, also have equipment rental outlets.

reefs. Not all beaches have lifeguards and warning flags, and unattended beaches are not necessarily safe. Look for other bathers, but whatever your experience elsewhere don't assume you'll be able to cope with the same conditions as the local kids. Always ask for advice and above all follow the cardinal rule – **never turn your back on the water**.

The beaches that experience the most accidents and **drownings** are those where waves of four feet or more break directly onto the shore. This varies according to the season, so beaches such as Hāpuna or White Sands, which are idyllic in summer, can be storm-tossed death traps between October and April. If you get caught in a rip current or undertow and find yourself being dragged out to sea, stay calm and remember that the vast majority of such currents disappear within a hundred yards of the shore. Never exhaust yourself by trying to swim against them, but simply allow yourself to be carried out until the force weakens, and swim first to one side and then back to the shore.

Sea creatures to avoid include *wana* – black spiky **sea urchins** – Portuguese men-of-war **jellyfish** and **coral** in general, which can give painful, infected cuts. **Shark attacks** are much rarer than popular imagination suggests; those which do occur are usually due to "misunderstandings",

Emergency numbers
Police, fire and ambulances ☎911
Ocean Search and Rescue ☎1-800/552-6458
Big Island **hospital** numbers are on p.35.

such as spear-fishers inadvertently keeping sharks from their catch or surfers idling on their boards looking a bit too much like turtles from below.

Sun Safety

Assuming that you're self-destructive enough to want a **tan**, expose yourself to the harsh tropical **sun** in moderation; a mere fifteen to thirty minutes is the safe recommendation for the first day. The hours between 10am and 3pm are the worst and be aware that even on overcast days human skin still absorbs harmful UV rays. Use plenty of **sunscreen** – doctors recommend Sun Protection Factor (SPF) 30 for Hawaii – and reapply after swimming. Note that some marine life sanctuaries, such as Lapakahi State Park, forbid the use of sunscreen by bathers, which should be enough to discourage you from swimming altogether. Drink lots of (non-alcoholic) liquids as well, to stave off dehydration.

Hiking and Camping

The Big Island is one of the most exciting **hiking** destinations imaginable. Well-maintained trails guide walkers through scenery that ranges from dense tropical rainforest to remote desert and, above all, offer the chance to experience at first hand the splendour of the world's most active volcanoes. If you're planning to do any hiking, however, it's essential to remember that Hawaii is more than a vacation playground and you may find yourself in some pretty uncompromising **wilderness**.

That doesn't mean that **camping** on the island has to be a battle with the elements; there are several lovely oceanfront campgrounds where you don't have to do anything more than drive in and pitch your tent, and some offer cabins for rent so you needn't even do that.

The majority of hiking trails, and all the campgrounds, are in the various public **parks** scattered across the island. There's a complicated hierarchy of county, state and national parks, each with different authorities, so it's not always obvious whom to contact for permission to camp in a particular spot. However, one thing you cannot do is simply set up your tent on some unoccupied piece of land; only camp at designated sites.

Camping

If you're on a **camping** vacation, then you'll almost certainly spend most of your time staying at the dozen or so **County Beach Parks** along the shoreline. There's a long stretch of the coast to either side of Kailua with no campgrounds at all, but otherwise you should find plenty of choice. **Spencer Beach Park** near Kawaihae in Kohala, with its white sandy beach and coconut palms, is the most popular – so booking in advance is a good idea – while the one by the black sand beach at **Punalu'u** is equally attractive and memorable. Several of the others, especially on the east side of the island, aren't really beaches in the usual sense, being set in clifftop woodlands or simply near the edge of a jagged lava shoreline.

All county parks offer showers, toilets and drinking water and are administered by the Dept of Parks & Recreation, 25 Aupuni St, Hilo HI 96720 (☎961-8311). Permits are required for all stays, with fees of $1 per day (50¢ for ages 13–17); they're also available in theory from offices in the Yano Center in Captain Cook (☎323-3046) and at Waimea Park in Waimea (☎885-5454), but call to check. County authorities are engaged in a constant struggle to prevent semi-permanent encampments of homeless local people developing at certain sites, so precise regulations on maximum lengths of stay, and even whether a particular park is open at all, tend to vary at a moment's notice.

In addition, the **state** provides eight-bed cabins with linen and cooking facilities at several of its own parks, including Mauna Kea (not the summit, but the state park on the Saddle Road; see p.130) and Kalōpā (p.120). Precise rates depend on the park and the size of your group; contact the Division of State Parks, 75 Aupuni St, Hilo HI 96720 (☎933-4200) for details.

Information about camping at the popular Hāpuna Beach is given on p.80.

Hawaii Volcanoes National Park has a number of campgrounds of its own, as detailed in Chapter Four. The most accessible of these are the free, first-come, first-served sites at Nāmakani Paio and Kīpuka Nēnē; it's also possible to book cabins at Nāmakani Paio through *Volcano House* (☎967-7321; see p.144). In addition, the park is the island's prime location for **wilderness camping**, with an assortment of very remote backcountry sites including Keauhou, Halapē and Ka'aha along the Puna Coast Trail (see p.157), and the Red Hill Cabin and Mauna Loa Cabin on the Mauna Loa Summit Trail (see p.157). Backpacking here has its own perils, so it's important to register with the park authorities before doing so.

Finally, you can also make arrangements to camp in a couple of out-of-the-way places on the Hāmākua coast. Camping in **Waipi'o Valley** – see p.127 – is now controlled by the *Bishop Estate* (PO Box 495, Pa'auilo HI 96776; ☎776-1104), while **Waimanu Valley** beyond – see p.126 – is under the jurisdiction of the Dept of Forestry in Hilo (1643 Kilauea Ave, Hilo HI 96720; ☎933-4221).

Hiking

All the best **hiking trails** on the Big Island are described in detail in the relevant chapters of this book. Other than the route down to **Kealakekua Bay** (p.62) and the **Pu'ako Petroglyph Trail** (p.78), the Kona coast is short of interesting trails, but the rest of the island has plenty to keep you occupied. Favourites include the descents into **Waipi'o** (p.124) and **Pololū** (p.96) valleys, the coastal walks to **Green Sand Beach** (p.166) and **Kamehameha's Birthplace** (p.94) and the loop to **Akaka Falls** (p.116).

National Parks Admissions

The Big Island has four parks that belong to the federal National Park Service. Admission to both Pu'ukoholā Heiau National Historic Site (p.81) and the undeveloped Kaloko-Honokōhau National Historic Park (p.56) is free, while Pu'uhonua O Hōnaunau National Historical Park (p.67) charges $4 and Hawaii Volcanoes National Park (p.138) $5.

The park system's **national passes** – the *Golden Eagle*, *Golden Access* and *Golden Age* passports – can be obtained at Hōnaunau and the Volcanoes, and give the holders free access into all the sites. The *Golden Eagle* passport is available to anyone, US citizen or otherwise, for $25 and is valid for one year. Both the *Golden Access* passport, free to US citizens or residents with disabilities, and the *Golden Age* passport, available to US citizens or residents aged over 62 for a $10 one-off fee, offer unlimited admission for life to all national parks in the US.

However, the most unique and fascinating feature of the island has to be **Kīlauea volcano**, in Volcanoes National Park. It would be easy to spend a week day-hiking the trails to the sites of the current and recent eruptions, without the thrill of being inside an active volcano wearing off, and there's potential for countless longer backpacking expeditions. See Chapter Four for full accounts.

Equipment and Safety

Like all the Hawaiian islands, but more obviously so thanks to its relative youth, the Big Island is basically a large pile of rough lava, and any **footwear** except sturdy boots is likely to be torn to shreds. Other equipment should include rain gear, a torch, insect repellent, sunscreen and sunglasses and a basic first-aid kit; if you're backpacking, of course, you'll need a waterproof tent and sleeping bag, and if you're heading up Mauna Kea or Mauna Loa take warm clothing as well, as there's a real risk of hypothermia.

Never drink untreated water when you hike. **Leptospirosis**, a bacterial disease carried by rats and mice in particular, can be contracted through drinking stream water (filtering alone will not purify it) or even from wading through fresh water if you have any cuts or abrasions. Symptoms range from diarrhoea, fever and chills through to kidney or heart failure and appear in anything from two to twenty days. In case of infection, seek treatment immediately; for more information, contact the Big Island's District Health Office on ☎933-4276.

Sports

Competitive sports are not very much in evidence on the Big Island, although the University of Hawaii in Hilo boasts some enthusiastically supported basketball and baseball teams. A number of showpiece events take place each year, however, with the highlight of the calendar being the **Ironman Triathlon**, held on October 15 and centred on Kailua. Its superhuman participants have to undergo a 2.4-mile ocean swim across Kailua Bay, a 112-mile cycle ride and a full 26-mile marathon, all on the same day.

In August, Kailua plays host to the **Hawaiian International Billfish Tournament**, when sports fishermen from around the world hunt the high seas for blue marlin weighing up to 1000 pounds, while early September sees the Queen Liliuokalani World Championship Long-Distance **Canoe Races**, once again held in Kailua (for details call ☎323-2565). Two of the Big Island's more unexpected spectacles are **rodeo**, best seen on July 4 at the Parker Ranch Rodeo in Waimea (☎885-7655) and **skiing**, in the shape of the Hawaii Ski Cup, Mauna Kea, snow permitting (☎737-4394 for details).

You're unlikely to see any **sumo** on the Big Island. All Hawaii's renowned wrestlers come from Oahu; grand champion *yokozuna* Akebono was born Chad Rowan from Waimānalo, Konishiki is Salevaa Atisanoe from Nānākuli and Musashimaru is Fiamalu Penitani from Wai'anae.

As for **participant sports**, many of the most popular activities are ocean-related (see p.28). Most of the larger hotels have **tennis courts** for their guests and there are public courts in Hilo, Kailua and elsewhere (call the Dept of Parks & Recreation for details: ☎961-8311).

There are also plenty of **golf courses** on the Big Island; a complete list appears overleaf. The courses at the major Kohala resorts, designed to tournament specifications, have the highest reputations, but they also have the highest **green fees** – all cost well over $100 and the reductions for hotel guests are not all that significant. Rates at Hilo's municipal course, by contrast, start around $10.

Big Island Golf Courses

	Location	Holes	Type	Phone
Alii Country Club	Kailua	18	Resort	☎322-2595
Discovery Harbor Country Club	Nā'ālehu	18	Public	☎929-7353
Hamakua Country Club	Honoka'a	9	Public	☎775-7244
Hapuna Golf Course	Kohala	18	Resort	☎882-1035
Hilo Municipal Golf Course	Hilo	18	Municipal	☎959-9601
Kona Country Club	Kailua	18	Resort	☎322-2595
Makalei Hawaii Country Club	Kona	18	Semi-private	☎325-6625
Mauna Kea Beach Golf Club	Kohala	18	Resort	☎882-7222
Mauna Lani Resort				
Francis H I'i Brown; North	Kohala	18	Resort	☎885-6655
Francis H I'i Brown; South	Kohala	18	Resort	☎885-6655
Naniloa Country Club	Hilo	9	Semi-private	☎935-3000
Sea Mountain Golf Course	Punalu'u	18	Resort	☎928-6222
Volcano Golf & Country Club	Volcano	18	Public	☎967-7331
Waikoloa Golf Club				
Beach Course	Waikoloa	18	Resort	☎885-6060
Kings' Course	Waikoloa	18	Resort	☎885-4647
Waikoloa Village Golf Club	Waikoloa	18	Resort	☎883-9621
Waimea Country Club	Waimea	18	Semi-private	☎885-8053

Crafts and Shopping

Many Big Island residents think nothing of flying to Honolulu for the day to shop in Ala Moana mall, and unless you're going to Oahu as well, you may find you come home from your vacation with fewer gifts and souvenirs than you expected. To put it simply, **shopping** is not one of the Big Island's strong points. The prints, posters and T-shirts on sale in Kailua and the major tourist areas are OK if you think that whales are interplanetary voyagers from another dimension, or that a gecko on a surfboard is neat, but stores and galleries selling high-quality indigenous arts and crafts are few and far between.

Shops and Galleries

Devoting your days to the search for the perfect gift is probably not a good idea, but it's worth knowing about some of the more interesting places to call in on as you explore the island.

Hōlualoa, immediately above Kailua, has the main concentration of **galleries** and you never know what locally produced paintings or ceramics might catch your eye in the co-operative *Coffee Mill Workshop* (see p.59). The *Kohala Collection* in **Kawaihae** (p.112) is expensive but offers a wide range of fine arts, as does the better known *Volcano Art Center* in the national park (p.145). As well as serving good food, **Hāwi's** *Bamboo Restaurant and Gallery* (p.95) usually has some nice *koa*-wood furniture and the bizarre *Hawaiian Shop* in **Honoka'a** (p.121) stocks an amazing tangle of genuine Pacific artefacts and absolute rubbish.

Big Island **bookstores** are listed on p.189 and **music** stores on p.187.

Hawaiian Crafts and Produce

Some of the most attractive products of Hawaii are just too ephemeral to take home. That goes for the orchids and tropical flowers on sale everywhere, and unfortunately it's also true of **leis**.

Leis (pronounced *lays*) are flamboyant decorative garlands, usually composed of flowers such as the fragrant *melia* (the plumeria or frangipani) or the Big Island's own bright-red *lehua* blossom (from the *'ō'hia* tree), but sometimes also made from feathers, shells, seeds or nuts. They're worn by both men and women, above all on celebrations or gala occasions – election-winning politicians are absolutely deluged in them. The days are gone when every arriving tourist was festooned with a *lei*, but you'll probably be way-*leied* at a *l'ūau* or some such occasion, while if you're around for Lei Day (May 1)

everyone's at it. If you want to buy one, most towns have a store or two with a supply of flower *leis* kept in refrigerated cabinets.

Colourful Hawaiian clothing, such as **aloha shirts** and the cover-all "Mother-Hubbard"-style **mu'umu'u** dress, is on sale everywhere, though classic designs are surprisingly rare and you tend to see the same stylized prints over and over again. Otherwise, the main **local crafts** to look out for are **lau hala weaving**, in which mats, hats, baskets and the like are created by plaiting the large leaves (*lau*) of the spindly-legged pandanus (*hala*) tree, and **wood turning**, with fine bowls made from native dark woods such as *koa*.

Directory

AREA CODE The telephone area code for the whole state of Hawaii is ☎808.

CLIMATE For details of the climate in Hawaii, see the *Introduction* on p.v.

ELECTRICITY Hawaii's electricity supply, like that on the US mainland, uses 100 volts AC. Plugs are standard American two-pins.

FISHING Full details of Hawaii's complex fishing regulations can be obtained from the Division of Aquatic Resources, Department of Land and

Natural Resources, Kalanimoku Building, 1151 Punchbowl St, Room 330, Honolulu HI96813.

GAY AND LESBIAN LIFE Much the greatest concentration of gay activism in Hawaii is in Honolulu, though the state as a whole is liberal on social issues. It's one of 25 states to allow consensual "sodomy", with no criminal laws against private sex acts and a guarantee of privacy in the constitution. Hawaii hit the national headlines in May 1993 when a decision of its Supreme Court was seen as clearing the way for the legalization of same-sex marriages, but no such marriages have yet taken place.

HOSPITALS Big Island hospitals can be contacted on the following numbers: Hilo ☎969-4111; Honoka'a ☎775-7211; Ka'ū ☎928-8331; Kohala ☎889-6211; Kona ☎322-9311. In emergencies call ☎911.

INOCULATIONS No inoculations or vaccinations are required by law in order to enter Hawaii, though some authorities suggest a polio vaccination.

PUBLIC TOILETS Doors in some public toilets are labelled in Hawaiian: *Kanes* means Men, *Wahines* means Women.

QUARANTINE Very stringent restrictions apply to the importation of all plants and animals into

Hawaii, mainly to protect the state's many endangered indigenous species. Cats and dogs have to stay in quarantine for 120 days; if you were hoping to bring an alligator or a hamster into the country, forget it. For full regulations on animals call ☎483-7151, for plants call ☎586-0844.

SENIOR TRAVELLERS The University of Hawaii at Hilo runs *Elderhostel* programmes each summer, in which senior citizens join courses in various aspects of Hawaiian culture and history, with fees covering board, lodging and tuition; for details contact the Program Director, University of Hawaii CCECS, 523 W Lanikaula St, Hilo HI 96720 (☎933-3555). *Elderhostel's* national headquarters is at 75 Federal St, Boston, MA 02110 (☎617/426 8056). US residents aged 50 or over can join the *American Association of Retired Persons*, 601 E St NW, Washington DC 20049 (☎1800/424 3410), for discounts on accommodation and vehicle rental. For details of the *Golden Age* passport to US national parks, see p.32.

TIME All US states *except* Arizona, part of Indiana, Puerto Rico, the Virgin Islands, American Samoa and Hawaii adjust their clocks to Daylight Saving Time from 2am on the last Sunday in April to 2am on the last Sunday in October. Between those dates the difference between Hawaii and the West Coast is three hours, not the usual two; the difference from the mountain region is four hours not three, and from the East Coast it's six hours not five. Hawaii varies between ten and eleven hours behind the UK. In fact it's behind just about everywhere else on earth because, although New Zealand and Australia might seem to be two and four hours respectively behind Honolulu time, they're on the other side of the International Date Line, so are actually almost a full day ahead of Hawaii.

TIPPING Waiting staff in restaurants expect tips of fifteen percent, in bars a little less. Hotel porters and bellhops should receive around $1 per piece of luggage and housekeeping staff $1 per night.

TRAVELLERS WITH DISABILITIES Copies of the *Aloha Guide to Accessibility in the State of Hawaii* and additional information on facilities for travellers with disabilities on the Big Island can be obtained from the *State Commission on Persons with Disabilities*, PO Box 1641, Hilo HI 96720 (☎933-4747). Wheelchairs and other equipment can be rented from *Medi-Home Care* (☎969-1123) and *Pacific United Rent-All* (☎934-2974) in Hilo, or *Kona Coast Drugs* (☎329-8886) and *Kona Rent-All* (☎329-1644) on the Kona side. Beach wheelchairs, designed for use on sand and in shallow water, are available free of charge from the *Beach Connection* at the Kuakini Center in Kailua (☎329-1038).

WEDDINGS To get married in Hawaii, you need to have a valid state licence, which costs $16 from Dept of Health, Marriage Licence Office, 1250 Punchbowl St, Honolulu HI 96813 (☎586-4545), and is valid for thirty days. You also have to show proof of rubella immunization or screening, which can be arranged through the Dept of Health. The Hawaii Visitors Bureau keeps a full list of companies who arrange weddings and will send you the *Weddings in Hawaii* booklet on request; most of the major resorts offer their own marriage planners, or contact *Paradise Weddings Hawaii*, PO Box 383433, Waikoloa HI 96738 (☎1-800/428-5844).

Part 2

The Island

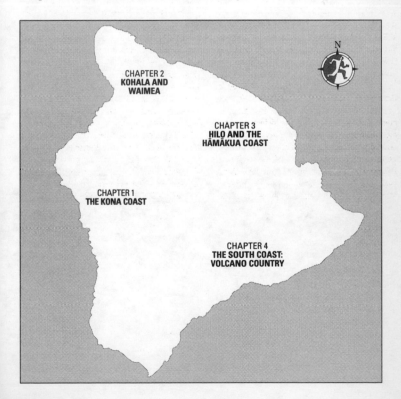

Chapter 1

The Kona Coast

On first impressions, the **KONA COAST** of the Big Island conforms to few conventional ideas of beauty. As you drop towards Keāhole airport, the grey tarmac runway appears as a tiny blemish on an unrelenting field of black lava, and the gap-toothed straggle of coconut palms at the edge of the ocean provides the only flash of colour. Travellers eager for a glimpse of a Hawaiian volcano may find it hard to believe that the long low ridge ascending into the mists really is Hualālai, at just over eight thousand feet third in rank of the island's peaks. Scars from its most recent eruption, early in the nineteenth century, still trail down to the sea, though they're barely distinguishable from generations of earlier flows.

Technically, most of this area is desert, and under American domination it was largely neglected until around thirty years ago, very much playing second fiddle to the sugar plantations of the Hāmākua coast. Then the virtues of being consistently dry and hot began to be appreciated. Resort development took off, and the region came into its own as one of Hawaii's prime tourist destinations, an increasingly crucial part of the Big Island economy. A five-mile strip of hotels and condos now stretches along the coast from its one sizeable community, **Kailua**, which has retained an attractive historic core despite the encroachment of fast-food restaurants and souvenir shops. The beaches may not be as broad and sandy as you would wish, but there are plenty of them, and a short drive can usually guarantee a private slice of paradise. Small boats run daily excursions to snorkelling and diving spots, or cruises in search of whales, while just a few miles offshore, some of the world's largest game fish – including giant marlin – wait to be hauled from the deep Pacific.

Although you'll hear the word "Kona" used to refer to Kailua, it literally means "leeward", and names a district that extends for roughly seventy miles, from the bleak flatlands north of Kailua to the rich coffee-growing hillsides in the south. Once this was the epicentre of the kingdom of Kamehameha the Great, who ruled the entire Hawaiian chain of islands from his palace at Kailua. The

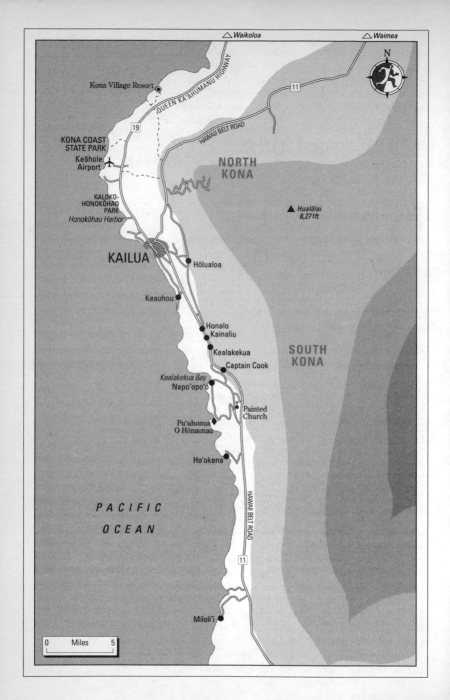

northern coast is dotted with ancient villages and fish ponds that have escaped successive lava flows and is riddled with hidden caves, some of which are thought to hold the bones of Kamehameha and the canoes of his war fleet. Southwards, reached by a gorgeous road through the lush coffee groves, lies **Kealakekua Bay**, site of the settlement where Captain Cook met his end. Now all but uninhabited, its dramatic past, spectacular scenery, and abundant marine life attract scores of day-trippers – including the dolphins who feast on its shoals of protected fish. Nearby, the **Pu'uhonua o Hōnaunau** or "Place of Refuge" bears atmospheric witness to a vanished Hawaiian way of life and death.

Kailua

Considering that **KAILUA** is the oldest Western-style community on the Big Island – it was here that Hawaii's first Christian missionaries arrived from New England in 1820 – and had before that been a favourite home of Kamehameha I, it took a surprisingly long time to grow to its present size. Before its recent spurt, things had stood still for more than a century, which leaves the town with an oddly dual personality. The harbour area remains dominated by the simple palace and church built in the 1830s, but increasingly it's being surrounded by gleaming new malls. The conspicuous high-rise hotels on the headlands to either side of the harbour form just a small part of the ribbon of beachfront properties capable of accommodating several thousand visitors per day.

Kailua is still a very long way indeed from the overkill of Waikīkī, however. When Mark Twain called it "the sleepiest, quietest, Sundayest looking place you can imagine" he meant to be pejorative, but if you've come to relax you'll probably find its low-key pleasures appealing. At least one of the beaches in the area is bound to suit you and, if not, there are plenty of alternative activities. In particular, sitting on the *lanai* of one of the many waterfront cafés and bars, for a blast of Kona coffee in the morning or for a cocktail at sunset, is enough to make anyone feel that all's right with the world.

Accommodation price codes

If you know in advance that you want to stay in Kailua for your entire vacation, then you're likely to get better accommodation rates by booking an **all-inclusive package** before you leave home; see p.20. Prices have been graded with the symbols below, according to the quoted rate for the least expensive double room for most of the year, not including state taxes of 10.17 percent.

①	up to $30	④	$75–100	⑦	$170–225
②	$30–50	⑤	$100–130	⑧	$225–300
③	$50–75	⑥	$130–170	⑨	over $300

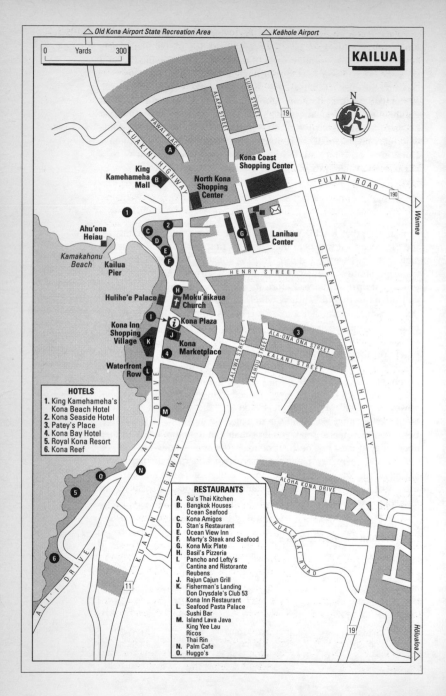

KAILUA

Old Kona Airport State Recreation Area △   △ Keāhole Airport

0   Yards   300

N

Kona Coast
Shopping Center

PULANI ROAD
190
△ Waimea

King
Kamehameha
Mall

North Kona
Shopping
Center

Lanihau
Center

Ahu'ena
Heiau

Kamakahonu
Beach

Kailua
Pier

HENRY STREET

Hulihe'e Palace

Moku'aikaua
Church

Kona Inn
Shopping
Village

Kona Plaza

Kona
Marketplace

ALA-ONA ONA STREET

KALANI STREET

Waterfront
Row

KUAKINI HIGHWAY

QUEEN KA-AHUMANU HIGHWAY

ALI'I DRIVE

ALOHA KONA DRIVE

HUALALAI ROAD

11

19

△ Holualoa

HOTELS
1. King Kamehameha's
   Kona Beach Hotel
2. Kona Seaside Hotel
3. Patey's Place
4. Kona Bay Hotel
5. Royal Kona Resort
6. Kona Reef

RESTAURANTS
A. Su's Thai Kitchen
B. Bangkok Houses
   Ocean Seafood
C. Kona Amigos
D. Stan's Restaurant
E. Ocean View Inn
F. Marty's Steak and Seafood
G. Kona Mix Plate
H. Basil's Pizzeria
I. Pancho and Lefty's
   Cantina and Ristorante
   Reubens
J. Rajun Cajun Grill
K. Fisherman's Landing
   Don Drysdale's Club 53
   Kona Inn Restaurant
L. Seafood Pasta Palace
   Sushi Bar
M. Island Lava Java
   King Yee Lau
   Ricos
   Thai Rin
N. Palm Cafe
O. Huggo's

Many new arrivals assume that Kailua, not Hilo, is the island's capital. Infuriated residents of Hilo console themselves with the thought that hardly anyone seems to get the name of their rival right. Officially, it's called Kailua, hyphenated by the post office to "Kailua-Kona" to distinguish it from the Kailuas on Oahu and Maui. Most tourists, however, have only heard of Kona and not of Kailua. Compound that with the fact that most of the businesses and other facilities that people generally refer to as being "in Kona" are in fact in Kailua, and you have a recipe for confusion.

Arrival and information

Keāhole Airport, the Big Island's laid-back main airport, sprawls across the lava nine miles north of Kailua. Most arriving passengers rent a car immediately from the usual outlets – detailed on p.16 – or arrange to be picked up by their hotels. Alternatively, you can ride into town in a shared *Gray Line* limousine (☎329-9337) for around $14 per person, or take a cab for more like $30.

The only **public transport** in Kailua town is the *Ali'i Shuttle* bus, which runs the five-mile length of Ali'i Drive every ninety minutes (7.45am–9.15pm; $1 flat fare). In addition, a free shuttle service (contact ☎322-3500 for details) will pick up passengers from any of the major hotels and ferry them to the Keauhou Shopping Village (see p.55). From Monday to Saturday, a daily bus run by the Hilo-based *Mass Transportation Agency* (☎935-8241) follows the Belt Road all the way to Hilo, leaving the Lanihau Center at 6.45am and arriving back at 4.30pm; for a full timetable see p.18.

Mauka and makai

Remember *mauka* means away from the sea and towards the mountain, and *makai* means away from the mountain and towards the sea.

Information and services

The helpful Kona-coast office of the **Hawaii Visitors Bureau** is in Kona Plaza, just south of Moku'aikaua Church on the *mauka* side of Ali'i Drive (Mon–Fri 8am–noon & 1–4.30pm; ☎329-7787). Most of the brochures they have on offer are also available from the abundant "**activities desks**" in the seafront malls and hotels – such as the *Activity Information Center* (☎329-7700 or 1-800/626-7771) – whose primary function is to book tourists onto snorkel cruises, helicopter rides, and the like. In addition, pick up any of the free listings glossies such as *This Week*, *Guide to the Big Island*, and *Big Island Gold*, which are available all over town (see p.26).

There are **post offices** in the Lanihau Center in downtown Kailua and in the Keauhou Shopping Center, five miles south at the far end of Ali'i Drive. As for getting **money**, the branches of the

Kailua

Bank of Hawaii, *First Hawaiian Bank*, and *American Savings Bank* in the Lanihau Center hold virtually every ATM under the sun.

Activities

See p.30 for a summary of the many operators organizing tours, excursions and adventures along the Kona Coast, as well as throughout the rest of the Big Island.

One of the most popular activities for visitors to Kailua is to take a cruise along the Kona Coast. A wide assortment of boat trips is available, including snorkelling cruises, diving trips, whale-watching and even submarine excursions. Most of the **ocean trips** start from Honokōhau Harbor, a few miles up the coast from Kailua town. A pricier but more exhilerating option is to take one of the many **helicopter** and fixed-wing **aircraft** tours, which leave from Keāhole airport, and fly around the island, giving stunning views of the volcanos and coastline.

If you want to explore under your own steam, **bicycles** can be rented from *Hawaiian Pedals* (☎329-2294) in the Kona Inn Shopping Village (see p.17). *Snorkel Bob* has an outlet of his inimitable **snorkelling equipment** rental service (daily 8am–5pm; ☎329-0770) opposite *Huggo's*, near the *Royal Kona Resort* (see p.30). A wider assortment of **beach** paraphernalia, including beach wheelchairs for the disabled, is rented out by *Beach Connection* (☎329-1038), in the Kuakini Center behind the *King Kamehameha* hotel.

Accommodation

For pleasant nearby alternatives to the Kailua hotels, see the sections on Hōlualoa (p.60) and Captain Cook (p.61).

Well over half of all the hotel and condo rooms available on the Big Island are concentrated in or near Kailua, the vast majority of them along the roughly five-mile oceanfront stretch of Ali'i Drive that runs south from Kailua proper as far as Keauhou. If money is no object, the *King Kamehameha*, the *Royal Kona Resort* and the *Kona Surf Resort* are the best of the bunch, though if you prefer a more resorty atmosphere, Keauhou, with its golf course and upmarket mall, may suit you better.

Aston Royal Sea Cliff Resort, 75-6040 Ali'i Drive; ☎329-8021, 1-800/922-7866 (US), 1-800/445-6633 (Canada) or 1-800/321-2558 (HI); fax 922-8785 (*Aston Reservations*); ⑤–⑤.
White multi-level complex of rooms and luxurious condos, dropping down to the coast roughly a mile south of central Kailua, and laid out around a lush courtyard garden to maximize ocean views. You can't swim in the sea from the resort, but it has fresh- and saltwater pools, plus a sauna and jacuzzi.

Keauhou Beach Hotel, 78-6740 Ali'i Drive; ☎322-3441, 1-800/367 6025 (US) or 1-800/448-8990 (HI); fax 322-6586; ⑤–⑤.
A seven-storey hotel jutting into the ocean on a black-lava promontory at the southern end of Kahalu'u Beach Park, a few miles south of central Kailua. Facilities include tennis courts and a small swimming pool, exposed to the gaze of diners in the *Kuakini Terrace* restaurant (see p.54), while signposted trails around the grounds lead past a couple of ruined temples and some scattered petroglyphs. The largely open-air *Makai Bar* is a good venue for an evening drink; Wednesday is comedy night, otherwise there's usually live Hawaiian music.

King Kamehameha's Kona Beach Hotel, 75-5660 Palani Rd; ☎329-2911 or 1-800/367 6060 (US/Canada); fax 329-4602; ⑤–⑦.
Long-established upmarket hotel at the northern end of oceanfront Kailua, set slightly to the right as Ali'i Drive heads off southwards and centred around the picturesque, sandy Kamakahonu Beach (see p.51). You can swim in the pool or from the beach, and canoes, pedaloes and other water-sports equipment are available for rent. Most mornings see performances and exhibitions of Hawaiian music and crafts in the lobby, while the attractive gardens provide a perfect setting for the *lū'au* (Tues, Wed, Thurs & Sun, 5.30–8.45pm; $51; open to non-residents), which features whole baked pigs, as well as live music and dancing.

Kona Bay Hotel, 75-5739 Ali'i Drive; ☎329-6488, 1-800/367-5102 (US/ Canada) or 1-800/442-5841 (HI); fax 935-7903; ③.
Friendly hotel in the centre of Kailua, run by the same family as the *Hilo Bay* in Hilo (see p.104); reservations for both are handled in Hilo. Simple but comfortable rooms, all fully air-conditioned with private bathrooms, are arranged in a crescent around a small pool and the *Banana Bay* restaurant (see p.52). The parking lot, at the back, is entered off Hualālai Rd, and discounts on car rental are available.

Kona Makai, 75-6026 Ali'i Drive; ☎329-6488, 1-800/367-5168 (US), 1-800/ KONA CAN (Canada) or 1-800/321-2558 (HI); fax 329-5480; ④.
Two rows of pink condos surrounded by palm trees, a mile out of Kailua, next to the *Royal Sea Cliff*; minimum stay of three nights.

Kona Reef Hotel, 75-5888 Ali'i Drive; ☎329-2959; 1-800/367-5004 (US/ Canada) or 1-800/272-5275 (HI); fax 329-5480; ⑤.
Fully equipped one- and two-bedroom condos right on the ocean, a few hundred yards out of Kailua proper, just beyond the *Royal Kona Resort*. Up to two children (under 18) free in parents' room, and a choice of free car rental or a sixth night free.

Kona Seaside Hotel, 75-5646 Palani Rd; ☎922-5333, 1-800/367-7000 (US) or 1-800/654-7020 (Canada); fax 922-0052; ③.
Six floors of reasonable air-conditioned rooms, each with its own balcony looking down on a small pool, a hundred yards from the sea just up from the *King Kamehameha*. Part of a small Hawaiian-owned chain, for which reservations are handled in Honolulu.

Kona Surf Resort, 78–128 Ehukai St; ☎322-3411, 1-800/367-8011 (US); fax 322-3245; ⑤–⑦.
Imposing white edifice, set in colourful gardens on a lava promontory at Keauhou, six miles south of Kailua. There's no beach, but the resort has two swimming pools, one filled with salt water, and its own boat harbour for marine excursions.

Patey's Place, 75-195 Ala-Ona Ona St; ☎326-7018 or 1-800/972-7408 (Big Island only); ①/②.
This somewhat chaotic hostel, popular with backpackers and surfers, is Kailua's cheapest option. It's a few hundred yards *mauka* of the town centre, reached by taking Kalani St up from Kuakini Hwy at *McDonald's*, and then the second turning on the left. It has minimally furnished, thin-walled, but reasonably clean doubles, or 4-bed dorms for $15 a bed, plus a communal kitchen and TV room, but no restaurant. As well as the occasional $5 barbecue, it runs its own cheap tours and beach excursions and can arrange discounts on car rental and even on air fares from other Hawaiian islands.

Royal Kona Resort, 75-5852 Ali'i Drive; ☎329-3111 or 1-800/774-5662 (US/ Canada); fax 329-9532; ⑤–⑦.
The gleaming white pyramids of the *Royal Kona Resort* (formerly the *Kona Hilton*), where each room has its own private balcony, dominate the headland at the southern limit of Kailua town, a few minutes' walk from the central malls. Its principal restaurant, the dinner-only *Lanai*, is renowned for its

All the properties listed here share the zip code Kailua-Kona HI 96740.

Hotels in this section are marked on the maps on pages 42 or 50.

Asian and Pacific cuisine, and the "Drums of Polynesia" *lū'au* (Mon, Tues, Fri & Sat; $51), open to non-residents, is one of the best in town.

The town

Central Kailua still retains something of the feel of a seaside village. Every visitor should set aside an hour or two to take a leisurely oceanfront stroll along the old Seawall, whose scenic route runs for a few hundred yards around the bay from the **Ahu'ena Heiau** to the **Hulihe'e Palace** and **Moku'aikaua Church**, jutting into the ocean in front of the *King Kamehameha* hotel.

At its heart is the jetty of **Kailua Pier**, a small expanse of asphalt popular with anglers, courting couples and surf bums. Until as recently as the 1960s there were still cattle pens on the pier. These days the mood tends to be slightly aimless, as most of the commercial boat operators – fishing charter vessels, snorkelling or whale-watching expeditions and so on – now leave from the larger and better-sheltered marina at Honokōhau Harbor, three miles north. Construction of a new information centre here may enliven things a little, and at least the time-honoured tradition of fishermen displaying their catches in the early evening still persists. The biggest fish of all usually weigh in during the International Billfish Tournament held each August, while more gleaming flesh is on show in October, when the pier is the starting point of the 2.4-mile swimming leg of the Ironman Triathlon (see p.33).

The resort area stretches away to the south. The higher you climb from the shoreline in modern Kailua, increasing numbers of malls appear each year, progressively catering more to the needs of local residents and less to those of tourists. Just to the north, Kailua's small industrial area is creeping farther up the coast, its expansion boosted by the arrival of several superstores.

Ahu'ena Heiau

The Ahu'ena Heiau is open daily 9am–4pm; free.

The **Ahu'ena Heiau**, guarding the mouth of Kailua Bay in a too-good-to-be-true setting beside a sandy little beach, looks as though it was built yesterday to provide an ersatz Polynesian backdrop for the *King Kamehameha* hotel. Few visitors spare it more than a passing glance, but this genuine Hawaiian temple, dedicated to the god Lono, deserves at least a few minutes of your attention. Kamehameha the Great held sway from a village focused on this shrine, between his return from Honolulu in 1812, and his death here on May 8, 1819. This was also the site where soon afterwards his son and heir Liholiho, spurred on by his mother Keopuolani and Kamehameha's principal queen, Ka'ahumanu, broke the ancient *kapu* system and thereby inadvertently cleared the way for the missionaries (see p.48).

As the *heiau* still possesses great spiritual significance, all access to the platform is forbidden. However, you can get a close-up view of it by walking to the end of the *King Kamehameha* beach – officially Kamakahonu Beach (see p.51) – or by swimming out a short way.

The *heiau* itself is small, but follows the conventional Hawaiian template, consisting of three distinct structures set on a platform (*paepae*) of black volcanic rock. The largest hut is the *hale mana* or "house of spiritual power", a place of prayer and council that also served as a schoolroom for the young Liholiho. The smaller *hale pahu*, "house of the drum", alongside, is thatched with leaves from the *hala* tree, while the ramshackle, strangely tapering structure nearby is the *anu'u*, or "oracle tower" used by the priests to intercede with the gods. In addition, half a dozen *ki'i akua*, carved wooden images symbolizing different gods, stand on the platform; the tallest, a god of healing known as Kōleamoku, has a golden plover on his head.

After his death, Kamehameha's bones were prepared for burial on a similar rock platform on the land adjacent to the *heiau*, then interred in a location that remains secret. The platform still exists, though the *hale iohaku* that stood upon it, in which the ceremonies took place, has long since disappeared.

Hulihe'e Palace

Though the four-square, two-storey **Hulihe'e Palace**, facing straight out to sea from the centre of Kailua, was built in 1838 as the residence of Governor John Adams Kuakini, it soon passed into the hands of the Hawaiian royal family. It was constructed using lava rock, coral and native hardwoods, though you wouldn't know that from a glance at its white-plastered exterior now. Visiting the palace, which is little more than a quaintish Victorian private residence, is not a very enthralling experience, nor is it helped by the ponderous reverence of the staff. The interior is notable mainly for its massive furnishings, made of wood from the *koa* tree to fit the considerable girth of such dignitaries as the four-hundred-pound Princess Ruth, while the bewhiskered King David Kalakua and his stately relatives are commemorated in countless fading photographs along the walls.

The Hulihe'e Palace is open daily except holidays 9am–4pm; $4.

The room immediately to the left of the entrance holds a small but interesting collection of ancient Hawaiiana, with bone fish hooks and stone adzes and hammers. Alongside a small cape made from yellow feathers and several wooden bowls, there's a narrow replica sled, once raced by the *ali'i*, down artificial slides made of rock carpeted with grass.

The master bedroom upstairs holds the King's mighty four-poster bed, a beautiful inlaid table and a colossal and highly ornate wardrobe, all fashioned from dark hardwood. The other bedroom is lighter and less formal, containing a child's crib, a collection of hats and a giant calabash gourd.

Pleasant *lānais* run the full length of the ocean side of both the first and second floors. Visitors are free to wander into the well-maintained gardens which, on the fourth Sunday of each month (except June & Dec), play host to free *hula* performances.

Moku'aikaua Church

The Moku'aikaua Church is open daily, dawn–dusk; free; congregational services Sun 8am & 10.30am.

Dating from 1820, the original **Moku'aikaua Church**, directly opposite the palace, was the first church to be built on the Hawaiian islands. At that time it closely resembled a traditional *heiau*, being no more than a thatched hut perched on a stone platform. The current building was erected immediately before the palace by the same craftsmen, using the same methods, and incorporates large chunks of lava into a design clearly related to the clapboard churches of New England.

The church itself is not of great interest, though part of it has been set aside as a museum of the early days of Hawaiian Christianity. Displays include a large model of the ship *Thaddeus*,

---

The Coming Of The Missionaries

The first organization to send missionaries to Hawaii was the Sandwich Islands Mission, which was formed largely as a result of the death of Henry 'Opukaha'ia. Having trained to become a *kahuna* (or Hawaiian priest) at the Hikiau *heiau* at Nāpo'opo'o in Kealakekua Bay (see p.66), he converted to Christianity and became a student of the Foreign Mission School in Cornwall, Connecticut. In 1818, when still in his early twenties, he caught typhus and, in his dying breath, lamented his failure to return to Hawaii to convert his benighted brethren.

Moved by the young man's untimely end, New England worthies provided heartfelt prayer and hard cash, enabling the mission's first two ministers, **Rev Hiram Bingham** and **Rev Asa Thurston**, to set sail from Long Wharf, Boston in the brig *Thaddeus*. Their 18,000-mile journey, via Cape Horn, started on October 23, 1819 and took more than five months, ending eventually in Kailua Bay on April 4, 1820.

Asa Thurston did not immediately take to Hawaii – he described Kailua as "a filthy village of thatched huts . . . on which the fervent sun poured its furnace heat every day of the year". But then, neither did the Hawaiians take to him, and there was considerable debate as to whether the missionaries should be permitted to land at all.

By coincidence, Thurston and Bingham arrived at a turning point in Hawaiian history, when **Queen Ka'ahumanu** had defied the all-pervasive *kapu* system and succeeded in breaking the hold of the priesthood. Therefore, when the missionaries arrived, the Hawaiian monarchy was reluctant to replace its previously powerful religious leaders with a new set of stern, moralizing clergy.

In the end, the counsel of the ageing John Young (see p.84) played a decisive role, but only Thurston was allowed to remain in Kailua. Bingham was obliged to settle in Honolulu, where, scurrilously known as "King Bingham", he took pleasure in denouncing his flock as the "stupid and polluted worshippers of demons". Liholiho never did quite take to the imposition of the new faith, but Ka'ahumanu became an enthusiastic promoter of Christianity after she was nursed through a grave illness by Bingham's wife Sybil.

See p.173 for the full story of how Queen Ka'ahumanu defeated the defenders of the old religion.

Hawaii's equivalent of the *Mayflower*, and an exhibition on traditional Polynesian navigational techniques featuring a fascinating Micronesian "stick chart", in which an intricate latticework of pandanus (*hala*) twigs and cowrie shells depicts ocean currents, swells and islands. Such charts were committed to memory rather than carried on board, and served to guide canoes across thousands of miles of the open Pacific.

Kailua

For more on Polynesian navigation, see Contexts, p.184.

A bizarre "sausage tree" grows in the grounds of the church. A native of Mozambique, it's named after the pendulous and foul-smelling elongated fruit that dangles on long cords from its branches. One of only two on Hawaii, it was planted here on a whim in the 1920s.

South along Ali'i Drive

Heading south from both the church and palace, **Ali'i Drive** is at first fringed with modern malls housing T-shirt stores, boutiques and restaurants. Beyond Kailua proper, the drive stretches five miles along a rugged coastline scattered with tiny lava beaches and lined all the way with hotels and condos. The only thing you could really call a "sight" along here is the tiny, blue, highly photogenic St Peter's Church, built in 1880; it takes perhaps a minute to admire its waterfront setting, on a tiny patch of lawn at the north end of Kahalu'u Bay, and glance in through the open door at the etched glass window above the altar.

The beaches along Ali'i Drive are described on p.51.

Beaches

Considering its reputation as a resort, central Kailua is surprisingly short of beaches. There are enough patches of sand along Ali'i Drive to satisfy families with young children, who like the convenience of being able to walk to and from their hotels, but most visitors tend to drive north when they fancy a swim. The Big Island's best beaches – such as the Kona Coast State Park (p.57), Hāpuna Beach (p.79), and Spencer Beach Park (p.81) – start a good ten miles or more up the coast, but a good nearby alternative is the Old Kona Airport park, just a few minutes from town.

Note that **camping** *is not permitted on any of the beaches covered in this section.*

Old Kona Airport State Recreation Area

When Keāhole airport opened in 1970, the lands of its predecessor on the northern outskirts of Kailua, which had become too small to meet the requirements of the tourist trade, were set aside for public use as the **Old Kona Airport State Recreation Area**.

This is now Kailua's most extensive and popular beach, although it's not as attractive as some of the island's other beaches. Driving in along the long former runways, which run parallel to the sea a few yards away, is either hair-raising or fun depending on your state of mind, as no one ever seems sure which, if any, of the plentiful road markings to follow.

The gates of the airport park are closed daily at 8pm to prevent night-time gatherings.

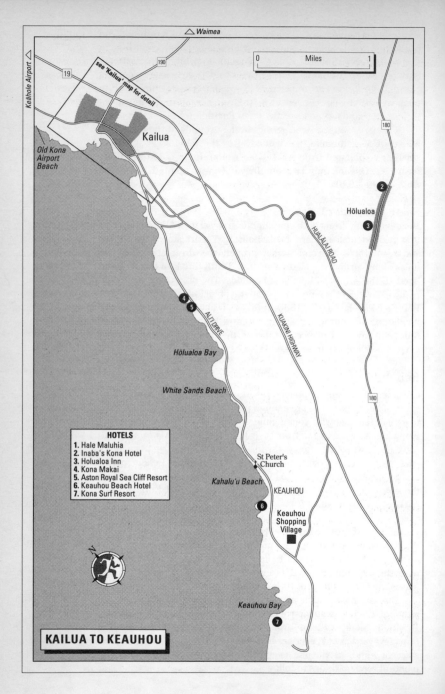

KAILUA TO KEAUHOU

HOTELS
1. Hale Maluhia
2. Inaba's Kona Hotel
3. Holualoa Inn
4. Kona Makai
5. Aston Royal Sea Cliff Resort
6. Keauhou Beach Hotel
7. Kona Surf Resort

A strip of fairly coarse, white-ish sand lies beyond the fringe of low palm trees, while the shoreline itself consists almost entirely of flat, smooth *pāhoehoe* lava, indented with calm shallow pools that are ideal for children to splash in. Sheltered pavilions and barbecue facilities are scattered all the way along and, despite the complete lack of food or drink outlets, there always seems to be plenty of locals and tourists around.

Kamakahonu Beach

Many first-time visitors to Kailua glance at pretty little **Kamakahonu Beach** – the name literally means "Eye of the Turtle" – and assume that it belongs to the *King Kamehameha* hotel. However, non-guests are entirely at liberty to sunbathe here, or swim out for a closer look at the Ahu'ena Heiau (see p.46). It can be a delightful spot, but you're not permitted to swim beyond the mouth of the tiny inlet, and in terms of size, calmness and crowds it often feels more like a swimming pool, so only small children are likely to want to linger for any length of time.

Ali'i Drive beaches

The coast along Ali'i Drive south of central Kailua is predominantly made up of black lava flats interspersed with the odd sandy cove. Very few of the hotels or condos have adjacent beaches, so the designated beach parks tend to be the only places it's possible to swim.

See p.30 for a list of operators who rent out snorkels and other beach equipment for use anywhere on the island.

If you visit in winter or early spring, you probably won't even be able to find the small **White Sands Beach Park**, immediately north of St Peter's Church (see p.49), four miles south of central Kailua. The dramatic waves that make this Kona's most exhilarating boogie-boarding and body-surfing beach are capable of washing it away altogether – hence the name by which it's more commonly known, **Magic Sands**. For most of the year, bathing is safe for children in the inshore area, while experienced divers can investigate a network of submarine lava tubes. So long as the beach is not devoid of sand, the snorkelling is superb, especially if you head off to the right.

The largest of the beaches along Ali'i Drive, and even better for snorkelling, is **Kahalu'u Beach Park**, just south of St Peter's Church. It's more of a slight indentation in the coastline than a bay, but that's enough for it to hang on to a fair-sized spread of white sand. Children play in the lava hollows to either side, snorkellers explore deeper but still sheltered pools, and strong swimmers and scuba divers use the shelving sand to access the open waters of the bay. Large segments remain of a long breakwater, which originally protected the whole area and was supposedly constructed by early Hawaiians – the *menehune* who, according to legend, were here long before the main Polynesian migration of the twelfth and thirteenth centuries – to aid fish-farming.

Generally this is a safe spot, but high surf conditions can create a devastating rip current. Don't venture into the water if you're in any doubt; if you get caught by the current, your best strategy, as ever, is to allow yourself to be swept out beyond its reach rather than exhaust yourself trying to fight it.

Restaurants

Thanks to its large numbers of visitors, Kailua is filled with **places to eat**, though it's surprisingly short of anything that could be considered fine dining. Each of its many malls has at least a couple of restaurants, while those that stand more than a block or so up from the ocean, such as the Lanihau Center, also house outlets of every imaginable fast-food chain. Asian cuisines, especially Thai, are strongly represented, and there are plenty of raucous heavy-drinking pseudo-Mexican options.

The restaurants along Ali'i Drive tend to be pricier, but most offer views of the bay and tend to serve slightly better quality food. Even along the waterfront, however, there are still some determinedly old-fashioned, inexpensive diners, such as the venerable *Ocean View*.

Inexpensive

Banana Bay Buffet Restaurant, *Kona Bay Hotel*, 75-5739 Ali'i Drive; ☎329-1393.
A palm-fringed and vaguely Polynesian open-air terrace, beside the pool of this central Kailua hotel, is the venue for plain but good value all-you-can-eat buffets, served in the morning and evening but not midday. The $4.95 breakfast is dished up Mon–Sat 7–11am and Sun sees a 7am–1pm $6.95 brunch; dinner is available nightly 5.30–9pm for $8.95.

Don Drysdale's Club 53, Kona Inn Shopping Village; ☎329-6651.
Predominantly a bar, but also serving an extensive and unimaginative range of nachos, chilis, wings, sandwiches and salads. A well-positioned if not exactly tranquil spot from which to watch the sun go down.

Island Lava Java Bakery & Bistro, Ali'i Sunset Plaza, 75-5799 Ali'i Drive; ☎327-2161.
Cafe/bakery facing the sea at the front of a new mall just south of central Kailua, with the shared use of some open-air tables. Open from early morning until late at night for delicious Kona coffee, plus exotic juices, fresh-baked breads, cookies, cakes and snacks. The perfect place for a light ocean-view breakfast or an after-dinner coffee; there's often live acoustic music – folk, blues, classical or Hawaiian – in the evening.

King Yee Lau, Ali'i Sunset Plaza, 75-5799 Ali'i Drive; ☎329-7100.
Large Chinese restaurant set back at the rear of this modern plaza, not far south of the *Kona Bay Hotel*. Most meat main courses, such as lemon chicken and crisp pressed duck, are $6–7, while sweet and sour *mahi-mahi* and other dishes cost slightly more. You can also get fresh lobster and crab, as well as budget lunch buffets.

Kona Mix Plate, Kopiko Plaza; ☎329-8104.
Very popular local Hawaiian-style diner, serving assorted daily specials, in one of Kailua's older shopping malls, a couple of blocks up from the sea. Dishes such as Korean chicken and mixed breaded seafood are around the $6 mark, various *teriyakis* and rice or noodle dishes are cheaper still. Open Mon–Sat, 10am–8pm.

Marty's Steak and Seafood, Kailua Bay Inn Shopping Plaza, Ali'i Drive; ☎329-1571.

Second-floor terrace restaurant in the centre of Kailua, with predictable steaks from $10 upwards. The assorted combos culminate in the Aloha Platter, at $66 for two people, which offers *sashimi*, crab, lobster, and shrimp followed by New York steak.

Ocean Seafood, King Kamehameha Mall, 75-5626 Kuakini Hwy; ☎329-3055.
Indoor Chinese dining in a small mall one block back from the sea, behind the *King Kamehameha* hotel. No views, and the food is served at plain glass-topped tables, but it's tasty and inexpensive: the weekday lunch buffet is $6.25, while set meals in the evening start around $10, as do the sizzling platters. Lots of shrimp and scallop dishes are on offer, as well as a small vegetarian selection.

Ocean View Inn, 75-5683 Ali'i Drive; ☎329-9988.
Old-style Hawaiian diner, facing the jetty on the *mauka* side of Ali'i Drive between the *King Kamehameha* hotel and Hulihe'e Palace, with magnificent views of the bay. Crowds flock for $8–12 dinner plates, plus breakfasts and lunches, and a wide range of good value sandwiches with fries, as well as all-day cocktails. Closed Mon. The attached *Hawaiian Angel*, up the stairs to the right of the entrance, serves espresso Kona coffee on a tiny open-air terrace if you don't want a full breakfast.

Pancho & Lefty's Cantina and Ristorante, Kona Plaza, 75-5719 W Ali'i Drive; ☎326-2171.
Lively Mexican place whose open-sided dining room runs the full length of the second floor of Kona Plaza. Breakfast specials and standard Mexican food throughout the day, though the lurid cocktails are what draw most of the evening crowd.

Rajun Cajun Grill, Kona Marketplace, W Ali'i Drive; ☎334-0615.
Simple open-air Cajun diner-cum-takeout, serving seafood gumbos and jambalayas in small and large portions. Open daily 11am–9pm.

The restaurants listed here are marked on the map on p.42

Reubens, Kona Plaza, 75-5719 W Ali'i Drive; ☎329-7031.
Mexican specialties served either on a sidewalk terrace or in an indoor dining room. In the evening, main dishes such as chicken *flautas* and *chiles rellenos* are around $8, but the same meals often appear as lunch specials, costing more like $5.

Ricos, Ali'i Sunset Plaza, 75-5799 Ali'i Drive; ☎885-0654.
Atmospheric and intimate Mexican restaurant in a modern mall a block or so beyond the *Kona Bay Hotel*; no sea views, but appealing red-check decor. For once the emphasis is more on eating than drinking, but the prices are still low; *tacos*, *tamales*, *tostadas* and *chimichangas* all cost $6–8, while mixed plates are a bit pricier.

Stan's Restaurant, 75-5685 Ali'i Drive; ☎329-4500.
Open-sided dining area, facing the sea in the centre of Kailua's most attractive stretch, next to the *Ocean View*. Serves full breakfasts, including Royal Hawaiian Hotcakes with banana, pineapple, papaya and coconut syrup, as well as an extensive dinner menu, featuring "Granny's 50-year Fish Recipe" and stuffed *mahi-mahi*.

Moderate

Bangkok Houses, King Kamehameha Mall, 75-5626 Kuakini Hwy; ☎329-7764.
Light and airy second-floor Thai restaurant where lunch (served Mon–Fri only) features $5 specials, plus slightly pricier fish and meat salads. Dinner, served nightly, includes a delicious mixed seafood curry, New Zealand mussels in spicy sauce, plus plenty of Thai curries prepared with and without coconut milk.

Basil's Pizzeria, 75-5707 Ali'i Drive; ☎329-4455.
Unadventurous Italian joint, immediately north of Moku'aikaua Church. Seated near the open doorway you can enjoy sea views; farther back there's

little to do but get your head down and eat the individual pizzas for $6–9, a variety of pasta dishes or tasty Italian daily specials.

Kona Amigos, 75-5669 Ali'i Drive; ☎326-2840.
Large, open-air deck, immediately opposite the *King Kamehameha* hotel. Serves a huge array of drinks, plus the usual reasonably priced Mexican dishes, including *chimichangas*, crab *enchiladas* and *fajitas*.

Kona Inn Restaurant, Kona Inn Shopping Village, 75-5744 Ali'i Drive; ☎329-4455.
Conventional waterfront fish place, with open-air *lanai* by the sea, and a plusher and more formal dining room inside. Clam chowder, *sashimi* and deep-fried oysters feature among the appetizers, while main courses – mostly assorted combinations of scampi, fresh fish and other seafood – cost around $15.

Su's Thai Kitchen *has another branch in Waimea; see p.88.*

Su's Thai Kitchen, 74-5588A Pawai Place; ☎326-7808.
Kailua's best Thai restaurant is hard to find, but also hard to beat. Not far from the centre, it's tucked away in the (light) industrial district behind the North Kona mall. Delicious Thai food served on an attractive and breezy (if view-less) *lanai*. Lunch (daily except Sun) features red or green curry specials for around $6. Dinner (served daily) includes Thai soups, Pad Thai noodles and plenty of vegetarian dishes for under $10.

Thai Rin, Ali'i Sunset Plaza, 75-5799 Ali'i Drive; ☎329-2929.
Smart, somewhat minimalist Thai restaurant, facing the sea in front of a modern mall, south of central Kailua towards *Huggo's*. Try satay or *poocha* (crab and pork patties) to start, for around $6, followed by one of the many Thai curries costing $7–10.

Expensive

Fisherman's Landing, Shipwreck Point, Kona Inn Shopping Village; ☎326-2555.
Modern, attractive waterfront restaurant, once a hotel, and entered via a bridge over a pool of carp. Dishes include fresh-caught Hawaiian fish prepared to your specification, or shrimp, scallop and other imported seafood, for around $15, plus Hawaiian Fried Ice Cream to round things off. The *Captain's Deck* alongside (same phone) serves simpler and cheaper fish dishes and sandwiches, as well as full breakfasts.

The restaurants listed here are marked on the map on p.42.

Huggo's, 75-5828 Kahakai St; ☎329-1493.
Large wooden *lanai* right on the ocean opposite *Snorkel Bob's* and next to the *Royal Kona Resort*. Lunch, served only on weekdays, includes salads, burger and sandwiches, all for around $6–8. The dinner menu, nightly until 10pm, features a range of Pacific-Rim cuisines, including fish stuffed with prawns, grilled lamb chops, and island-grown Maine lobster, all costing between $20–30. There's often live entertainment in the evenings, usually an easy-listening local band.

Kona Beach Restaurant, *King Kamehameha's Kona Beach Hotel*, 75-5660 Palani Rd; ☎329-2911.
This completely enclosed, not very atmospheric dining room does daily breakfast specials for just $1.99. Lunch and dinner cost in the region of $16–20 for most main courses, such as Alaskan King Crab legs, steaks and prime rib. There's a $16 seafood buffet on Friday and Saturday nights, and Sunday's $20 champagne brunch buffet, served 9am–1pm, is the best meal of the week; alternatively, for around $50, you could treat yourself to a place at the *lū'au* on Sun, Tues, Wed or Thurs (see p.45).

Kuakini Terrace, *Keauhou Beach Hotel*, 78-6740 Ali'i Drive; ☎322-3441.
Pleasant, partly open-air hotel dining room, best known for its copious $13 all-you-can-eat Chinese buffets (Mon–Thurs 5–9pm) and the spectacular $20 spread of seafood (Fri–Sun 5–9pm). You can also choose from a full *à la carte* menu, on which the standard of preparation is a bit more reliable.

Shopping

Generally speaking, there's little to chose between the individual malls, but as a rule those closer to the sea tend to be more firmly geared towards tourists, with the predictable array of T-shirts, sun hats, postcards and sundry souvenirs on sale, and the odd *ABC* convenience store thrown in. For everyday shopping and services, locals tend to head for *Costco* or *Kmart*, on the northeastern edge of town, or the **Lanihau Center** near the main stoplights on the highway.

As well as being the current Kailua base of the *Hawaii Visitors Bureau* (see p.43), **Kona Plaza Shopping Arcade**, near Moku'aikaua church, is home to the *Middle Earth Bookshoppe*, with its copious selection of Hawaiiana; *Hawaiian Island Gems* with its gold and silver marine mammals; and a *Lapperts Ice Cream* outlet. The larger **Kona Marketplace**, immediately south, has a two-screen movie theatre, plus more galleries and jewellery stores, trinket shops such as the *Eclectic Craftsmen* and *Incredible*, and the *Kona Flea Market*.

Across Ali'i Drive on the seafront, **Kona Inn Shopping Village**, the largest and most tourist-oriented of all, has ranks including several clothing stores and the self-explanatory *Big Island Hat Company* and *Bag Man*.

Perched above the sea at the far southern end of Ali'i Drive, the modern **Keauhou Shopping Village** centres on a *KTA* superstore. It also houses a post office, the *Keauhou Village* bookstore, a *Kona Kai* coffee bar, and a couple of pizza and sandwich places.

Big Island bookstores are listed on p.189, and music stores on p.187.

La Bourgogne, Kuakini Plaza S, 77-6400 Nalani St #101; ☎329-6711.
Intimate and authentically French restaurant with a high reputation, three miles south of Kailua on Hwy-11. Appetizers include snails, baked brie, French onion or lobster soup and extortionately priced *pâté de foie gras*; among the main courses are scallops, fresh fish, *filet mignon* and saddle of lamb with garlic and rosemary, all in the $20–30 region. Open for dinner only, Mon–Sat 5.30–10pm.

Palm Café, Coconut Grove Marketplace, 75-5819 Ali'i Drive; ☎329-7765.
Sophisticated, pleasant restaurant, with clear views of the bay, serving its own eclectic and highly inventive blend of Pacific cuisines. Typical appetizers include blackened *ahi* or Waimea green salads, for $5–7, and each day there's a choice of fish specials with ginger, Thai spices, tropical fruits, or other Asian or Polynesian ingredients. Open for dinner only, 5.30–10pm.

Seafood Pasta Palace, Waterfront Row, 75-5770 Ali'i Drive; ☎329-4436.
Oceanfront open-deck pasta restaurant, in a modern mall to the south of central Kailua. Full breakfasts and a lunch menu of $6 pizzas or all-you-can-eat pasta, plus sandwiches, salads and daily specials. There are no pizzas in the evening, but a full range of fresh fish prepared in different ways and served with pasta marinara, for around $20.

Sushi Bar, Waterfront Row, 75-5770 Ali'i Drive; ☎326-5653.
Classic sushi bar, where you eat at a long counter, so there are no views and you're not expected to linger. The food is good, but expensive; individual *sushi* rolls cost around $5, while a Sushi Combination is $19.50. Closed Sun.

North Kona

Until the 1970s, it was barely possible to travel overland along the coast north of Kailua – and few people had any reason to do so. Then

North Kona

Queen Ka'ahumanu Highway, Hwy-19, was laid across the lava, serving the new airport and granting access to previously remote beaches. Many of these were swiftly engulfed by plush resorts – especially in the South Kohala district (see p.72) – but with the road running on average a mile in from the ocean, the beaches remain occasional, distant bursts of greenery in an otherwise desolate landscape. North of Honokōhau's boat harbour and the airport, there is little in Kona to lure you off the highway. Unless you're a guest you're unlikely to notice the *Kona Village Resort*, while the **Kona Coast State Park** houses perhaps the least spoiled beach on the island but lies at the far end of a deliberately difficult dirt road.

Despite the huge sums spent on all this construction, Big Island tourism is still not on the scale that was originally envisaged. As a result, the highway system is unusual for Hawaii in that it's more than adequate to handle the volume of traffic. The one potential hazard for drivers is posed by the unpredictable "Kona Nightingales", scrawny descendants of the donkeys that once hauled loads to and from the shoreline, which roam wild across the barren slopes.

Honokōhau Harbor

You'll find more details of Honokōhau Harbor boat operators, plus other Big Island activities, on p.30.

A couple of miles north of Kailua, a short avenue leads down to narrow **HONOKŌHAU HARBOR**, which provides safe moorings for the town's pleasure boats while leaving the jetty in Kailua itself free from congestion.

This is a functional rather than a decorative place, and the only reason for coming here is to take one of the many boat trips which leave from the far end of the quay. The most appealing spot to sit and watch the proceedings is the open-air deck of the *Harbor House* (Mon–Sat 11am–7pm, Sun 11am–5.30pm; ☎326-4166), a bar-cum-restaurant in the central Kona Marina complex. To its left is a line of fishing charter vessels, beyond which an information kiosk details the different expeditions available, together with a deli selling snacks, sandwiches and drinks.

If you have an hour or two to kill before or after an excursion, a small secluded sandy beach, ideal for snorkellers, can be reached by hiking south for ten minutes across the lava, while a five-minute walk around to the north of the harbour brings you out at the southern access to the Kaloko-Honokōhau National Historic Park.

Kaloko-Honokōhau National Historic Park

Kaloko-Honokōhau Park is open daily 9am–3pm; free; ☎329-6881.

The **KALOKO-HONOKŌHAU NATIONAL HISTORIC PARK**, north of the harbour and south of the airport, was established in 1978 to preserve one of the state's last surviving natural wetlands. Despite being administered by the National Park Service, it remains almost entirely undeveloped, and the goal of re-creating ancient techniques of aquaculture and farming, protecting endangered Hawaiian water birds, and returning the area to its pre-contact appearance, seems as distant as ever. What few human visitors it attracts are usually, like the birds, here to fish, and it will probably disappoint anyone other than naturalists.

Even the entrance is almost impossible to find, via a barely discernable driveway on the *makai* side of the highway between mileposts 96 and 97. The rough track down ends beside the tranquil Kaloko Fishpond, sealed off from the ocean by a massive stone wall which is now popular with anglers. The wetlands stretch away from the seafront picnic area, while a coastal footpath leads south to Honokōhau Harbor via the 'Aimakapa Fishpond. You can also walk in from the southern end, having driven as far as possible round to the right-hand side of Honokōhau Harbor.

Scattered across the mostly trackless expanse of the park are several *heiaus*, of which the least ruined is the Pu'uoina, as well as a *hōlua* ("land-surfing") slide and fields of petroglyphs. Descendants of Kamehameha the Great took pains to reserve this area for themselves, which suggests that one of its countless caves may still hold his bones.

Kona Coast State Park

One of the Big Island's least known but most beautiful beaches, designated not long ago as the **KONA COAST STATE PARK**, lies a couple of miles north of Keāhole airport. Once again, you need to keep your eyes peeled to spot the driveway, and then be prepared to bump your vehicle for 1.5 miles over rippling *pāhoehoe* lava, on a virtually unsurfaced track.

The Kona Coast State Park is open daily except Wed, 9am–8pm; free.

At the bottom of the track, there's a parking lot; from its *mauka* end take the obvious path which sets off northwards across 200 yards of bare lava towards a dense grove of coconut palms. When you come to a single portable toilet, you can either cut in through the trees to reach the beach directly, or follow the path round until it emerges in the middle of a perfect horseshoe-shaped bay. All around you is an exquisite beach of coarse golden sand, lightly flecked with specks of black lava – what the locals call "salt and pepper" sand. Each of the headlands jutting to either side is a spur of rougher '*ā'ā* lava, topped with its own clump of palms. Immediately behind the beach is the looming bulk of Hualālai, and at this point Mauna Kea becomes visible far inland, as does Haleakalā across the sea on Maui. The calm waters of the bay itself provide sheltered swimming, local surfers ride the tumbling waves offshore, and divers burrow their way into submarine caves and tunnels.

As yet Kona Coast State Park has no food and drink facilities for day users, and is closed at night and on Wednesdays, although it seems to be being groomed as a sort of substitute for the recently developed Hāpuna Beach farther north. The only **accommodation** in the vicinity is well up from the highway, at the *Three Bears B&B*

North Kona   (72-1001 Pu'u Kala, Kailua-Kona HI 96740; ☎ and fax 325-7563 or 1-800/765-0480; ④), which offers comfortable en-suite rooms set in bright ocean-view gardens.

Kona Village Resort

PO Box 1299, Kailua-Kona HI 96745; ☎325-5555, 1-800/367-5290 (US) or 1-800/432-5450 (HI); fax 325-5124; ⑨.

If you cherish a fantasy of undisturbed days in a paradise where your every whim is anticipated – and have unlimited funds – then your best bet is to stay at the *Kona Village Resort*, the oldest of the Big Island's luxury resorts. Supposedly it's a re-creation of the Polynesian past, but its main appeal is that it bears so little relation to reality of any kind.

Set in the black desertscape five miles north of the airport, the resort consists of 125 thatched South Pacific-style *hales*, or huts, most of which are surrounded by bright flowers. The huts have no phones, TVs, or radios, but each has a private *lanai*, a hammock and even an alarm clock that wakes you up by grinding fresh coffee beans. Beach gear, such as masks, fins and even kayaks is provided free for guests and scuba equipment and instruction is also available.

The daily rates of $390–680 include all meals at the *Hale Moana* and *Hale Samoa* restaurants; for non-residents a five-course dinner at the *Hale Moana* costs $54 and consists of a seafood appetizer, soup, salad, and fresh fish prepared to your exact specification. Most outsiders visit on *lū'au* nights, Monday and Friday, when $63 buys an atmospheric beachside feast plus Polynesian entertainment; advance reservations are essential.

The resort sits on the sandy **Ka'ūpūlehu beach**, which is superb for snorkelling; stately turtles cruise by and manta rays billow in at night. Anyone can visit this isolated beach; although the resort's security guards do their best to discourage non-residents, don't be put off – everyone has right of access.

A more conventional hotel, the *Four Seasons*, has been under construction for several years on land adjoining the *Kona Village Resort*. Work was greatly delayed when archeologists discovered that the hotel was being built on the site of an ancient *heiau*; by the time court proceedings allowed the project to recommence, work had to start again from scratch, as the existing foundations had rusted away.

South Kona

South of Kailua and Keauhou, the Belt Road, now called **Hwy-11**, sets off on its loop around the island by rising away from the sea, to run through attractive verdant uplands. Trees laden with avocados, mangos, oranges and guavas stand out from the general greenery, and the route is characterized by the blossom of coffee bushes and the occasional aroma of the mills.

Kealakekua Bay, along the south Kona coast, is where Captain Cook chose to anchor, as it was the best harbour and the main population centre on the island. However, within a century the seafront slopes were largely abandoned, and these days even the area higher up is inhabited only by a sparse scattering of old-time farmers and New-Age newcomers. Most tourists scurry through as they head to and from the volcanoes, put off perhaps by the lack of beaches and the uninviting look of the small towns that sprawl along the highway. However, many of these hold one or two welcoming local cafés or intriguing stores, and it's certainly worth dropping down to visit the restored **Pu'uhonua o Hōnaunau**, the "Place of Refuge" that once offered sanctuary to fleeing *kapu*-breakers.

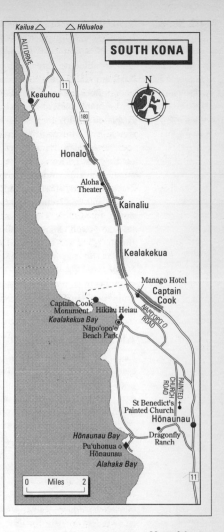

Hōlualoa

HŌLUALOA, the first and nicest of the coffee-growing towns, stands well above the Belt Road, scarcely three miles out of Kailua, and feels a long way removed from the hurly-burly below. This sleepy village consists of a single quiet road (Hwy-180) that meanders across the flanks of Hualālai, 1400 feet up from the ocean, and is lined on either side with small galleries and workshops, as well as orchards brimming with tropical blooms.

The production of **art** in Hōlualoa remains essentially a cottage industry, though more galleries open each year and several now also display pieces by mainland artists. Prices are not low and the place is geared more towards selling to tourists than *kama'āinas*. Nonetheless, half a day can enjoyably be spent admiring the prints and paintings of the *Kim Starr Gallery*, the furniture and woodcarvings in the *County Frame Shop* and the general creative free-for-all that is the *Coffee Mill Workshop*, also known as the *Kona Arts Center*.

Most of the galleries and workshops in Hōlualoa are closed on Saturday afternoons and Sundays (some take Mondays off as well).

North Kona

The accommodation in Hōlualoa is marked on the Kailua to Keahou map, on p.50.

Practicalities

Accommodation possibilities in the village include *Inaba's Kona Hotel* (PO Box 342, Hōlualoa HI 96725; ☎324-1155; ①), a rusty relic of bygone days, whose Japanese owners let out extremely basic single, double and twin rooms at low prices. More salubrious accommodation is available lower down the hill, on the ocean side of the main road, at the exquisite *Holualoa Inn B&B* (PO Box 322, Holualoa HI 96725; ☎324-1121; 2-night min; ④). Reservations are essential if you want to savour its tasteful guest rooms, Japanese-style open-plan living room and the incredible views, looking down on the rest of Kona from the crow's-nest seating area on top of a small central wooden tower. There's another B&B, the *Hale Maluhia* (76-770 Hualalai Rd, Kailua-Kona HI 96740; ☎329-5773; 1-800/559-6627; fax 326-5487; ③–④), on the minor road back down to Kailua. Guests stay in individual cottages, of varying standards and capable of sleeping up to six, on a large garden estate that has its own stream and waterfalls.

At the top end of the village, the friendly German-owned *Holuakoa Cafe* (Mon–Sat 6.30am–5pm) serves **coffees and snacks**, such as spinach or curry pasties, in a pleasant garden with a relaxed ambience. On Thursday evenings it also opens from 7pm until 10pm for live music.

Along Hwy-11: the coffee towns

In theory there are four separate towns within the first four miles south of the junction of Hwy-180 and Hwy-11, though where one ends and the next begins is far from obvious. Any points of interest can be easily spotted as you drive through, be they wayside coffee stalls, antiquated general stores, local diners or simply junkyards.

If you want to sample the atmosphere, the best stop comes just south of tiny Honalo, in the shape of **KAINALIU**'s friendly *Aloha Café* (open Mon–Sat 8am–8pm, Sun 9am–2pm; ☎322-9924). Housed in the lobby of the 1930s *Aloha Theater* – still an active community theatre, with performances by local groups and visiting musicians, and occasional movie shows – this all-day town forum serves coffees, snacks, fresh-baked pastries and a limited dinner menu.

The Kona Historical Society Museum is open Mon–Fri 9am–3pm, alternate Saturdays 10am–2pm; admission by donation.

To the south of Kainaliu, set back from the highway in a century-old former general store in **KEALAKEKUA**, is the **Kona Historical Society Museum**. This low-key assortment of photographs and family heirlooms documents Kona's history from the perspective of its immigrant farmers, but time is probably better spent sitting in the *Kona Kai Café* (81-6739 S Kona Belt Rd; ☎323-2115), watching growers come in to sell sacks of raw "cherry" and drinking the freshest coffee you're ever likely to taste. The only other reason to visit Kealakekua – as distinct from Kealakekua Bay, down below – is to hire horses from the barn-like headquarters of the *King's Trail Rides* (see below).

Kona Coffee

Succulent, strong-smelling **Kona coffee** – one of the world's most highly prized gourmet coffees – has been grown on the Kona coast ever since 1828, when the first seedlings arrived from Brazil. Strictly speaking, the Kona name only applies to beans grown between the 800ft and 2000ft elevations on the western slopes of Hualālai and Mauna Loa – a narrow strip that extends roughly from Hōlualoa to Hōnaunau. Here the combination of bright, sunny mornings, humid, rainy afternoons and consistently mild nights, create perfect greenhouse conditions for the colourful tropical plants to flourish.

Kona boasts an enviable reputation, and demand always outstrips supply, but coffee-growing is an unpredictable business, with prices forever subject to the vagaries of the world commodity market. Large corporations have long tended to leave the labour-intensive processes of planting and tending the coffee bushes, and harvesting the ripe red "cherry" from the intricate tangle of branches, to small-scale family concerns. The total area under cultivation in Kona is now only 1300 acres, although in recent years the predominantly Japanese farmers have been joined by an influx of back-to-the-land *haoles*.

Independent Kona farmers are currently campaigning to obtain a federal patent to restrict use of the word "Kona" only to coffee consisting of one hundred percent pure Kona beans. That would supercede a Hawaiian state law that allows any coffee containing at least ten percent of Kona-grown beans to be sold as Kona coffee; and it would threaten the profits of the mainly Californian bulk buyers who use a smattering of Kona beans to improve the flavour of lesser coffees. Such misleading "blends" are far more widely available – even on the Big Island – than the real thing, and sell at inflated prices despite packing a fraction of the punch of the undiluted Kona bean.

Roadside outlets in the "coffee belt" along highways 11 and 180 serve fresh Kona coffee in whatever form may take your fancy – as *espressos*, *cappucinos* or *lattes*, flavoured with vanilla or macadamia nuts, the list is endless. In addition, visitors are welcome at working farms such as Hōnaunau's **Langenstein Farm**, between mile markers 104 and 105 on Hwy-11 (visits by appointment; ☎328-8356); the **Bay View Farm**, off the highway nearby half a mile north of the Painted Church (daily 9am–5pm; free; ☎328-9658 or 1-800/662-5880); and the **Old Hawaiian Coffee Plantation**, reached via a one-track rutted road 400 yards from marker 105 outside the town of Captain Cook. On the road down to Napoʻopoʻo Beach, the **Mauna Loa Royal Kona Coffee Mill and Museum** (daily 9am–5pm; free), is run by *C Brewer*, one of Hawaii's original "Big Five". The story of coffee cultivation in Kona is illustrated here by old photos and a short video, and they give away small paper cups of long-brewed coffee.

Coffee prices range from around $11 per pound for the lowest ("prime") grade up to as much as $20 for the gourmets' favourite Peaberry. You can also buy mail-order through *Coffee Times* (PO Box 1092, Captain Cook, HI 96704; ☎326/7637 or 1-800/750-KONA).

Captain Cook

The town of **CAPTAIN COOK** lies just past the point where the minor road down to Kealakekua Bay branches off the highway. It is noteworthy primarily as the site of the long-established *Manago Hotel*

(PO Box 145, Captain Cook, HI 96704; ☎323-2642; ①–②), whose wooden facade dominates what there is of a town centre. Established around eighty years ago by the Japanese Manago family, it offers some of the best-value, most "Hawaiian" lodging on the island. The cheapest rooms share a bathroom and have minimal facilities, but all the rooms in the newer three-storey motel-like building at the back face the ocean, with the rates rising floor by floor; there's also one special deluxe Japanese room. Each of the faintly musty conventional suites has a small *lanai*, a strong hot shower and a period-piece radio, but no phone. The hotel's great appeal is its views of lush gardens, the hillside beyond sloping down until the *pali* suddenly drops away, and the shoreline stretching away south.

The *Manago*'s panelled dining room (Tues–Thurs 7.30am–7.30pm, Fri–Sun 5–7pm only) is pretty much the social centre of Captain Cook, coooled by whirring ceiling fans and breezes wafting up from the bay. A full breakfast costs $4, and the highlight of the simple lunch and dinner menu is the lightly breaded pork chops, of which you get a couple for $7.50.

Kealakekua Bay

For a full account of the last days of Captain Cook and the legends surrounding his death, see p.64.

KEALAKEKUA BAY may be familiar because of Captain Cook's fatal encounter with the rulers of old Hawaii – as well as the *Little Grass Shack* of the song – but it's a surprisingly inaccessible spot. Very few visitors make it as far as the actual site of Cook's death, on the north shore of the bay, and most of those who see the obelisk to the navigator's memory do so from the south side, across a mile of shark-infested sea. **Nāpo'opo'o** here is the only point that can be reached by car; to see the bay otherwise, you either have to undertake a strenuous hike, or come by boat.

The name Kealakekua, which means "pathway of the god", refers to the five-hundred-foot cliff that backs the sheltered crescent bay. It was said that this *pali*, which slopes down from north to south, was used as a slide by the god Lono when he needed to leave his mountain home in a hurry. When Cook was here, around 80,000 Hawaiians are thought to have lived on the coastal lava plain that extends to the north and south. Though the mummified bodies of their chiefs, and possibly that of Cook as well, remain entombed in lava-tunnel "caves" high on the cliff face, all that remains below are overgrown walls and ruined *heiaus*.

Tentative plans have been put forward to restore the area around Cook's monument as a state park, but at present only the waters of the bay itself are formally protected. As a Marine Life Conservation District, it offers some of the best snorkelling on the island.

Walking to the bay

Walking down to Kealakekua Bay – or, more accurately, back up again – is a serious undertaking, though well worth it for keen

Kealekekua on horseback

Four-wheel-drive vehicles are out of the question on the narrow track down to Kealakekua Bay, and the only alternative to walking is to go on **horseback**. Individual or group trips can be arranged, with advance notice, through *King's Trail Rides O Kona*, based at mile marker 111 in Kealakekua (PO Box 1366, Kealakekua HI 96750; ☎323-2388). The cost for the enjoyable half-day round trip is around $90 per person.

hikers. With no facilities at the bottom, not even water, you have to carry everything you need, and allow a total walking time of at least four hours for the round trip.

The unmarked trail starts a mere hundred yards down the Nāpo'opo'o road, which leaves Hwy-11 a quarter-mile before Captain Cook. First take a dirt road that drops to the right, and then keep going straight when that road veers off to the right within a couple of hundred yards. A rutted track, fringed with bright purple and red flowers, continues down for about a mile through open pastureland and avocado orchards. Eventually the vegetation thins out and you find yourself on very exposed black lava fields, picking your way over jagged rocks. You should avoid climbing this stretch in the baking midday sun.

From this high vantage point you can discern the worn path of the old King's Trail that once encircled the entire island, paved with river-rounded boulders carried down the hillside by toiling commoners. The trail you're on is the former county road, shored up in places following landslides; it drops abruptly from here onwards.

Ka'awaloa and the Captain Cook Monument

Safely back on level ground at the foot of the hill, the path pushes its way into a tangle of scrubby undergrowth. Soon, half submerged by twisted pandanus trees and low vegetation, you can make out the solid black walls that delineate the homesteads of the long-vanished Hawaiian village of **KA'AWALOA**. Somewhere in the village stood the house of the high chief Kalaniopu'u, whose attempted kidnapping by Captain Cook precipitated the final drama of Cook's life (see overleaf).

The trail reaches the waterfront at the precise spot where Cook died; a small bronze **plaque** reposes in a rocky pool under a couple of inches of water. Fifty yards away to the left, on what is legally a small patch of England, stands the better-known white marble **obelisk**, 27 feet high, that was raised to Cook's memory in 1884. Visiting ships, especially from Commonwealth countries such as Australia and Great Britain, traditionally set their own small plaques in the cement at its base. An equally well-established tradition is for such plaques to be prised away by souvenir hunters, which is why the most interesting ones, together with all earlier memorials to Cook, have long since disappeared.

South Kona

The death of Captain Cook

When Captain James Cook sailed into Kealakekua Bay on January 17, 1779, he was on his second visit to the Hawaiian islands, on his way home after a year spent searching in vain for the fabled Northwest Passage. His ship, the *Resolution*, had circled the Big Island for seven weeks, trading with canoes that came alongside but not allowing anyone ashore. Finally Cook anchored in this sheltered bay, where a vast crowd of Hawaiians had gathered to greet him. For three weeks, he was feasted by chief Kalaniopu'u and his priests, attending temple ceremonies and replenishing his supplies.

The departure of the *Resolution*, amid declarations of friendship, might have been the end of things, had it not been forced to return just a week later, following a violent storm. This time the islanders were not so hospitable and far from keen to part with further scarce resources. On February 14, Cook led a landing party of nine men in a bid to kidnap Kalaniopu'u and try to force the islanders to return a stolen small boat. In an undignified scuffle, surrounded by thousands of hostile warriors including the future Kamehameha the Great, Cook was **stabbed** and died at the water's edge. His body was treated as befits a dead chief; the skull and leg bones were kept, and the rest cremated (though supposedly his heart was eaten by children who mistook it for a dog's).

The **interpretation** of Cook's death has always been surrounded by controversy. It became widely believed by Europeans that the Hawaiians had taken Cook to be the great god Lono. The legend goes that, by chance, Cook had arrived at the temple of the god Lono at the height of the Makahiki festival and the billowing sails of the *Resolution* were taken to be Lono's emblems, while the ship itself was believed to be the floating island of tall trees on which Lono was expected to voyage around Hawaii.

This story, however, is based very much on a *European* view of Cook and of primitive people in general, rather than on Polynesian perceptions of the man. The European mentality of the time assumed that a noble figure of the Enlightenment such as Cook must appear god-like to the superstitious "natives". His voyage was perceived by the British as bringing civilization and order to heathen lands, while Cook saw himself as a stern father forever having to chastise the islanders who were his "insolent" children. His last recorded words are "I am afraid that these people will oblige me to use some violent measures; for they must not be left to imagine that they have gained an advantage over us". Cook would have been shocked had he realized that the Hawaiians surmised that "Brittanee" must be suffering from a severe famine, judging by the hunger of its sailors.

While Cook may have wanted to be seen as the representative of a superior civilization and creed, to Pacific islanders his superiority was largely a matter of **fire power**. A common theme in European contacts with the peoples of Polynesia is the attempt to draw well-armed foreigners into local military conflicts. Ironically, Cook had sailed away from Tonga in 1777, having named it one of "the Friendly Islands", without ever knowing that in doing so he had narrowly avoided a plot to kill him and seize his ships. Similarly, the elaborate ceremonies at Hikiau Heiau in Kealakekua Bay (see p.66), during which Cook was obliged to prostrate himself before an image of the god Kū, can be interpreted as an attempt to incorporate him into the *kapu* system (see p.180) as a man of equal ranking with the high chiefs. This would have enabled Kalaniopu'u to seek Cook's aid in the imminent renewal of hostilities with Maui.

The process of **myth-making** draws on many sources. For example, the supposed "Hawaiian" legend that the god Lono was due to return may owe more to the English desire to make Cook into a hero to rival the Spanish *conquistador* Hernan Cortés, said to have been seen as the returning Quetzalcoatl by the Aztecs of Mexico. Furthermore, annual celebration of the Makahiki festival in the form described may only have been instigated by Kamehameha twenty years later.

The major anomaly in the Cook-as-Lono legend is quite why the Hawaiians would have killed this "god". Some proponents say it was a ritual sacrifice, while others argue that the man who struck the final blow had only just arrived from upcountry, and "didn't know". The usual explanation, that it was simply an accident, serves both to perpetuate the idea of Hawaiians as "innocent" savages, and to absolve Cook himself of any responsibility for his fate. Though the British version of the dismantling of Hikiau Heiau has the priests eager to co-operate in return for iron trinkets, other sources, including Hawaiian tradition, have Cook's peremptory behaviour seen as outrageous, sacreligious enough to merit his death. That suggests that while Cook might have appeared a valuable potential ally to the chiefs, the priests and commoners viewed him as a blasphemer; and when he antagonized the chiefs by seizing Kalaniopu'u, deference gave way to defiance.

Snorkellers from the cruise boats will probably ensure that you don't have the place to yourself, although they're not allowed to leave the water. Kayakers, however, tend to use the surround of the monument as a convenient place to haul in their vessels. As there's no proper beach, it's also the easiest launching point if you want to snorkel yourself.

Fifty yards farther along the coast towards the cliff, look out for the inconspicuous **Queen's Pool**. This spring-fed pool of slightly brackish fresh water, originally lined with gentle river rocks and sealed off from the ocean, makes an ideal spot to rinse off after a swim.

Kealakekua Bay Marine Life Conservation District

The whole of Kealakekua Bay has been designated by the state of Hawaii as an **underwater state park**, to protect its varied stocks of multi-hued fish. Much of it is very deep, as the sheer *pali* simply drops beneath the surface of the ocean. The shallowest and most sheltered spot is in the immediate area of Captain Cook's monument, where the reef provides perfect conditions for snorkellers. Swarms of intensely yellow butterfly fish and tangs, plus parrotfish, triggerfish and hundreds of other species, can always be found circling near the edge.

For centuries, this area has been a favourite haunt of **"spinner" porpoises**. Marine biologists have yet to explain why, but the porpoises gather here in schools of up to a hundred individuals to

Kealakekua Snorkel Cruises

Snorkelling cruises to Kealakekua Bay are among the most popular
tourist activities on the Big Island, so much so that the number of visitors
who can enter the marine conservation district each day is strictly limited.
The going rate is around $55–65 for the standard four-hour trip, including
some form of food plus use of basic snorkelling equipment. By shopping
around Kona-side activity centres a few days in advance you may be able
to get the price down to below $50. If possible, choose a boat that starts
from Keauhou, as this gives you more time at Kealakekua and a shorter
journey. Note that passengers are forbidden to set foot ashore, so
snorkelling must be your priority.

The following operators run two trips daily:

Captain Cook VI (☎329-6411). Luxury glass-bottom motor yacht,
leaving Kailua Pier at 8.30am and 1.30pm.

Fair Wind (☎322-2788). This large catamaran sails from Keauhou Pier at
9am (4hr 30min) and 1.45pm (3hr 30min).

while away the afternoons by arching in and out of the water. Mark
Twain described them as "like so many well-submerged wheels", but
they do vary their routines by rotating on their own axes and even
flipping the occasional somersault. At the end of the day, they head
out once more to the open sea, to feed on the deep-water fish that
come to the surface at night.

Nāpo'opo'o Beach County Park

To drive to the south shore of Kealakekua Bay, follow the road
down from just before Captain Cook as it twists for four miles
around the great *pali*. It comes to an end in the small, usually
crowded, parking lot of NĀPO'OPO'O BEACH COUNTY PARK.

Until recently Nāpo'opo'o was a reasonably pleasant beach, but
virtually all its sand has now been whipped away, a process started
by Hurricane Dot in 1959 and completed by Hurricane Iniki in
1992. The snorkelling remains as good as ever, once you've eased
across the rocks at the water's edge; there are more fish on the far
side, near the monument, but you may be swimming with the sharks
for a mile to get there.

Immediately beside the parking lot rise the stout black-lava tiers
of the **Hikiau Heiau**, the temple where Captain Cook was formally
received in January 1779. During a baffling ceremony that lasted
several hours, he was fed putrefied pig, had his face smeared with
chewed coconut and was draped with red *tapa* cloth. Shortly
afterwards, it was also the site of the first Christian service on the
islands – the funeral of William Whatman, an elderly member of
Cook's crew who died of a stroke.

Nothing remains of the structures that once stood on the
platform; in fact, Cook may well have precipitated his own death by
ordering the dismantling of the wooden palings that surrounded it,
for use as firewood.

Pu'uhonua O Hōnaunau National Historical Park

A featureless road runs south from Nāpo'opo'o for four miles, across the scrubby coastal flatlands, before meeting another road down from the main highway. The two converge at the entrance to **PU'UHONUA O HŌNAUNAU**, the single most evocative historical site in all the Hawaiian islands.

This small peninsula of jagged black lava, jutting out into the Pacific, holds the preserved and restored remains of a royal palace, complete with fish pond, beach and private canoe landing, plus three *heiaus*, guarded by large carved effigies of gods. However, it's most famous for the *pu'uhonua* sanctuary that lies firmly protected behind the mortarless masonry of its sixteenth-century Great Wall.

Pu'uhonua O Hōnaunau park is open daily 7.30am–5.30pm; $4 per vehicle or $2 per person. US National Park passes, such as the $25 Golden Eagle passport (see p.32 for further details) are both sold and valid.

Visiting the park

Visits to the Pu'uhonua O Hōnaunau, which was declared a National Historical Park in 1961, start at the small information desk at the far end of the parking lot. A schedule of daily talks by rangers is posted, while immediately to the right are three large, informative wall panels.

Next you descend along paved walkways through the black lava field, into a grove of rustling giant palms. Here an assortment of reconstructed houses stand on individual lava platforms, ranging from small tent-like shelters for storage to the larger houses of the *ali'i* (chiefs). To one side is a perfect small sandy beach that once served as the royal canoe landing. Picnicking, sunbathing and smoking are all forbidden here, though swimming and snorkelling are permitted. Away to the left is the King's Fishpond, as placid as a hotel swimming

---

Cities of Refuge

Pu'uhonuas used to be known as "Cities of Refuge", for their alleged parallels with the cities mentioned in the Bible. That term is now discouraged, as these were not cities but sacred precincts, and unlike the Jewish model they served not to protect the innocent but to absolve the guilty. The idea was that any condemned criminal who succeeded in reaching a *pu'uhonua* would undergo a ritual lasting a few hours – at the very most, overnight – and then be free to leave. As *pu'uhonuas* always stood near strongly guarded royal enclaves, however, they had first either to run a gauntlet of armed warriors by land, or to dodge canoeists and sharks by sea.

The survival of the fittest was one of the fundamental principles of ancient Hawaiian law, in which might was generally considered to be right. The laws were determined by gods, not men, and they were concerned not with acts such as theft and murder but with infractions of the intricate system of *kapu* – for which the penalty was always death. *Pu'uhonuas* provided a sort of safety valve to spare prime citizens from summary execution. In addition, non-combatants, loaded with provisions, could come here to sit out the conflict in times of war, while defeated armies might flee to the nearest *pu'uhonua* to avoid death on the battlefield. Each island had at least one, and the Big Island is thought to have had six, with other sites including Waipi'o Valley, and what's now called Coconut Island in Hilo.

---

pool, where a few fish live undisturbed except by the occasional wading bird. Various lava boulders nearby have been hollowed out to serve as bowls or salt pans, and one levelled in order to play the game *kōnane*, in which black and white pebbles served as counters.

A simple A-frame thatched structure serves as a carving shed, and usually holds one or two idols on which work is still in progress. Master craftsmen also fashion outrigger canoes here, from mighty trunks of beautiful dark *koa* wood; you may see the *Mauloa*, a 26-foot coastal canoe equipped with a *lau hala* (pandanus leaf) sail, or the larger *Miloli'i*, completed in 1993, which sailed to Tahiti in 1995 (see p.185).

Beyond the royal area is the L-shaped **Great Wall**, which is 10 feet high, up to 17 feet wide, and runs across the tip of the promontory to seal off the sanctuary itself. Its northern end is guarded by the **Hale O Keawe** *heiau*, once used to house the bones of powerful chiefs. At the time when this was dismantled and stripped by Lord George Byron in July 1825, it was the last *heiau* in the islands to remain in perfect condition. Now, like the houses, it has been reconstructed. All the fearsome wooden idols that surround it are modern reproductions, but they're still eerie in their original setting.

The tide at Hōnaunau generally fluctuates by two or three feet; in February, however, the seas are sometimes rough and flooding can cause the whole area to be closed off.

Few buildings now stand beyond the wall. Apart from a couple of bare *heiau* platforms, there's just a sparse scattering of trees on the rippling *pāhoehoe* lava that runs into the ocean. One especially large grey stone, supposedly the favourite spot of the chief Keoua, is surrounded by six holes in the rock that may have held the wooden poles of a canopy. Black crabs scuttle across the waterfront rocks and countless pools are alive with tiny multi-coloured fish. You can snorkel here if you want, but the water is so clear and shallow that you can see everything anyway.

As you can't linger on the beach in the main part of the park, you may want to walk a short way south around the bay to a long stretch of public beach. This is one of the best snorkelling spots on the island, as well as a good place for a picnic. The only parking is in the *pu'uhonua* lot, however, which means you can't really get here without paying the admission fee for the park proper.

St Benedict's Painted Church

Mass is held at St Benedict's on Mon, Tues, Thurs & Fri at 7am, Sat 4pm & Sun 7.15am. Hawaiian mass is held every second Sun.

When you visit the *pu'uhonua*, be sure also to make the slight detour north from Hwy-160, the spur road to Hwy-11, to see **St Benedict's Painted Church**. This small wooden church, an intriguing hybrid of medieval Europe and Hawaii, was decorated between 1899 and 1904 by a Belgian priest, Father John Velge, with brightly coloured Biblical and allegorical scenes. Columns with Hawaiian texts erupt into palm leaves on the vaulted ceiling of a tropical sky, and the walls behind the altar are painted with a *trompe-l'oeil* Gothic cathedral modelled on that in Burgos, Spain. Orchids and *leis* festoon the altar and statuary within, while purple bougainvilleas fill the lush tropical gardens outside. The spectacular views down the hillside at sunset look out over the flat expanse of trees that line the coast between Hōnaunau and Nāpo'opo'o.

Immediately below the Painted Church on the road down to the
pu'uhonua – and within easy reach of the beaches – is one of the
Big Island's most distinctive **B&Bs**. *A Dragonfly Ranch* (PO Box
675, Hōnaunau HI 967226; ☎328 2159 or 1-800/487 2159; fax
328 9570; ③–⑤) is a self-styled tropical retreat, geared to
alternative travellers, but still offering a high degree of luxury. The
owners have a New Age approach and offer traditional Hawaiian
massage and aromatherapy among other treatments.

Ho'okena State Park

Continue south along Hwy-11, for just under three miles from the
Hwy-160 turn-off, and another small road leads to the sea at
HO'OKENA STATE PARK. The vegetation thins out as you drop the
two miles down the hillside, but the park itself is pleasant enough. It
consists of a genuine, if greyish, sandy beach, pressed against a small
pali, and shaded with coconut palms and other trees. Getting in and
out of the water across the sharp lava can be a bit gruelling if you
don't have water shoes, but the **snorkelling** is once again excellent.

This sheltered, south-facing bay was once a regular port of call
for inter-island steamers, but now houses very few buildings,
although it does have toilets and a picnic area. It's also the only
beach in South Kona that allows **camping**; permission, as usual,
must be obtained from the Department of Parks and Recreation in
Hilo (☎961-83411) at a cost of $1 per day. *Neoki's Corner* at the
foot of the road sells soft drinks, and has public showers.

Miloli'i

The last point in South Kona at which access to the sea is practical
is another twelve miles beyond Ho'okena, where a very tortuous
five-mile single-lane road winds down the steep, exposed ridge of
Mauna Loa. Having reached the sea at **Ho'opuloa** – no more than a
few houses on bare rock – the road follows the coastline south, to
drop to the small bay of **MILOLI'I**.

The tiny stretches of beach here are mere indentations in the
black lava along the shore, filled with a random scattering of white
coral and black lava pebbles, and backed by groves of coconut
palms. The thick tongue of the most recent lava flow (in 1926) can
be seen spilling over the sparse slopes above; it obliterated
Ho'opuloa, and disputes over the allocation of land to rehouse the
victims lasted for well over fifty years thereafter.

At the south end of the cove there's a **beach park**, with a
thatched picnic shelter and a rest room, near an especially sheltered
pond that's a favourite with children. Here too the main appeal is to
snorkel around the rocks. A short way back from the sea, the
Miloli'i Grocery Store sells snacks and sodas. The road ends next
to the pastel yellow, red-roofed **Hau'oli Kamana'o Church**.

Chapter 2

Kohala and Waimea

T he northernmost spur of the Big Island is its oldest segment, named after the first of its five volcanoes to appear above the ocean – the long-extinct **Kohala Mountain**. With five million years longer to scour its slopes than in the rawer, newer south, the wind and the rain have combined to produce the kind of heavily eroded scenery familiar from other Hawaiian and Pacific islands. The Big Island's largest **coral reefs** – albeit small by most standards – lie just offshore and as a result the island's only sizeable **white-sand beaches** have been washed into nearby sheltered coves.

Although the landscape gets more dramatic the further north you go, facilities for tourists are almost entirely restricted to **South Kohala**. At first glance, this might seem a volcanic wasteland, criss-crossed by the massive trails of black lava that flowed down to the ocean during assorted nineteenth-century eruptions. However, it has undergone an amazing transformation since the 1960s, when Laurance Rockefeller spotted the potential in its average annual rainfall figures of just 8.7 inches, which make it the sunniest area on the entire archipelago. Some entrepreneurs have lost heavily on the sheer scale of the investment needed to build artificial oases in the empty lava lands, but the exclusive self-contained resorts that now line the coast have become the showpieces of the Big Island's tourist industry.

North Kohala, which spreads across both sides of the mountain, is a microcosm of the whole island, with its dry leeward side separated by rolling uplands from the precipitous wet valleys of the eastern coastline. The road that curves around the north comes to an end at **Polulū Valley**, the last of a chain of valleys that begins with Waipiʻo (see p.122). Like Waipiʻo, Polulū was home to generations of ancient *taro* farmers; in fact two centuries ago, this region was the original powerbase of Kamehameha the Great. Several crucial sites associated with Hawaii's first monarch can still be seen, ranging from the Kamehameha birthplace at the northern extremity of the island to his huge war temple at **Puʻukoholā**, overlooking Kawaihae Harbor. The traditional Hawaiian way of life

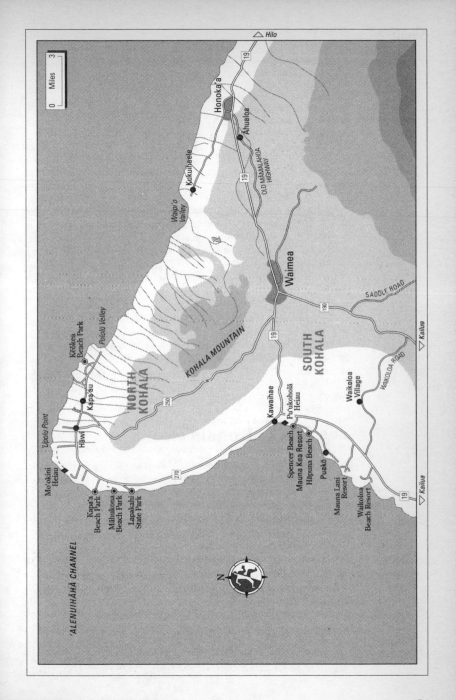

△ Hilo

0 — Miles — 3

19

Honoka'a

Āhualoa

19

Kukuihaele

OLD MĀMALAHOA HIGHWAY

19

Waipi'o Valley

Waimea

19

SADDLE ROAD

190

Kailua

Kōhea Beach Park

Pōlolū Valley

KOHALA MOUNTAIN

SOUTH KOHALA

NORTH KOHALA

Kapa'au

250

WAIKOLOA ROAD

Waikoloa Village

'Upolu Point

Hāwī

Kawaihae

Pu'ukoholā Heiau

Mo'okini Heiau

270

Spencer Beach

Mauna Kea Resort

Hāpuna Beach

Puakō

Kapa'a Beach Park

Māhukona Beach Park

Lapakahi State Park

Mauna Lani Resort

Waikoloa Beach Resort

19

Kailua

'ALENUIHĀHĀ CHANNEL

N

Accommodation price codes

Note that the prices shown here for **accommodation** in the resort hotels are the regular "rack rates". You should be able to get much better rates by booking an all-inclusive package before you leave home; see p.3 for details. Prices have been graded with the symbols below, according to the quoted rate for the least expensive double room for most of the year, not including state taxes of 10.17 percent.

①	up to $30	④	$75–100	⑦	$170–225
②	$30–50	⑤	$100–130	⑧	$225–300
③	$50–75	⑥	$130–170	⑨	over $300

came to an end in 1906, when the waters from Pololū were diverted along the Kohala Ditch to irrigate sugar plantations. However, the last of those closed down twenty years ago and these days the area is relatively unpopulated, scattered with tiny characterful communities that are attempting to diversify into coffee and macadamia nut production. A few tourists pass through on day trips, mainly to enjoy the spectacular hilltop views along **Hwy-250**, but have to return south at night, because of the scarcity of accommodation.

The only town of any significant size in Kohala, **Waimea**, is poised between north and south, a dozen miles up from the sea on the cool green plains between Kohala Mountain and Mauna Kea. After more than a century as the epicentre of the mighty Parker Ranch, with its own distinct version of cowboy culture (imported by the *paniolos*), it has become one of the most in-demand residential areas on the island, with a selection of good restaurants, but few hotels or sights.

The South Kohala Coast

See p.58 for details of the Kona Village Resort, the southernmost of the luxury resorts.

Though the whole of the western seaboard of the Big Island tends to be referred to as the Kona coast, the most famous of its resorts are in fact situated in the district of **South Kohala**, which starts roughly 25 miles north of Kailua. Overlooked by the volcanoes of Mauna Kea, Hualālai and Kohala – and on clear days by Mauna Loa, to the south, and even Haleakalā on Maui – this region was all but inaccessible by land, until the 1960s. The only visitors to the inlets along the shore were local fishermen and the occasional intrepid hiker or surfer. The Hawaiian villages that had once flourished here were long gone and only wealthy landowners maintained a few private enclaves.

Mauka **and** *makai*

Remember *mauka* means away from the sea and towards the mountain, and *makai* means away from the mountain and towards the sea.

Since the sixties, the landscape has been reshaped; holes large enough for giant hotels were blasted in the rock and turf laid on top of the lava to create lawns and golf courses. **Queen Ka'ahumanu Highway** (Hwy-19) pushed its way across the bare lava slopes and multi-property resorts appeared in quick succession at **Waikoloa** and then **Mauna Lani**, a couple of miles farther north.

Most of the beaches that may once have existed along the southern stretches of South Kohala were probably destroyed by lava early in the 1800s – so the *Hilton*, for example, had to build its own beach from scratch – but as you head further north towards Kawaihae you come to some of the finest expanses of sand on the island. These were prime targets for the developers; the first of the luxury hotels was the *Mauna Kea Beach Hotel*, which went up at Kauna'oa in the 1960s and, despite strong opposition, it has recently been joined by the *Hāpuna Beach Prince Hotel*.

Since it's illegal for anyone to deny access to the Hawaiian shoreline, local people, and visitors who are not staying at the Kohala resorts, are entitled to use all the beaches along the coast. Some hotels make things more difficult by restricting the number of parking permits they issue to non-guests – as few as ten per day – but as long as you can make your way to the sea, you're entitled to stay there.

Waikoloa

The fundamental division of land for the ancient Hawaiians was the *ahupua'a*, a wedge-shaped "slice of

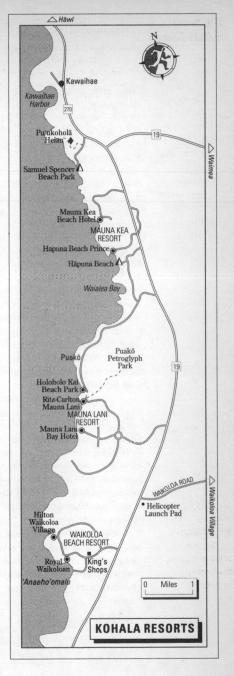

*At present the
Waikoloa Beach
Resort does not
have its own gas
station; the
nearest are in
Kailua or
Waikoloa Village.*

*The King's
Shops are open
daily 9.30am–
9.30pm.*

cake" reaching from the top of the mountain down to a stretch of
the sea (see p.178). The name **WAIKOLOA** originally referred to
such a division, which is why modern visitors are often confused as
to where exactly "Waikoloa" is.

The community called Waikoloa, generally referred to as
Waikoloa Village (see p.76), is six miles *mauka* of Queen
Ka'ahumanu Highway, half-way up to the Belt Road. The **Waikoloa
Beach Resort** – reached by a mile-long approach road that leaves
the highway a little way south of mile-marker 76, 25 miles north of
Kailua and a mile south of the turning up to Waikoloa Village – is,
unsurprisingly, down by the sea. It holds little other then the
Hilton and *Royal Waikoloan* hotels and the 32-store *King's
Shops* mall, which is set back from the sea, just before the
approach road splits off to the different hotels. The mall consists
of upscale clothes stores, a small Food Court and a couple of fully-
fledged restaurants.

Hilton Waikoloa Village

69-425 Waikoloa Beach Drive, HC02 Box 5500, Waikoloa HI 96743; ☎885-
1234; 1-800/HILTONS; fax 885-2902; ⑦–⑨.

The *Hilton Waikoloa Village* is almost a miniature city; guests
travel between its three seven-storey towers on a light railway
system, a mile-long network of walkways or in boats along the
canals. It boasts a four-acre artificial lagoon, equipped with
waterfalls, and a beach of imported sand as well as rows of
coconut palms, some of which were flown here by helicopter from
Kalapana on the south coast, just before it was engulfed by lava
(see p.137).

This synthetic tropical paradise, which consumes seven percent
of all the energy used on the Big Island, cost a fortune to build and
opened in 1988, as the *Hyatt Regency* – just in time to be hit by the
Gulf-War economic downturn. When *Hilton* bailed out the original
developers in 1993, they bought it for a rumoured 25¢ *on* the
dollar. It's now one of the most popular of the Kohala resorts and if
you book through a package-tour operator, can work out as one of
the cheapest. However, it feels a bit like staying in a theme park and
would probably appeal most to families with young children, or
those who are quite happy to see nothing of the rest of the island.

One of the resort's highlights is its "swim with a dolphin"
programme; although an hour in the lagoon with your favourite
mammal can cost up to $100, the experience is so much in demand
that a lottery is held to decide which guests can take part. You can
also take a free guided tour through the network of underground
tunnels, used by staff to ensure unobtrusiveness.

Surprisingly, neither of the more formal of the *Hilton*'s six
restaurants – the north Italian *Donatoni's*, and the Japanese *sushi*
and *teppanyaki* specialists *Imari*, both of which serve dinner only
– offers sea views, though the food is as good as you'd expect. The

best casual alternative is the breezy *Palm Terrace*, which presents a different bargain buffet every night.

Royal Waikoloan

69-275 Waikoloa Beach Drive, HC02 Box 5300, Waikoloa HI 96743-9743; ☎885-6789; 1-800/688-7444; fax 1-800/622-4852 (US & Canada); ⑤–⑨ depending on room.

In contrast to its showy neighbour, the *Royal Waikoloan* is restrained, pleasantly comfortable and relatively price-sensitive. The hotel's main attraction is the adjacent 'Anaeho'omalu beach (see below), where available watersports include snorkelling, kayaking, scuba diving and excursions in glass-bottomed boats and catamarans.

Prices at the resort range from $750 for a suite down to $120 for a simple garden-view room, making it the cheapest accommodation along this stretch of coast. If you simply want to swim and soak up the sun, the *Royal Waikoloan* is the best value in Kohala. Only if you plan a lot of extra "activities" is it worth considering the hotel's all-inclusive rates of $354 to $478 per couple per night, which cover all water sports, all meals, including the *lū'au*, and service.

Of the resort's three restaurants, the dinner-only candle-lit *Tiare Room* (daily except Wed & Sun, 6–9.30pm) is the most formal. The *Royal Terrace* (open for all meals) has a nightly entertainment programme, usually of light Hawaiian music, and a $19.75 champagne brunch on Sundays, while the poolside *Lava Tube* serves alfresco sandwiches and salads in an informal setting. There's also a twice-weekly *lū'au*, open to all (Wed & Sun 6pm; $42 adults, $22 children under 12).

'Anaeho'omalu

The *Royal Waikoloan* stands at the northern end of a sheltered white-sand beach, which shelves very gradually out to sea. This is a favourite spot with snorkellers and windsurfers, and bathing is generally considered safe. Hawaiians named the area 'ANAEHO'OMALU, or "protected mullet", in recognition of the fact that the mullet raised in its two fish ponds were reserved for the use of chiefs alone; *ali'i* voyaging around the island could stop here to pick up supplies. The beach also witnessed one moment of high

---

Waikoloa Condos

You can enjoy the facilities of the Waikoloa Beach Resort without staying in its mega-hotels by renting a **condo** at either the *Bay Club* (☎885-7979; fax 885-7780; ⑦–⑧), or the *Shores at Waikoloa* (☎885-5001, 1-800/922-7866 US, 1-800/445-6633 Canada, 1-800/321-2558 HI; fax 922-8785; ⑦). Both properties are near the beach, with their own pools and tennis courts.

---

drama, when an unpopular king of Hawaii, Kamaiole, was slain by his rival Kalapana. The ambushers took advantage of the tradition that when the king set off on an expedition, his canoe was always the last to leave the beach.

Waikoloa Village

Most visitors to the Waikoloa resorts never need to head the eight miles up to **WAIKOLOA VILLAGE** itself. Should you want to, however, you can take the road which leaves Queen Ka'ahumanu Highway a short distance north of the resort turn-off, half-way to Mauna Lani. A small lot at this otherwise desolate intersection is the base for **helicopter** trips (see p.19), run for resort guests by *Kenai Helicopters* (☎885-5833) and *Papillon Hawaiian Helicopters* (☎329-0551) among others.

Apart from a supermarket and a gas station, there's nothing really to the village, which is basically a dormitory community for the people who work in the resorts. However, keen golfers or those wanting to self-cater may consider staying here at the good-value *Waikoloa Villas* (☎531-7595, 1-800/535-0085 US & Canada, 1-800/219-9700 HI; fax 922-2421; ⑤) or the *Elima Lani* (☎883-8288, 1-800/367-5004 US & Canada, 1-800/272-5275 HI; fax 883-8170; ⑤). These condos are attached to a new golf course, with excellent facilities including its own restaurant.

Commanding panoramic views down the slopes from the south end of the roadside **Waikoloa Highlands Village** mall, the *Highlands Restaurant & Night Club* (☎883-8132) is one of the island's major concert venues, the small stage in its central bar hosting reggae, country and touring bands. It serves lunch dishes for around $6; the least expensive item on the dinner menu is the seafood gumbo, while main courses such as skate are more like $18. Also in the mall, *Straw Hat Pizza* (☎883-8181) prepares gourmet pizzas to your specifications, or you can pick up snacks or burgers at the open-air *Aloha Deli* (☎883-8246) and Mexican fast food at *El Gecko's* (☎883-8137).

Mauna Lani Resort

A mile or so north of the Waikoloa Village turn-off, another approach road *makai* of Queen Ka'ahumanu Highway heads through lurid green lawns down to the plush **Mauna Lani Resort**. This area once belonged to the Parker Ranch; then for forty years it was the secluded oceanside retreat of Francis Hyde I'i Brown, before being snapped up by developers in the early 1970s. The name *Mauna Lani* means "mountains reaching heaven", and refers to the misty volcanoes that loom in the distance to the north, south and east.

Two major resorts face the sea in splendid isolation, sharing the use of two golf courses. Around the *Mauna Lani Bay Hotel* in particular, where the beach is backed by several scenic fish ponds, traces of ancient occupation are everywhere. An informative map, available from the hotel reception, explains various sites along the **Kalāhuipuaʻa Trail**. This disappointing two-mile walk starts out well as an attractive seaside stroll, but rapidly turns gruelling as you head inland across craggy *āʻā* lava in pursuit of rudimentary caves and some faint depressions where tools were ground. Farther up the coast at **Puakō** is a more easily intelligible relic of the past – one of the Big Island's largest fields of petroglyphs (see p.78).

Mauna Lani Bay Hotel

1 Mauna Lani Drive, Kohala Coast HI 96743; ☎885/6622, 1-800/327-8585 (US/Can), or 1-800/992-7987 (Hawaiʻi); fax 885-6183; ⑨.

The gleaming, white *Mauna Lani Bay* is an unabashed resort hotel, with its central building thrusting like a gigantic arrow straight into the Pacific and an oceanfront golf course to either side. This classic resort has attracted guests such as Kevin Costner, who is said to have insisted his villa was entirely re-decorated when he stayed here during the filming of *Waterworld*. However, it offers little in the way of activities for children and, apart from golf or the beach, not much for adults either; this is a place to simply lie back and take it easy or to use as a luxurious base for explorations further afield.

Of the four **restaurants**, the *Bay Terrace* commands ocean views from its indoor and outdoor dining room. On Sundays, there's a champagne brunch, but Friday and Saturday are the best nights to come when, in place of the usual unadventurous menu of American favourites, there's a delicious $35 all-you-can-eat seafood buffet. The expensive *Le Soleil* (closed Fri & Sat) is stuffy in every sense, compared to the open-air Polynesian-style *CanoeHouse* (closed Tues & Wed), set in the grounds close to the sea and surrounded by fish ponds. Finally, the *Gallery*, away from the sea in the hotel's tennis complex, may not be atmospheric, but the food is superb – a mixture of Pacific-Rim delicacies such as lobster ravioli-cum-wontons and grilled lamb chops with *ohelo*-berry sauce.

Kohala Coast Adventures

The concessionaire for water sports and other activities for the *Ritz-Carlton*, *Hapuna Beach Prince* and *Hilton Waikoloa* is *Red Sail Sports*, 69-425 Waikoloa Beach Drive, Kamuela HI 96743-9791; ☎885-2876 or 1-800/255-6425; fax 885-4169. It runs snorkel ($55–65) and sunset ($45) cruises, cycle trips such as the *Paniolo Cycle Adventure* down Hwy-250 (see p.91) from Kohala Ranch to Kapaʻau ($70), an introductory Scuba Dive package (one hour's instruction in a swimming pool plus a one-tank dive for $100 or a two-tank dive for $120) and full diving certification courses for $650 for one person or $395 per person in groups of two or more.

Ritz-Carlton Mauna Lani

1 North Kaniku Drive, Kohala Coast HI 96743; ☎885-2000, 1-800/241-3333
(US/Canada) or 0800/234000 (UK); fax 885-1064; ⑧–⑨.

*Mauna Lani's
Francis I'i
Brown golf
course is the
scene each
January of the
Senior Skins
tournament,
when the likes
of Arnold
Palmer, Jack
Nicklaus and
Lee Trevino
contest a
$450,000 purse.*

As you might expect from the prestige name, this is the most
sophisticated and elegant of the Kohala giants, although the
traditional *Ritz-Carlton* dress code and atmosphere has been
greatly relaxed. The resort offers all the usual facilities, including a
seafront swimming pool and jacuzzi as well as a wide range of
healthy pursuits, catering for children as well as adults, with golf
being the keynote. All the rooms have marble bathrooms and
extensive views either over the sea or across a golf course to the
volcanoes. Staying here makes an ideal rest cure or sybaritic break,
though your funds need to be unlimited to make the most of it.

The showpiece *Dining Room*, spreading across a terrace,
serves "contemporary Hawaiian" cuisine, with a strong Pacific tinge.
A full meal costs $40–50, but dishes such as guava-smoked
pheasant and *nori*-wrapped salmon roulade are worth every penny.
The *Grill Restaurant*, with its *koa*-wood fittings, serves a more
conventional assortment of less expensive, traditional grilled dishes.

Mauna Lani Condos

Once again, the Mauna Lani Resort also offers a small selection of condos
for those who prefer self-catering. The luxurious *Mauna Lani Point*
development is well to the south of the Mauna Lani Bay, very close to the
sea (☎885-5022 or 1-800/642-6284; fax 661-0147; ⑦–⑨).

Puakō

*See p.155 for
details of the
most extensive
collection of
petroglyphs on
the Big Island,
at Pu'u Loa.*

This collection of ancient **petroglyphs** is located a short walk back
from the sea between the *Ritz-Carlton* and the small community of
PUAKŌ. Laboriously etched into bare *pahoehoe* lava, the carvings
range from matchstick warriors to abstract symbols and simple
indentations, where the umbilical cords of new-born babies were
reverentially buried.

The Malama Trail to **Puakō Petroglyph Park** starts from the
mauka end of the Holoholo Kai Beach Park parking lot. If you're
staying at the *Ritz-Carlton*, it's an easy walk along the shore, first
along the edge of the golf course and then over the rocks. Driving
from elsewhere, follow the signs for the *Ritz-Carlton* and turn right
just before the hotel. The only facilities are at the beach; there's no
water along the mile-long trail which, though not difficult, traverses
some rough terrain.

For the first 150 yards, the trail is paved, leading across open
lava to some modern replica petroglyphs set up for visitors who
want to take rubbings. From there you plunge into a tinderbox-dry
forest of creaking, thorny *kiawe* trees; a single spark would set the
whole thing ablaze, so smoking is forbidden. Five hundred yards in,
a sign indicates a system of shallow lava caves and a few

petroglyphs can be discerned on nearby rocks. Many visitors turn back here under the impression that they've seen all there is to see, but you should continue another 250 yards and cross an unpaved track. A short way beyond that a fenced-off viewing area brings you to a halt in front of a slightly sloping expanse of flat reddish rock, covered with simple stick figures, most a couple of feet tall, still lying where they were left to bake centuries ago. A total of three thousand designs have been identified, many of them in areas closed to the public; those on view are easiest to see early in the morning or late in the evening, when the sun creates shadows.

Holoholo Kai Beach Park is a mixture of black lava and white coral, not especially good for swimming. **Puakō** itself is beyond it to the north, but there's no through road from here and the connecting path from the petroglyphs has long been closed. To reach Puakō, take the next road *makai* off Hwy-19, after the Mauna Lani turning. It's more of an exclusive residential area than a town, with the long Puakō Beach Drive lined for three miles by private villas. The occasional gap permits public access to the thin strip of sand beyond, where the tide pools are interrupted at one point by a small concrete jetty and boat landing.

Waialea, Hāpuna and Kauna'oa beaches

Much the best of the natural white-sand beaches of South Kohala are along the coast just south of Kawaihae Harbor. Such beaches are formed from the skeletal remains of tiny coral-reef creatures, which explains why they're found here in the most sheltered areas of the oldest part of the island. They're now at the foot of Mauna Kea rather than Kohala Mountain, because lava from Mauna Kea has progressively swamped its venerable neighbour.

Of the three best-known beaches, separated each from the next by short stretches of *kiawe* forest through which public access is legally guaranteed, only the southernmost, **Waialea**, remains in anything approaching a pristine state. Comparatively small, and sheltered by jutting headlands, it's a perfect base for recreational sailing, while the gentle slope into the sea makes it popular with family groups.

The magnificence of both **Hāpuna** and **Kauna'oa** to the north has undoubtably been impaired by the addition of mighty resort hotels. During the *Mauna Kea Beach Hotel*'s recent closure for refurbishment, the sweeping crescent of Kauna'oa beach reverted to something like its old self, used by locals but few tourists. All these beaches offer superb conditions for much of the year, but are exposed to very strong winds and high surf in winter, when much of the sand is washed away and swimming becomes very hazardous.

Hāpuna Beach

Broad, sandy **HĀPUNA BEACH** has often been called the most beautiful beach in the United States. Though in summer it's the widest beach on the Big Island, capable of accommodating large crowds of day-trippers, it always seems to retain an intimate feel. This is partly due to the promontory of black lava that splits it down the middle; how much is also owed to the lack of development will become apparent over the next few years, as the impact of the controversial new *Hapuna Beach Prince Hotel* becomes clear. Campaigners fought bitter battles first to stop its construction, and later to limit the influence it exerts; the hotel is not permitted for example to serve food or alcohol on the beach, to leave unoccupied furniture on the sand or to discourage public access to any area below the tree line.

For the moment, most of Hāpuna Beach remains a delightful public park, well equipped with washrooms and pavilions. In deference to the safety of body-surfers, who consider this the best spot on the island, surfboards are forbidden. With a potential for unruly weather any time between October and March, look for the warning flags that fly outside the hotel before you enter the water.

Six simple and slightly run-down A-frame shelters at Hāpuna are available for rent. Contact *Hapuna Beach Services*, PO Box 44318, Kamuela HI 96743 (☎882-1095). Tent camping is not permitted.

Hapuna Beach Prince Hotel
62-100 Kauna'oa Drive, Kamuela HI 96743; ☎880-1111 or 1-800/882-6060; fax 880-3200; ⑨.

After much debate, the ultra-modern *Hapuna Beach Prince Hotel* opened in August 1994. Standing roughly six miles north of Mauna Lani, with the approach road unexpectedly *mauka* of the highway, it occupies most of the northern end of Hāpuna Beach. Despite being moulded to the contours of the hillside, it's undeniably intrusive. The prospect from the inside looking out is superb; the hotel's giant central lobby is open to cooling sea breezes, while the turquoise pool is set flush with a broad patio, complete with a whirlpool spa giving excellent sunset views. Few resorts in the world can offer the same combination of luxurious accommodation and idyllic situation, though if you're on the outside looking in, it's considerably less appealing.

Of three gourmet **restaurants**, all of which serve dinner only, the *Coast Grille*, above the pool, specializes in adventurous Pacific fish dishes. Appetizers include crispy scallops in a lemon-grass and lobster broth, while a typical main course is *opah* in a ginger and pistachio crust. At the authentically Japanese, minimally furnished, but view-less, *Hakone* (Fri–Tues), you can get full *sashimi* dinner with scallop, prawns and tuna for $30, or choose from a separate *sushi* bar. The most formal option is the *Bistro* (Wed–Sat, dinner only), which requires men to wear jackets to eat fine French and Mediterranean cuisine.

> **Mauna Kea Beach Hotel**
>
> The *Mauna Kea Beach Hotel*, which opened for business in 1965 as the
> first of the Kohala resorts, was closed for refurbishment when this book
> went to press. For current information, contact 1 Mauna Kea Beach Drive,
> Kohala Coast HI 96743 (☎882-7222 or 1-800/882-6060; fax 882-7657).

Kawaihae

For the ancient Hawaiians, the natural harbour at **KAWAIHAE**, a
couple of miles north of Hāpuna Beach, was one of the most
important landing points along the coast of the Big Island, providing
access to the whole Kohala region. Over the last fifty years, massive
earth-moving projects have destroyed any beauty that it once
possessed, though in terms of population it remains no more than a
tiny settlement. The entire area is still dominated by a great war
temple, built by Kamehameha to show that the gods looked with
favour on his plans for conquest.

Spencer Beach Park

The last significant beach along the Kohala coast, 'Ohai'ula Beach,
is one of the nicest and virtually the only one still geared towards
low-tech, low-budget family fun. It's better known as the **SAMUEL
M SPENCER BEACH COUNTY PARK**, which offers the best
oceanfront **campground** on the island, as well as full day-use
facilities. No cabins are available; visitors are expected to bring
their own tents or trailers and to obtain the necessary permit in
advance by contacting the Hawaii County parks office in Hilo
(☎961-8311; see p.32).

The beach itself, sheltered by a long reef, is popular with
recreational swimmers as well as more serious snorkellers and
scuba divers; it takes a major storm to render bathing unsafe.

Pu'ukoholā Heiau National Historic Site

PU'UKOHOLĀ HEIAU is the single most dramatic and imposing
Hawaiian temple still standing on any of the islands; its construction
between 1790 and 1791, by the future Kamehameha I, is one of the
greatest – and most horrific – epics of Big Island history.

*Pu'ukoholā
Heiau is open
daily except
hols
9.30am–4pm;
free;
☎882-7218.*

The story of this *luakini*, a "war temple", fed by human sacrifice,
began in 1782, when the young warrior Kamehameha seized control
of the northwest segment of the Big Island. Over the years that
followed, he conquered Maui, Lanai and Molokai, but failed to defeat
his rivals on the rest of his home island of Hawaii. Eventually, he
heard that his cousin Keōua wanted to expand out from Ka'ū in the
southwest, so Kamehameha sent his aunt to consult the prophet
Kapoukahi of Kauai, who suggested that building a *luakini* at
Pu'ukoholā and dedicating it to his personal war god Kūkā'ilimoku
would guarantee success in the coming conflict.

Kapoukahi himself came to the Big Island to oversee the construction of the new temple, on the site of a ruined *heiau* erected two centuries before by the legendary Lonoikamakahiki. The process was accompanied throughout by precise, exacting ritual; in the words of an old Hawaiian proverb, "the work of the *luakini* is like hauling *ohia* timber, of all labour the most arduous". First of all, the entire island had to be purified, by means of clearing the circle road and erecting altars at regular intervals.

For Kamehameha's rivals, the start of work was a clear announcement of impending war. They set out to sabotage the project, knowing that its completion would give Kamehameha irresistible *mana*, or spiritual power. Not only Keōua, but also the defeated chiefs of Maui, Lanai and Molokai, and even the rulers of Kauai and Oahu, joined forces to attack; but Kamehameha managed to hold them all off and pressed on with construction.

When the *heiau* was completed, in the summer of 1791, the prophet ordained that a great feast should be held, involving the sacrifice of 400 pigs, 400 bushels of bananas, 400 coconuts, 400 red fish, 400 pieces of *oloa* cloth and plenty of human beings, preferably themselves possessing considerable *mana*. Kamehameha therefore invited Keōua to attend the dedication, and make peace; like a figure from Greek tragedy, Keōua accepted the invitation.

The moment Keōua stepped ashore on the beach, he was slain with a spear thrust by Kamehameha's trusted warrior Keeaumoku (the father of Ka'ahumanu). All his companions were also killed before Kamehameha, who insisted that he had not sanctioned the slaughter, called a halt upon recognizing the commander of the second canoe as his own son Kaoleioku. Keōua's body was the main sacrifice offered, together with those of ten of his associates (the war god, who did not like blood on his altar, preferred his victims to have been killed elsewhere).

As sole ruler of the Big Island, Kamehameha went on to reconquer first Maui, Lanai and Molokai, then Oahu, which had been recaptured by their original rulers during the building of the temple. Finally he exacted tribute from Kauai, whereupon the whole archipelago took on the name of Kamehameha's native island and thus became known as Hawaii.

Their purpose served, the altar and idols at Pu'ukoholā were destroyed in 1819 on the orders of Kamehameha's successor Liholiho, shortly after the breaking of the ancient system of *kapus* (see p.173).

Visiting Pu'ukoholā Heiau
The parking lot for the *heiau* stands just off Hwy-19, at the start of the approach road to Spencer Beach Park and next to a small visitor centre, which hands out the informative Park Service booklet. The temple's three colossal tiers of black stone are not immediately

visible from here, so follow the signed trail for a couple of hundred yards down towards the sea.

As the path rounds "the hill of the whale" after which the *heiau* was named, the vast platform of the temple – 224 feet long by 100 feet wide – looms above you, commanding a long stretch of coastline. Disappointingly, this is as close as you'll get; access is forbidden, in part because this remains a sacred site but also because recent earthquake damage has rendered it unstable. No trace survives of the thatched houses and other structures that originally stood upon it – the Hale Moi, the smaller Hale Kahuna Nui for the priest, the oracle tower and drum house, or the lava altar that once held the bones of human sacrifices.

A little farther down the slope towards the sea stands the subsidiary **Mailekini Heiau**, narrower but longer, and much older than the main temple. It too is inaccessible to visitors. Both *heiaus* loom large above **Pelekane Beach**, which you are free to walk along, although nowadays it's not all that spectacular. In Kamehameha's era the beach was far longer and there was a royal compound in the palm grove just back from the sea; the land that now lies immediately to the north is infill created during the construction of Kawaihae Harbor, when the beach itself was largely obliterated.

Appropriately enough, breeding sharks still circle the site of the **Haleokapuni Heiau**, dedicated to the shark deities, which is submerged beneath the waves around 100 feet out. The voracious beasts would devour offerings beneath the watchful gaze of the king, standing beside the stone Leaning Post above the shore. Swimming is neither permitted, nor particularly desirable here; if the sharks aren't enough to put you off, the water is also clogged with gritty silt deposits, which have completely obscured, and probably damaged, the underwater *heiau*.

Kawaihae Harbor

Despite remaining without a wharf until 1937, **KAWAIHAE HARBOR** has long been the most important anchorage on the leeward coast of Hawaii. It was always the major port for the cattle of the Parker Ranch (see p.88); in the old days intrepid cowboys would swim both cows and horses from the beach out to sea, then lasso them in the water and lash a dozen of them to the outside of flimsy whaleboats, which in turn rowed them to larger vessels anchored offshore.

The bay was finally dredged by the military during the 1950s to create an extensive harbour area. Casualties of the process included an assortment of delightful, grassy islands, each of which held a thatched shack or two, and most of the Big Island's best coral reef. The port remains relatively low-key, however, poorly protected from occasional violent storms and with few services nearby, let alone a proper town. Its biggest flurry of activity for many years came with

John Young and Isaac Davis

Just off the beach at Kawaihae, in 1790, the tiny six-man schooner *Fair American*, belonging to the trading ship *Eleanora*, was stormed and captured by Hawaiians. They had been angered by the *Eleanora*'s captain Stephen Metcalfe, whose recent exploits included the slaughter of one hundred Hawaiians in the 'Olowalu Massacre, which took place near Lahaina in Maui. The islanders, therefore, exacted revenge by looting the *Fair American* for its valuable iron, and killing all its crew except Isaac Davis, who was spared because he put up such valiant resistance; among the victims was Metcalfe's own son, Thomas.

Ignorant of what happened, Captain Metcalfe set out to search the islands for his missing boat and crew. In due course, the *Eleanora* arrived at Kawaihae and first mate John Young was sent ashore to investigate. Kamehameha himself prevented Young from re-joining his vessel with the news of the murders, whereupon Captain Metcalfe concluded that his envoy had been killed and sailed away. Metcalfe himself died soon afterwards and never learned of the death of his son; both Davis and Young, however, remained on the islands for the rest of their lives, taking Hawaiian names and becoming valued advisors to the king. They were responsible for teaching the Hawaiians to fight with muskets and cannon – the royal arsenal began with two guns seized from the *Fair American* and was augmented by weapons traded with foreign ships.

Renamed Olohana ("all hands"), Young served between 1802 and 1812 as governor of the Big Island, during which time he fortified Mailekini Heiau. He made his home 500 yards inland from the beach at Pu'ukoholā; a difficult trail still leads there from the beach, although there's nothing to see as the remains of his original building are long gone. Young continued to oversee activities at Kawaihae – including the first shipments of cattle – until his death at the age of 90 in 1835. Isaac Davis, meanwhile, was poisoned mysteriously in April 1810.

As this book went to press, the word was that the futuristic Waterworld *set had been sold for scrap to a Japanese company.*

the much-troubled filming of the Kevin Costner blockbuster *Waterworld* in 1994–95, during which the movie's centrepiece, a floating slave colony, sank at least once to the bottom of the harbour. Shooting was plagued by hurricanes, anticipated *tsunamis* that never turned up and the mundane vagaries of the Hawaiian climate.

Kawaihae Shopping Center

Kawaihae's only shops and restaurants – there's no accommodation – are to be found in the KAWAIHAE SHOPPING CENTER, at the junction of Hwys 19 and 270.

This small two-storey mall is more upmarket than the location might suggest. As well as few clothes stores and an art gallery, there's a *Café Pesto* (Sun–Thurs 11am–9pm, Fri & Sat 11am–10pm; ☎882-1071), serving the same menu of delicious *calzones* and pizzas as the branch in Hilo (see p.112). Upstairs *LB's Snackorama* dishes up simple lunches and the Mexican *Tres*

Hombres (closed Wed; ☎882-1031), serves a $7 *burrito* or sandwich lunch and has a full dinner menu of various types of *tacos* and *fajitas*.

Waimea and the Kohala uplands

From Kawaihae, Hwy-19 heads abruptly inland, climbing for fourteen miles to **Waimea**. For many visitors, inland Hawaii comes as a surprise, with its pastoral meadows undulating across gentle plains where once stood forests of sandalwood. These rolling uplands are cowboy country, still roamed on horseback by the *paniolos* (or cowhands) of the United States' largest private cattle ranch, the **Parker Ranch**. Only when you look closely at the occasional rounded hills dotted across the landscape do you spot the telltale signs of their volcanic origin; many are eroded cinder cones, topped by smoothed-over craters. The fact that temperatures are distinctly cooler here than down by the sea is one reason why locals are moving to Waimea in ever-increasing numbers; visiting sun-worshippers tend not to be quite so keen.

Waimea

Kohala's largest community, **WAIMEA**, is not the company town it once was. The Parker Ranch, which at its peak in the nineteenth century extended across more than half a million acres, now covers only ten percent of the Big Island and employs just one hundred of Waimea's eight thousand inhabitants. While remaining proud of its

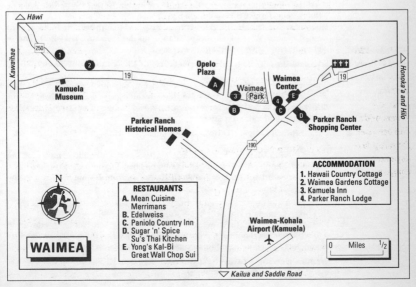

cowboy past, with memorabilia of the much-mythologized *paniolos*
(see p.89) prominent everywhere, Waimea has become more of a
sophisticated country resort and is now home to a diverse
community that includes international astronomers from the Mauna
Kea observatories and successful entrepreneurs from the mainland.

You may sometimes hear the town referred to as "Kamuela", by
the post office, for example. This is to avoid confusion with other
Waimeas on Kauai and Oahu; it's simply a nineteenth-century
corruption of "Samuel", one of the many scions of the house of
Parker.

There's not all that much to Waimea as a tourist destination;
most visitors simply while away an afternoon or so enjoying its
dramatic setting between the volcanoes. What town there is consists
of a series of low-slung shopping malls, lining Hwy-19 to either side
of the central intersection, where it makes a sharp right-angle turn
towards Honoka'a and Hilo. The largest of the malls, the **Parker
Ranch Shopping Center**, is home to the local post office and the
visitor centre for the ranch itself (see p.90); head a quarter-mile
east from there to see an appealing little cluster of clapboard
churches, set well back from the road.

Accommodation

Few visitors spend the night in Waimea, although it's one of the
pleasantest towns on the island; the only drawback is that the nights
here are significantly colder here than down by the ocean. For
Hawaiians, however, that's a plus point, and the attractive B&Bs in
the neighbourhood are often booked well in advance.

Hawaii Country Cottage, PO Box 1717, Kamuela HI 96743; ☎885-7441 or
1-800/262-9912; fax 885-0559; ③.
Modern, well-furnished B&B apartment, attached to a private home two miles
west of central Waimea, a short distance up the ravishing Hwy-250. Three-
night minimum stay; reservations essential.

Kamuela Inn, PO Box 1994, Kamuela HI 96743; ☎885-4243; fax 885-8857;
③–⑤.
Former motel refurbished to become part inn, part luxury hotel, a half-mile
west of the central intersection and within easy walking distance of
Merrimans and *Eidelweiss* restaurants. A wide range of modernized rooms,
plus a couple of more expensive suites.

Parker Ranch Lodge, PO Box 458, Kamuela HI 96743; ☎885-4100; fax 885-
6711; ③.
One of the Big Island's closest approximations to the ubiquitous motels of the
mainland. Simple, predictable red motel units backing onto the Kohala slopes,
at the very start of the road down to Kawaihae from the intersection in the
centre of Waimea.

Puu Manu Cottage, reserved through *Hawaii's Best Bed & Breakfast*, PO
Box 563, Kamuela HI 96743; ☎1-800/262-9912; fax 885-0559; ④.
Former horse barn, three miles east of Waimea, which has been converted
into an idyllic B&B cottage, enjoying splendid views of the meadows flanking
Mauna Kea. Three-night minimum stay; reservations essential.

Waimea Gardens Cottage, PO Box 563, Kamuela HI 96743; ☎885-4550 or
1-800/262-9912; fax 885-0559; ④.

Upmarket and extremely hospitable B&B, run by Barbara Campbell, who also coordinates the *Hawaii's Best Bed & Breakfast* agency (see p.21). The property is two miles west of central Waimea, immediately beyond the 59-mile marker and before the bridge as you head for Kawaihae. It has two large and comfortable guest cottages with private bathrooms, one with kitchen facilities. Both are furnished with antiques and a library of Hawaiiana, with views towards the green and rolling Kohala hills. Three-night minimum stay; reservations essential.

Kamuela Museum

For sheer entertainment value, the **Kamuela Museum** – two miles west of the central Waimea intersection, almost directly opposite the junction of highways 250 and 19 – is the best museum on the island. Its most memorable specimen is its owner and curator, Albert Solomon, who was in charge of the Honolulu police force motorcycle escort team when Franklin Roosevelt came to Hawaii in 1934, and can show you the great man's slippers to prove it. If you have an hour or two spare, both he and his wife Harriet can tell some great tales; she is a direct Parker descendant and their family anecdotes cover the period since Americans first arrived in Hawaii.

The museum is open daily 8am–5pm; $5 adults, $2 children under 12; ☎885-4724.

The museum itself spreads through several rooms of the Solomons' bungalow. Each of the dozens of display cases contains an unpredictable mixture of items and hand-written labels, which categorize the objects from "unique" (the rope used to haul the Apollo 11 astronauts out of the Pacific), through "quite rare" (a dessicated Hawaiian bat suspended by its feet), down to simply "old" (a motley assortment of toothpick holders, Japanese noodle-cutting machines, accordions, "historic reptile dung", chicken spectacles and can openers). An intriguing collection of Chinese and Japanese porcelain, costumes and weaponry culminates with a gun retrieved from the wreckage of a *kamikaze* plane that attacked the USS *West Virginia* in April 1945.

However, most visitors are drawn by the unusual and extensive range of ancient **Hawaiian artefacts**. Sinister-looking idols of wood and stone loom over rows of daggers, "death cups" used in magic rituals and lava knuckle dusters. Laid out for your inspection are all the daily implements of a world without metal, including wooden hooks that were baited with human flesh and used to catch sharks, as well as fish hooks made from human bone, *poi* pounders and *tapa* beaters, and colourful feather *leis* and helmets.

Restaurants

Having over the last decade or so become one of the Big Island's most exclusive residential areas, Waimea has begun to acquire the **restaurants** to go with it. In addition, there are still a few old-style cowboy places, piling up meaty mountains of ribs, while the Waimea Center mall, a couple of hundred yards down the road towards Hilo, is the place to head for **fast food**, with *McDonalds*, *TCBY* and *Subway* outlets.

Edelweiss, opposite *Kamuela Inn*, Hwy-19; ☎885-6800.
One of the Big Island's more incongruous spots, an expensive and very good restaurant serving filling German and Austrian cuisine (vegetarians beware) in a Hawaiian version of an Alpine chalet, constructed of broad planks of dark-hued wood. The basic lunch menu features burgers, sandwiches or *bratwurst* and *sauerkraut*, all for $5–6, while dinner options include *wiener schnitzel* (breaded veal cutlets), sautéed calf's liver, filet mignon or New York steak, for around $17–20. Most people, however, come here for the huge list of changing daily specials. Open Tues–Sat only, 11.30am–1.30pm & 5–9pm, but no reservations are accepted, so be prepared to wait in line for up to 45 minutes.

Great Wall Chop Sui, Waimea Center; ☎885-7252.
Extensive Chinese menu in a not very atmospheric mall. Dishes include *chop sui*, with chicken or duck; noodles and seafood start at around $6 and range up to a $13 lobster in black bean sauce. Open daily except Wed 11am–8pm.

Mean Cuisine, Opelo Plaza, 65-1227A Opelo Rd; ☎885-6325.
Unpretentious and popular bakery/diner in the same mall as *Merrimans*. Chowder with bread costs around $2, a sandwich is a little more, while substantial, tasty home-cooked stews and bakes, costing $6 or so, are prepared daily. There's lashings of fresh coffee to go with it all, and the cakes are sublime.

Merrimans, Opelo Plaza, 65-1227A Opelo Rd; ☎885-6822.
This gourmet restaurant, a few hundred yards down towards Kawaihae from the central crossroads, has a deserved reputation as one of the Big Island's top dining places, with an emphasis on organic produce. Although the dinners can be rich, the lunch menu is simple, with a $10 grilled shrimp salad being the most expensive dish. In the evening, appetizers include steamed clams and wok-charred *ahi*. Among the main courses, mostly priced around $22–25, are steak or Chateaubriand, veal T-bones, fresh fish in a myriad of styles and Thai seafood yellow curry. Open for lunch Mon–Fri only, 11.30am–1.30pm, and for dinner every night 5.30–9pm.

Paniolo Country Inn, next to the *Parker Ranch Lodge*; ☎885-4377.
Large steakhouse in central Waimea, which specializes in substantial portions of whatever you fancy at any time of the day. Breakfast is served from 7am, with *huevos rancheros* and eggs benedict. At dinner, main courses start at $5 for Mexican *burritos* and *quesadillas*, ranging through large pizzas for two people up to a 16oz Porterhouse steak costing $21.

Sugar'n'Spice, Parker Ranch Center; ☎885-0548.
Small bakery stocked to the rafters with all things sweet 'n' sickly, good for a fresh breakfast coffee if you're sure you can resist the home-made ice creams, jellybeans and candies.

Su's Thai Kitchen, Parker Ranch Center; ☎885-8688.
Another branch of Kailua's excellent Thai restaurant (see p.54), next to the visitor centre in the Parker Ranch Center. American breakfasts until 10am, then a full Thai menu. All the daily lunch specials, which include Chinese and Japanese dishes, cost $5.75; for dinner, try a delicious yellow or green curry, prepared as hot as you like, a whole *pomino* fish or the seafood special mix.

Yong's Kal-Bi, Waimea Center; ☎885-8440.
Fast food Korean-style, including chicken, pork, or beef ribs to take out or eat in, mostly barbecued and costing $5–7. Open Tues–Sun 10.30am–9pm.

The Parker Ranch

The Parker family history dates back to **John Palmer Parker**, a ship's clerk from Massachusetts, who jumped ship in Kawaihae Harbor in 1809. He soon came to the attention of King Kamehameha, who gave him the job of maintaining the fish ponds at Hōnaunau (see p.67). After a brief fit of wanderlust had seen him join the crew of a merchant ship and find himself detained in Canton for two years during the War of 1812, Parker returned to Hawaii at the end of 1814 and convinced the king that this time he intended to stay.

He returned at a fortuitous moment. On February 1793, Captain George Vancouver of the *Discovery* had presented Kamehameha with six cows and a bull and suggested that a *kapu* be placed on them, forbidding anyone to kill or harm the cattle and thus allowing a population to grow. Unchecked breeding, as well as subsequent imports, ensured that by 1815 wild cattle had become a serious problem on the island, destroying crops and terrorizing villages. Similarly, wild mustangs also roamed unmolested.

Kamehameha gave Parker permission to shoot the cattle and from his first base at Niuli'i near Pololū he set out to impose discipline on the unruly beasts. With the decline of the sandalwood trade, the supply of fresh beef and hides to visiting whalers became crucial to the Hawaiian economy. Parker managed the business for the king and, by taking his pay in live animals, swiftly built up his own herds. Marrying Kamehameha's granddaughter **Kipikane**, he soon integrated into local society and was one of only two foreigners present at the famous banquet in 1819 when Liholiho broke the age-old *kapu* on men and women dining together (see p.173). He moved to the village of Waimea in 1835, establishing his homestead at Mana and soon building a separate house for his son John Palmer Parker II.

Mexican, Native American, and Spanish cowboys were brought to the island to round up the horses and cattle. Their ponchos, bandanas and rawhide lassos were swiftly adopted by the Hawaiians they recruited, who called themselves *paniolos* (from *Españoles*, or Spaniards). By 1846, the Big Island held an estimated 25,000 wild and 10,000 domesticated cattle.

Like so many other outsiders, Parker seized his opportunity in the Great Mahele of 1847, when private land ownership was allowed for the first time. He was granted two acres and his wife Kipikane received 640 more. Soon he was in a position to buy another thousand acres and to lease the entire *ahupua'a* (region) of Waikoloa.

After a long period when the ranch was divided between Parker's immediate heirs and the high-living **Samuel Parker** frittered much of it away on lavish parties, the property was re-established on a firm footing under Thelma Parker in 1906. Attempts to diversify into sugar production and bee-keeping came to nothing, but the cattle ranch went from strength to strength for the remainder of the twentieth century, albeit with imported pedigree animals rather than the original Hawaiian stock.

The last Parker to control the operation, the sixth-generation **Richard Smart**, died in November 1992, leaving the ranch to a charitable trust. The ranch currently holds around 55,000 cattle on 227,000 acres of land, the bulk of which is divided into three huge parcels; one takes up most of North Kohala, one curves around the higher Hāmākua reaches of Mauna Kea and the main tranch runs for forty miles up the western slopes of Mauna Kea from the ocean at Kawaihae. Assorted schools and health-care facilities in the Waimea area are now among the beneficiaries of the ranch's profits.

The Parker Ranch Visitor Center

*The Visitor
Center and the
Historic Homes
are open daily
except Easter
Sun, July 4,
Thanksgiving &
Xmas. The
Visitor Center
opens
9am–5pm, last
admission 4pm;
$5. The Historic
Homes open
10am–5pm,
last admission
4pm; $7.50.
Combined
admission to
Historic Homes
and the Visitor
Center is $10;
tickets sold
9am–3pm only;
☎885-7655.*

The small **Parker Ranch Visitor Center**, located in the Parker Ranch Shopping Center in central Waimea, provides a fascinating overview of Parker family history as well as the general history of Hawaii. Its primary focus is on displays of old ranching equipment, with a slightly scaled-down but genuine hut from the ranch crammed with saddles, spurs, bottles and cowboy paraphernalia. A short video evokes the atmosphere of ranch life, with footage of cattle being swum out to waiting steamers, as well as modern action shots of a dawn round-up high on Mauna Kea.

The Historic Homes

You may find your interest in the Parker family flagging at the so-called **Historic Homes**, half a mile out of Waimea on Hwy-190 towards Kailua. The construction of the stately **Puʻuʻōpelu**, the more imposing of the two Parker dwellings preserved here, started in 1863, but it was completely remodelled in 1969 and now lacks any apparent connection with things Hawaiian. Its pastel yellow rooms are filled instead with a motley collection of minor European paintings, while through the air waft the melodious tones of its last owner, Richard Smart, in recordings made during his career as a Broadway musical star.

The **Mana House** alongside looks like an ordinary white clapboard house, but the interior is panelled throughout with gleaming, dark *koa* wood, the sheer weight of which groans under every step you take. In fact these timbers were the only components robust enough to be moved when it was decided to reconstruct the house here in 1970, twelve miles from the site where it originally went up during the 1840s. The walls of the tiny building are packed with family documents and fading photographs.

Five hundred yards beyond the Historic Homes towards Kailua, you come to **Paniolo Park**, the home each July 4 of the annual Parker Ranch Rodeo (information on ☎885-7655). Six miles beyond that is the turn-off for the Saddle Road.

Onwards from Waimea

Whichever direction you choose to head out of Waimea, there's spellbinding scenery to enjoy just a few miles down the road. Heading east towards Hilo on Hwy-19 brings you to Honokaʻa in less than twenty minutes, with the enticements of Waipiʻo Valley not far beyond (see p.122). From an intersection just six miles to the south of Waimea, the **Saddle Road** starts its dramatic climb across the heart of the island between Mauna Kea and Mauna Loa – a journey covered in detail on p.127. The most attractive drive of all is **Hwy-250** along Kohala Mountain to Hāwi. However, the transition from the dry to the wet side of the Big Island can be experienced at its most marked if you make a slight detour off Hwy-19 three miles east of Waimea and follow the atmospheric and little-used **Old Māmalahoa Highway**.

Old Māmalahoa Highway.

Once part of Kamehameha's protected round-island trail, the **Old Māmalahoa Highway** was known to the ancient Hawaiians as "mudlane" and was notorious as a site where '*oi'o*, or processions of the souls of the dead, heading for the underworld below Waipi'o (see p.123), might be encountered at night. Now it's a minor road, somewhat slow and sinuous, but not difficult, even for cyclists.

The road heads first through treeless volcanic uplands where the rolling meadows, misty when they're not windswept, are grazed by horse and cattle. After about eight miles, you abruptly plunge into a magnificent avenue of stately old ironwoods. Thereafter, the vegetation is tropical and colourful, and homes with glorious gardens dot the hillside. Soon after passing through the residential community of Āhualoa, you rejoin the Belt Road near Honoka'a.

North Kohala

The district of **North Kohala**, which officially starts four miles or so north of Kawaihae, to all intents and purposes comprises the low-rise flanks of Kohala Mountain itself. Though it holds some of the most beautiful of all the Big Island's scenery, it's an area that few visitors take the time to explore. The major drawback is that access to the sea is restricted, on both the leeward side, which is almost entirely devoid of beaches, and on the rugged windward coast, which is lined by the series of inaccessible valleys from Pololū down to Waipi'o. Add that to a complete lack of hotels and an economy deflated by the decline of agriculture, and perhaps it's not surprising that you may well have the roads and parks almost to yourself. Miss the drive along Hwy-250 from Waimea, however, and you've missed something very special indeed.

Across the mountain: Hwy-250

With a maximum elevation of 5408 feet, Kohala Mountain is considerably lower than its younger Big Island rivals. Its summit is always green, never covered by snow, and its smooth velvet knobs betray few traces of their violent volcanic past. Few people might recognize this landscape as being Hawaiian, but the varying views of it obtained from a trip along **Hwy-250** are among the most sublime in the entire state.

For the first four miles or so out of Waimea, as the highway climbs the west flank of Kohala, a panorama of the Kohala coast gradually unfolds. At first the rolling lava landscape is covered with wiry green turf; there's barely any other vegetation. Scattered tree cover starts to appear higher up, together with clumps of flat-bladed cactus, often growing straight out of bare outcrops of chunky black lava. Higher still you enter proper ranching country; for a while the road becomes an avenue lined with two rows of splendid ironwood trees, between which can be glimpsed undulating pastureland grazed by sleek horses. At various points along the way, vivid green turf-covered cinder cones bulge from the meadows, speckled with black and brown cattle.

Unfortunately, at no point do you get the opportunity to turn off the road and explore the magnificent scenery higher up the mountain. As well as large landholdings of the Parker Ranch, especially along the northern half, there are several other private estates and even one or two old-style cattle-ranching communities hidden away. The very top of the mountain is a surreal landscape of eroded hillocks, which as soon as you cross the watershed become so thickly forested as to be almost impenetrable. Rudimentary trails lead down to valleys such as Waipi'o, and the rough terrain is still cut through in places by irrigation channels such as the famous **Kohala Ditch**, constructed in the early 1900s to service the sugar industry.

The easiest and most enjoyable way to experience this unique area is on **horseback**, with either *Kohala Na'alapa Trail Rides*, (PO Box 992, Honoka'a HI 96727; ☎775-0330), who run daily half-day trips from the ironwoods of Kohala Ranch into the uplands above Kahua Ranch at 9am and 1.30pm for $65 per person, or the similarly priced *Paniolo Riding Adventures* (☎889-5354), based at Ponoholo Ranch.

Along the Coast: Hwy-270

The only alternative to Hwy-250 if you want to see North Kohala is the coastal **Hwy-270**, which heads north from Kawaihae Harbor. Most visitors drive a circular route that takes in both; the shoreline road is not as immediately attractive, but it does offer a handful of interesting historic sites, the occasional beach park and in winter at any rate a reasonable chance of spotting humpback whales in the waters of the 'Alenuihāhā Channel.

For its first dozen miles Hwy-270 has no access to the ocean; if you want to snorkel in the bays at the foot of the low cliffs, join one of the boat excursions organized by the Kohala resorts (see p.77).

Lapakahi State Historical Park
Fourteen miles north of Kawaihae, the first turning *makai* of the highway leads a short way down to **LAPAKAHI STATE HISTORICAL PARK**, where you'll find the ancient village of Koai'e,

– thought to have been inhabited for more than five hundred years until it was abandoned during the nineteenth century.

North Kohala

Lapakahi Park is open daily except hols 8am–4pm; free; ☎889-5566.

A hot, exposed but fascinating one-mile-long trail leads through what appears to have been a sizeable community inhabited by ordinary, subsistence-level Hawaiians. They probably chose this site as their home because of its white coral beach and absence of the usual cliffs, making it the safest year-round canoe landing for many miles. Sustaining a population on such barren land must always have been hard, and the struggle seems to have been defeated in the end by a combination of a drop in the water table and the economic changes taking place in the islands as a whole.

You pass the villagers' dwelling places – which weren't necessarily roofed and whose low walls served primarily as wind breaks – as well as assorted traces of their day-to-day life. Most of these are simply hollowed out rocks; some were used to hold lamps, others served as salt pans of differing depths, and there's even a little indented stone, holding scattered black and white pebbles, used to play the game *kōnane*. Beside a fish shrine, where offerings would be left to ensure a successful catch, a carved decoy rests on a open net; the shy *ahu* fish was captured when it attempted to make friends with its wooden counterpart.

The **beach** at Lapakahi is composed of medium-sized boulders rather than fine sand. This is a marine conservation area and the water is very clear, with parrotfish and darting yellow shapes visible in its turquoise depths. Visitors are only allowed to swim or snorkel north of the ancient village and even there the use of sunscreen and towels is forbidden. From the bluff near the end of the trail, you can see the towering Haleakalā volcano on Maui.

Māhukona and Kapaʻa Beach County Parks

A mile north of Lapakahi, another spur road connects Hwy-270 with North Kohala's first beach park, **MĀHUKONA BEACH COUNTY PARK**. In fact, there's no beach at all, just a nineteenth-century harbour hemmed in by yet more lava outcrops. The sea wall is still shored up, a mess of rust-streaked concrete pilings and jetties built to service the *Kohala Sugar Company* mill, which opened in 1863. For almost a century this was the shipping centre for raw sugar brought by train from the fields around Niuliʻi near Pololū; it closed down in 1956, after a final flurry of activity when the Hāmākua railroad was destroyed by the *tsunami* of 1946 (see p.114). The mill itself ceased to operate in 1975.

Māhukona is no place to swim; local divers join the swarms of yellow fish to explore the old railroad machinery beneath the waves, but conditions can get very stormy indeed, especially in winter.

Much the same goes for **KAPAʻA BEACH COUNTY PARK**, reached from another spur road off Hwy-270, a mile farther on. Once again there's no beach, and the rocky stretch of coastline is cluttered with overgrown ruins. All Kapaʻa has to offer is a pavilion equipped with rest rooms, a barbecue/picnic area and views across to Maui on clear days.

Mo'okini Heiau and the Kamehameha Birthplace

At the northernmost tip of the Big Island, a long straight road drops down to halt abruptly at the perimeter fence of 'Upolu airport, built by the military during the 1930s and now little used. From there an unpaved road winds west along the coastline, degenerating occasionally into big pools of mud. Though quite rutted, in dry conditions it should pose few problems for ordinary rental cars. There are no trees along this exposed and windy stretch, where the rolling meadows halt a few feet up from the black lava shoreline.

The prime reason to venture this way is to visit one of Hawaii's remotest but most significant ancient temples. The **MO'OKINI HEIAU** is roughly two miles from the airport, accessible from a rudimentary parking lot, via a short footpath up a small bluff. Though the gate is usually locked, visitors are welcome to go through the gap in the low walls. The *heiau* itself, in the centre of a large green lawn, is a ruined but impressive pile of lichen-covered rocks; you can enter the structure on one side and discern the traces of its separate rooms, as well as a boulder on which victims were prepared for sacrifice.

Two conflicting legends make the temple's origins somewhat obscure. Its current guardians state that it was built between sunset and sunrise on a single night in 480 AD by Kuamo'o Mo'okini, using water-worn basalt stones that were passed from hand to hand along a fourteen-mile human chain from Polulū Valley. Alternative sources suggest that it was created by the Tahitian warrior-priest Pa'ao seven centuries later, as a temple to Kū the god of battle. The most likely explanation, though, is that Pa'ao simply rededicated an existing temple to Kū; it may even have been the site where the practice of human sacrifice was first introduced to Hawaii. The Kahuna Nui, the hereditary priesthood of Kū, has maintained an unbroken descent; the traditional *kapu* barring female priests has long since been broken, however, and the current Kahuna Nui, Leimomi Mo'okini Lum, is the seventh woman to hold the position.

For more about the life of Kamehameha, see p.172.

A few hundred yards farther along, a low double-walled enclosure sloping down a little closer to the sea is known as the **KAMEHAMEHA AKAHI AINA HANAU**. Kamehameha the Great is said to have been born here in 1758 – the date is known thanks to the appearance of Halley's Comet – at a time when his parents were in the retinue of King Alapa'i, who was preparing to invade Maui. The baby was whisked away in secret and brought up in Waipi'o Valley, though he returned to live in Kohala in 1782 (see below). The entrance to the large compound is from the south, *mauka* side; you can't go into the central enclosure, which amounts to little more than a patch of scrubby soil scattered with a few boulders. One such rock is said to mark the precise birthsite; visitors still leave offerings to Hawaii's greatest ruler on the walls nearby.

Hāwī

Twenty years on from the closure of its principal *raison d'être* – the *Kohala Sugar Company* mill – the tiny town of HĀWĪ, a mile on from the 'Upolu turn-off, is hanging on as one of the nicest little communities in the state. It's an appealingly run-down place, with its all-purpose stores still connected by creaking boardwalks and every yard bursting with bright flowers.

Once you've filled up with fuel at the intersection of highways 250 and 270, there's nothing to see or do in Hāwī beyond stroll across the village green and up and down the hundred yards of its main street. However, the spacious *Bamboo Restaurant and Bar* (Tues–Sat all day, Sun 9am–2pm only; ☎889-5555), converted from a former hotel used by migrant Japanese sugar labourers, is among the most enjoyable **restaurants** on the Big Island, serving "island-style" cuisine in a dining room equipped with bamboo and rattan furniture and festooned with tropical plants. A lunchtime salad, burger or plate of stir-fried noodles costs $5–8, while dinner dishes, priced at $15–20, include prawns, shrimps and scallops as well as chicken, beef or lamb from local farms. There's sometimes live music on weekend evenings and an attached store-cum-gallery sells attractive *koa*-wood gifts and crafts.

If you're just looking for a light snack, the *Kohala Coffee Mill* across the road (☎889-5577) serves fresh Kona coffee and muffins, and sells coffee by the pound, while *Matthew's Place* (☎889-5500), next door to the *Bamboo*, is a tiny café with big breakfast omeletttes for $2.95 and dinner specials for $7–8.

Kapa'au

The main feature of the even smaller hamlet of KAPA'AU, a couple of miles east of Hāwī on Hwy-270 towards Pololū, is a **statue** of King Kamehameha, the original of an identical one in Honolulu. Commissioned from an American sculptor in Florence for the coronation of King David Kalākaua in 1883, it was lost at sea and then miraculously recovered after the insurance money had paid for a replacement. Kamehameha had established his headquarters in **Hālawa** in 1782, in order to prepare for the imminent contest over the right to succeed the ageing King Kalaniopu'u. All traces of Hālawa were ploughed over to plant cane many years ago, but as it was very close to where modern Kapa'au now stands Kapa'au seemed a reasonable alternative location for the surplus statue.

Opposite the statue in the centre of town, *Don's Deli* (☎889-5822) serves sandwiches, as well as delicious fruit smoothies and all sorts of ice creams.

Not far east of town, a narrow road *mauka* of the highway leads through some verdant countryside to the picturesque **Kalahikiola Church**, built in 1855. Its first preacher, Rev Elias Bond, established the adjoining Bond Estate, a complex including homes, farm buildings and a school.

Kēōkea Beach County Park

The road on from Kapaʻau runs past the site of Hālawa; a huge wayside boulder at this tight curve is known as **Kamehameha Rock**, as the future king is said to have demonstrated his right to rule by having sufficient *mana*, or spiritual power, to raise it above his head.

Immediately beyond, a lane leads via a Japanese cemetery dotted with small black steles down to **KĒŌKEA BEACH COUNTY PARK**. In the centre of a rocky bay, a small stream flows into the ocean, and the surrounding hillsides have all too evidently been pounded to pieces by endless high surf. An open-sided lookout shelter, exposed to the winds on a small hillock, makes a nice picnic spot, but there is no beach.

Pololū Valley

As Hwy-270 reaches its dead end at a tiny parking lot, you get a view over one final meadow to the open cliff face that abuts the sea. Stretching away into the distance, it's punctuated by a succession of valleys, only accessible to visitors on foot and each therefore progressively less frequented and wilder. The last of these, not visible from here, is Waipiʻo (see p.122); the first, spread out beneath you, is **POLOLŪ VALLEY**.

If not quite on the scale of Waipiʻo, Pololū was also once heavily planted by *taro* farmers. Regular *tsunamis* did little to encourage a stable population, however, and the death knell came when completion of the Kohala Ditch in 1906 drained its previously plentiful water supply off for use on the nearby sugar plantations.

Pololū Valley remains a magnificent spectacle, and nowhere more so than from the initial overlook. If you take the time to explore it close up you may well find the hike less strenuous, and more private, than its better-known equivalent farther east. The pedestrian-only trail down from the end of the parking lot takes twenty minutes without ever being especially steep, although when it's wet – which is almost always – it's an absolute quagmire of gloopy brown mud. Assessing whether you want to attempt the descent is easy; conditions are at their worst at the very start of the trail, which drops immediately into dense head-high grasses. From there you wind down the hillside among assorted ironwood, guava and *hala* trees. Occasional stretches of small loose lava pebbles come as a welcome relief from the prevailing mud, and offer glimpses of the shore below.

Once on the valley floor, the trail remains thoroughly squelchy as it approaches the broad river-cum-lake that meanders across the terrain, surrounded by marshy reeds. Hikers who try to head inland are swiftly confronted by "Private Property" signs warning you to go no farther.

Though Pololū's **beach**, like the one at Waipi'o, is commonly referred to as being black sand, it's basically grey grit, littered with decaying detergent bottles and pulverized detritus. A colourful touch is added by the yellow and purple blooms which back the black lava rocks. In winter, the shore is prone to strong winds and heavy surf; there's no question of swimming even at the best of times. Take care too as you wade across the shallow but fast-flowing stream to reach the longer segment of the beach; high water is capable of carrying hikers out to the sharks offshore. On the far side of the stream, the beach is lined by gentle woodlands of pine-needle-covered hillocks, grazed by mules and horses.

Onwards from Pololū

A conspicuous but virtually impossible-to-follow trail switchbacks eastwards from Pololu over to the next valley, Honokāne Nui, and on to Honokāne Iki beyond it. The track doesn't go all the way through to Waipi'o, so at some point the few suicidal hikers who attempt it have to double back. As a rule the path follows the contours of the hillsides and doesn't drop back down to the sea each time, but it's in roughly the same bedraggled condition as the trail down to Pololū and is certainly no easier. Only experienced wilderness backpackers should even consider an expedition into this uninhabited and remote terrrain.

Chapter 3

Hilo and the Hāmākua Coast

Visitors to the magnificent **Hāmākua coast**, on the northeastern flank of the Big Island, are confronted by archetypal South Seas scenery. This spectacular landscape has been carved by the great torrents of rain unleashed when the trade winds hit Mauna Kea, the highest peak in the Pacific, after crossing two thousand miles of open ocean. Countless streams and waterfalls cascade down the cliffs and gullies, nourishing dense jungle-like vegetation that is alive with multi-coloured blossoms and iridescent orchids. All in all, if you arrive on the dry Kona side of the island, and never cross over to this windward coast, you'll be left with a literally one-sided impression of Hawaii.

Even before the emergence of commercial agriculture during the nineteenth century, these slopes formed the fertile heartland of Hawaii; **Waipi'o Valley** in the north, the home of generations of ancient rulers, was said to be capable of feeding the entire island. Until recently, windward Hawaii's major city, **Hilo**, was the unchallenged economic and political powerhouse of the island. It's still the capital, though as the sugar mills close down and the significance of Kona-side tourism increases, it feels more like a rather traditional small town, and is seen by brasher recent migrants as something of a staid backwater. As a place to visit, it's relaxed and attractive, spread over a surprisingly large area but with an appealing old-fashioned downtown district where it's still possible to stroll between friendly cafés, street markets and historic sites.

As well as having the only **airport** along the Hāmākua coast, Hilo holds virtually all its **hotels**. In the absence of sizeable sandy beaches, however, those tourists who choose to come here are drawn largely by the beauty of the nearby coast, which can be admired at several viewpoints along the Hawaii Belt Road as it runs northwest. The full fifty-mile excursion up to Waipi'o Valley is irresistible, but nearer at hand you can enjoy the delightful Pepe'ekeo Scenic Drive, or the mighty Akaka and Rainbow Falls.

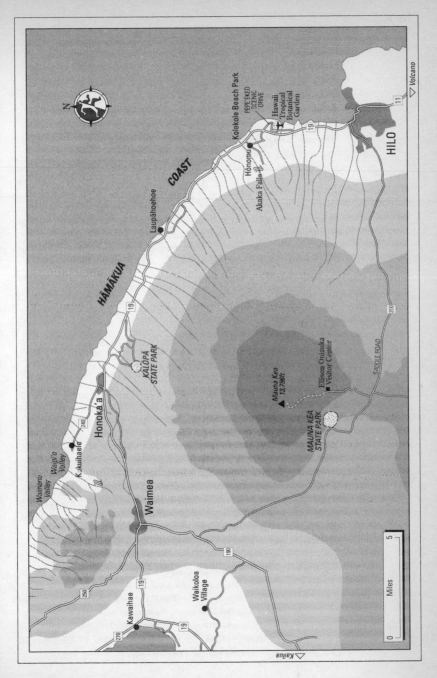

Accommodation price codes

Prices have been graded with the symbols below, according to the quoted rate for the least expensive double room for most of the year, not including state taxes of 10.17 percent (see p.20 for a fuller explanation).

① up to $30   ④ $75–100   ⑦ $170–225
② $30–50   ⑤ $100–130   ⑧ $225–300
③ $50–75   ⑥ $130–170   ⑨ over $300

Several botanical gardens offer the chance to inspect the extraordinary plants that flourish in this hothouse climate.

Although the Belt Road is very much the island's main thoroughfare, and the recommended route if you're heading between Hilo and Kailua, it is also possible to cut directly across the Big Island on the **Saddle Road**. Heading way beyond the clouds to pass directly between the volcanoes, it's one of the most unusual and memorable drives in all Hawaii.

Finally, if you plan to visit **Hawaii Volcanoes National Park** (which is covered in Chapter Four), note that while Hilo makes a much more convenient base than anywhere on the Kona side, it is also possible to stay in Volcano, on the park's very doorstep.

Hilo

The paradise of Hawaii . . . what Honolulu attempts to be, Hilo is without effort.

Isabella Bird, 1873

Although it's the Big Island's capital, and largest town, just 45,000 people live in **HILO** and it remains an endearing and unpressured place. In the early 1970s, it made a serious bid to become a major tourist centre, expanding its airport to accept jumbo jets direct from the mainland. Despite that, mass tourism has never taken off; quite simply, it rains too much. Statistics show that Hilo receives an average of 130 inches of annual rainfall, with fewer than 90 rain-free days per year. Most mornings, however, start out clear and radiant; the rain tends to fall in the afternoon or at night, and America's wettest city blazes with wild orchids and tropical plants.

Hilo stands where the Wailuku and Wailoa rivers empty into an enormous curving bay, named "Hilo" by ancient Hawaiians in honour of the first crescent of the new moon. By far the best natural harbour on the island, it was here in 1796 that Kamehameha the Great built his *peleleu*, a fleet of eight hundred war canoes for use in his campaigns against the other Hawaiian islands. Characterized by his enemies as "monstrosities", these hybrid Western-influenced vessels carried mighty armies of warriors; some say they were never destroyed and still lie hidden in caves along the Kona coast.

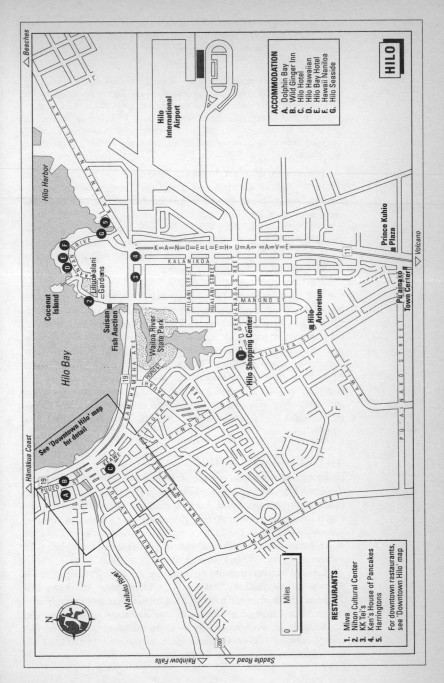

HILO

ACCOMMODATION

A. Dolphin Bay
B. Wild Ginger Inn
C. Hilo Hotel
D. Hilo Hawaiian
E. Hilo Bay Hotel
F. Hawaii Naniloa
G. Hilo Seaside

RESTAURANTS

1. Miwa
2. Nihon Cultural Center
3. KK Tei's
4. Ken's House of Pancakes
5. Harringtons

For downtown restaurants,
see 'Downtown Hilo' map

Hilo

The port prospered in the nineteenth century, when a strong missionary influence enabled it to present itself as a clean-living alternative to dissolute Honolulu. In the words of the evangelist Titus Coan in 1848:

> *No man staggers, no man fights, none are noisy and boisterous. We have nothing here to inflame the blood, nothing to madden the brain. Our verdant landscapes, our peaceful streets, our pure cold water, and the absence of those inebriating vials of wrath which consume all good, induce wise commanders to visit this port in order to refresh and give liberty to their crews.*

Historically, Hilo's role as the island's main port gave it an unusually radical labour force. From the Thirties onwards, local workers spearheaded successive campaigns against the "Big Five" companies that had long dominated the Hawaiian economy (see p.174). Fifty people were injured, though none died, in the "Hilo Massacre" of August 1, 1938, when strikers were attacked by armed police and strikes in 1946 and 1949 helped to end the long-term Republican domination of state politics.

The innermost segment of the bay, encompassing both port and town, is now protected by a long breakwater, whose construction began in 1908 at the expense of destroying a coral reef and a black-sand beach long popular with surfers. In principle, this is a very calm stretch of water, but its funnel shape means that during great storms it can channel huge waves directly into the centre of town. Cataclysmic *tsunami* killed 96 people in April 1946, and a further 61 in May 1960. Lava flows have also repeatedly threatened to engulf it; in 1881 Princess Ruth Ke'elikōlani summoned up all her spiritual power, watched by missionaries and journalists, to halt one on the edge of town, while as recently as 1984 another flow stopped eight miles short.

For more about Princess Ruth and the goddess Pele, see p.15.

Arrival and information

Compact and walkable, downtown Hilo focuses on the junction of the seafront Kamehameha Avenue and Waianuenue Avenue, which heads towards the Saddle Road across the island. However, the urban area extends for several miles, and the **airport** at General Lyman Field (☎935-4782), on the eastern outskirts, is well beyond walking distance. If you're not renting a car at the airport – see p.16 – a taxi into town will cost around $5.

Limited **bus** services are operated by the *Mass Transportation Agency* (25 Aupuni St; ☎935-8241). Their base, **Mooheau Bus Terminal**, is an open-air pavilion on Kamehameha Avenue, opposite the S. Hata Building between the two highways, where you can enjoy views of the bay as you wait. In addition to assorted city routes, scheduled to meet the needs of commuters and of little use to visitors, there are a few longer-distance services. On weekdays only, the "35 PAHOA/KAU" leaves Hilo at 2.30pm and reaches Pahoa, 20 miles southeast of Hilo, at 3.45pm; the "7 DOWNTOWN HILO" leaves Pahoa at 6.20am and arrives in Hilo at 7.30am. For a full timetable of the once-daily cross-island service between Hilo and **Kailua** (which leaves Mooheau Terminal at 1.10pm), see p.18; the service to **Hawaii Volcanoes National Park** and Ocean View, leaving Mooheau Bus Terminal at 2.40pm on Monday to Friday only, is detailed on p.142.

In addition, the *Hilo Sampan* runs hourly along two separate routes around the city, which coincide only at Hilo Shopping Center (Mon–Sat 8am–4pm; single fare $2, daily pass $7; ☎935-6955). Tourists may enjoy the ride in these converted 1930s-style taxi-cabs, complete with running boards, but again they're of no great practical use.

Information and services

The **Hawaii Visitors Bureau** is at 250 Keawe St, one block up from the front in the centre of downtown (Mon–Fri 8am–noon & 1–4.30pm; ☎961-5797; fax 961-2126). Helpful staff can advise on accommodation and tours and have piles of brochures to take away.

Hilo's main **post office** (Mon–Fri 9am–4.30pm, Sat 9am–12.30pm) is on the approach road to the airport, but there's another one downtown in the Federal Building on Waianuenue Avenue (Mon–Fri 8am–4pm). **Banks** are dotted all over town and in the malls, with the most central branch of the *Bank of Hawaii* being at 117 Keawe St.

City Tours

The Lyman House Museum (see p.105) organizes a free **walking tour** of downtown on the third Saturday of each month, setting off at 9am; if you're not around for that, it's well worth spending $1.25 on a copy of the museum's **historical map** of downtown Hilo.

Jack's Tours, 226 Kanoelehua Ave (☎961-6666), and the staff of *Arnott's Lodge* (see p.104) can arrange bus tours farther afield. Details of helicopter and fixed-wing **flight-seeing** operators based at General Lyman Field appear on p.19; Big Island boat trips are restricted to the Kona side of the island.

Accommodation

Downtown Hilo is extremely short of **hotels**; at least three were destroyed by the *tsunami* of 1946, and now only the *Hilo Hotel* remains in the centre of the city. However there's plenty of choice along the oceanfront crescent of **Banyan Drive**, a mile or so southeast, and a couple of welcoming and inexpensive inns can also be found north of the Wailuku River, a short walk from downtown.

Furthermore, room rates are significantly lower on this side of the island, in part because the hotels don't set out to be fully fledged resorts, assuming instead that you'll be out exploring the volcanoes or the Hāmākua coast during the day. If that *is* what you're going to be doing, there's no great reason to spend more than a couple of nights in Hilo; if you plan to spend most of your time on the beach, then it's probably the wrong side of the island for you altogether.

All the properties listed here share the zip code HI 96720.

Arnott's Lodge, 98 Apapane Rd; ☎969-7097, 1-800/368-8752 (US) or 1-800/953-7773 (HI); fax 961-9638; ①/②.
Laid-back budget accommodation in a two-storey motel-style lodge, tucked away in the woods a couple of miles southeast of downtown, just off the road that leads from Kalaniana'ole Ave to Onekahakaha beach. Call from the airport for free pick-up. The downstairs dorms have 12 beds for $15 each, while the second floor is divided into two-bedroom units. There's a treehouse and a bar, but no food apart from a twice-weekly barbecue. The management organizes good-value excursions in a four-wheel-drive van, including trips to the summit of Mauna Kea, Volcanoes National Park or South Point.

Dolphin Bay Hotel, 333 Iliahi St; ☎935-1466; fax 935-1523; ③.
Small and friendly 18-room hotel, within walking distance of downtown on the north side of the Wailuku River. Studios and one- and two-bedroom suites are all fully equipped with TV, bathroom, and kitchen. Free papayas and bananas dangle at strategic points around the building.

Hale Kai, 111 Honoli'i Pali; ☎935-6330; fax 935-8439; ④.
Small, comfortable and modern B&B, perched above the ocean a short distance *makai* of Hwy-19, a couple of miles north of downtown Hilo. Each of the three rooms in the main building (2-day minimum stay) has its own bath and shares a common living room, while the adjacent guest cottage (5-day minimum stay) comes with a living room and kitchenette. All rooms have use of the pool and jacuzzi. No credit cards; reservations essential.

Hawaii Naniloa Hotel, 93 Banyan Drive; ☎969-3333, 1-800/367-5360 (US & Canada) or 1-800/442-5845 (HI); fax 969-6622; ⑤–⑨.
Hilo's principal high-rise hotel, built in the 1970s and slightly showing its age. The 300-plus rooms are well equipped but a little thin-walled, and over-priced; the pool is good though. Restaurants include the formal *Sandalwood*, and the *Ting Hao* (see p.114), while as one of Hilo's premier live music venues, the *Crown Room* across the lobby tends to feature performers popular with locals rather than the usual somewhat sanitized tourist fare.

Hilo Bay Hotel, 87 Banyan Drive; ☎961-5818, 1-800/367-5192 (US & Canada) or 1-800/442-5841 (HI); fax 935-7903; ③.
The oldest of the Banyan Drive hotels, run by Uncle Billy and his family since its creation after the 1960 *tsunami*. From the thatched chandeliers in the lobby to the merchandise in the gift store, everything is relentlessly, but enjoyably, Polynesian. Two wings of fairly basic rooms spread to either side of a tropical garden, filled for an hour or so at sunset with raucous birdsong. There's a small pool near the ocean and the restaurant has a free nightly *hula* show (see p.114). A very popular spot with *kama'ainas* (off-islanders), it also offers car-rental discounts.

All these hotels are marked on the maps on p.101 or p.106.

Hilo Hawaiian Hotel, 71 Banyan Drive; ☎935-9361, 1-800/367-5004 (US & Canada), 1-800/272-5725 (HI), 0800/891834 (UK) or 0014-800/125659 (Australia); fax 961-9642; ⑤–⑨.
Upmarket, recently renovated luxury hotel, in a superb setting. The long white crescent of the 285-room building directly faces Coconut Island, a few yards out in the bay, but there's no beach. Ocean-view rooms cost a little extra. The excellent *Queen's Court* restaurant is reviewed on p.113.

Hilo Hotel, 142 Kinoole St; ☎961-3733; fax 935-7836; ③–④.
Originally built in 1884 on the site of Niolopa, a favourite residence of King David Kalākaua (his statue stands in the nearby park), this large, inexpensive Japanese-style hotel is in the heart of downtown, a block up from the HVB and

two blocks back from the bayfront highway. It offers conventional rooms or two-bedroom suites and is home to the good-value *Fuji Restaurant* (see p.112).

Hilo Seaside Hotel, 126 Banyan Drive; ☎935-0821, 1-800/367-7000 (US) or 1-800/654-7020 (Canada); fax 922-0052; ③/④.
Simple, reasonably priced rooms in low motel-style units, with the use of a small pool. Very near the intersection of Banyan Drive with Kamehameha Avenue, this is part of a small Hawaiian-owned chain, for which reservations are handled in Honolulu. Discounts for seniors and on car rental packages.

Wild Ginger Inn, 100 Puueo St; ☎935-5556 or 1-800/368-8752 (US mainland); ②.
Very nice modernized Hawaiian inn, near the *Dolphin Bay* in a quiet residential area just across the Wailuku River from downtown. One of the Big Island's best bargains, with around thirty simple but comfortable rooms arranged round attractive tropical gardens. A few slightly more secluded "deluxe" rooms have TV and all rates include a simple breakfast buffet.

The City

There is a simple and tragic reason why **downtown Hilo** looks so appealingly low-key, with its modest streets and wooden stores: all the buildings that once stood on the *makai* side of Kamehameha Avenue were destroyed by the two *tsunami* of 1946 and 1960. Furthermore, the large gap between downtown and Banyan Drive, now occupied by the Wailoa River State Park, is there because the city was literally cut in two by the inundation of 1946. The majority of the downtown businesses that were swept away were Japanese-owned family stores, which lined Kamehameha Avenue all the way to the Wailoa River. After the waters returned in 1960, all hope was abandoned of rebuilding "little Tokyo". Instead, Project Kaikoʻo cleared the destroyed area as a "buffer zone" against future deluges, using landfill to create a new administrative complex above the high-water mark.

Though little in central Hilo today bears witness to its long history – King David Kalākaua's former palace of Niolopa disappeared over a century ago, to make way for the *Hilo Hotel* – it's still a pleasant place to amble around. That's especially so on Wednesdays and Saturdays, when a colourful open-air **market** takes place at the bottom of Mamo Street, right across the highway from the open ocean. As you wander past stalls selling orchids, tropical fruits, and coffee fresh from the farm, it's hard to believe you're still in the USA.

The Lyman Museum and Mission House

The two-part **Lyman Museum** at 276 Haili St (☎935-502), a few blocks up from the ocean, is downtown Hilo's principal historic site, and offers an interesting introduction to the Big Island for first-time visitors. Its main focus is the original **Mission House** of Calvinist missionaries David and Sarah Lyman, built in 1839. Guided tours of the house – the oldest building in Hilo, and the oldest surviving wooden house on the island – start at regular intervals from the adjacent museum, which you can look around while you wait for the next tour to start.

The museum opens Mon–Sat 9am–5pm, Sun 1–4pm; adults $4.50, children 6–18 $2.50.

For more about
the Big Island's
first
missionaries,
see p.48.

The Lymans had been in Hilo for several years before building
the house. Their congregation numbered just twenty until the
charismatic Titus Coan arrived in 1835, and aided by a fortuitous
tsunami in 1837, started a Revival – complete with speaking in
tongues – which baptized thousands of ordinary Hawaiians but
antagonized his superiors. With Christianity firmly established, the
Lymans constructed the finest home in the city, fit to welcome
Hawaiian royalty and foreign dignitaries alike. It had neither kitchen
– for fear of fire – nor bathroom, but stood three stories high, with a
towering thatched roof, a roomy *lanai* running around the first two
levels and a spacious attic. Its original position was in what is now
the middle of the street; it was moved slightly and many of its
interior walls were taken down, shortly before it became a museum
in 1932. Most of the furniture inside is made of dark *koa* wood, as
are the floors, whose broad planks are up to nineteen inches wide.

The modern **museum** alongside traces the history of Hawaii
from its earliest settlers, with a map of the Pacific to show the
routes they followed, as well as a relief model of the Big Island,
complete with black lava flows. A thatched hut holds the basic tools

and utensils of the ancient Hawaiians, with stone tools and fish hooks, rounded calabashes of *kou* and *koa* wood, ornaments of dogs' teeth, whales' teeth and even human bone (believed to transmit the spiritual power of the original owner to the wearer).

After a detailed history of the missions comes a fascinating section on the different ethnic groups that make up Hilo's population, with artefacts brought and made by each wave of immigrants. The Japanese are represented by an ornate wooden "wishing chair", the Chinese by a resplendent red and gilt Taoist shrine rescued from a temple destroyed by the *tsunami* of 1960, and the Portuguese by the little four-string *braginha* guitar that was to become the *ukulele*.

Most of the space upstairs is occupied by the **Earth Heritage Gallery**, focusing on the geology and astronomy of the island. A model of the summit of Mauna Kea shows the various international observatories – computer-literate visitors can tap into their latest discoveries – while a brief account of Polynesian techniques of stellar navigation mentions that the Ahua'umi Heiau on Mauna Kea, now badly damaged, was probably the first observatory to be built up there. A huge sonar map of the entire archipelago shows how alarmingly prone Hawaii is to massive landslides, and pinpoints the fiery submarine volcano of Lō'ihi thrusting its way to the surface just off the southeast coast of the Big Island. A further collection contains corals, shells – including some unique indigenous land snails – a few stuffed birds and fossils and colourful minerals from around the world, some of which glow in the dark. The small **Shipman Gallery of Chinese Art**, also upstairs, consists mostly of delicately painted but uninspiring porcelain.

Wailuku River and Rainbow Falls

The **Wailuku River**, which defines the western limit of downtown Hilo, is at eighteen miles the longest river in the Hawaiian archipelago. Now safely channelled, and crossed by three road bridges, it once had a fearsome reputation; *wailuku* means "destroying water", as it was considered so dangerous to cross during periods of high rain.

A large rocky outcrop in the river bed, visible upstream from the bridge that connects Puueo and Keawe streets, is known as **Maui's Canoe**. The legend goes that it was abandoned here by the mighty warrior after he'd raced it back from Haleakalā on his namesake island (with just two paddle strokes). Maui was hurrying to rescue his mother Hina, who lived in a cave farther up the river and was trapped by rising waters engineered by a dragon.

Maui's route is now followed by Waianuenue ("rainbow seen in the water") Avenue, and the site of Hina's cave, just under two miles out from downtown, is known as **Rainbow Falls**. Sightseers drive out to admire this broad waterfall from a safe distance; various short trails lead to different viewpoints, but don't let you anywhere near the actual water. From the fenced-off viewing area immediately to the right of the parapet wall of the parking lot, you can see the falls square-on, as they shoot over a thick shelf of hard rock. In the pool down below, the power of the water has progressively scooped out the hollow where Maui's mother is supposed to have lived. Climb a small but often very muddy and slippery staircase off to the left, to draw level with the stream bed at the top of the falls, with the summit of Mauna Kea looming high in the distance. Follow the same trail slightly farther away from the falls, and you'll find yourself in the capacious shade of a gigantic banyan.

A little more than a mile farther up the road, beyond Hilo Memorial Hospital, the **Boiling Pots** are a succession of churning, foaming pools in the river as it drops towards the ocean, with another, smaller, set of falls. Here a treacherous ungraded path to the right of the viewing area allows you to approach the maelstrom, but you'd be crazy to swim.

Wailoa River State Park

Wailoa River State Park, created in the aftermath of the 1960 *tsunami* in the heart of what had been downtown Hilo, is a tranquil if often rather marshy landscaped park of lawns, coconut palms, and dazzling orange-blossomed *lehua* trees. It's a little hard to find your way in; the best approach is to turn down Pauahi Street, which runs between Kilauea and Kamehameha avenues (at the *Chevron* gas station), and then halfway along, take the curving Piopio Street which leads away southeast.

Paved footpaths cross the river and clear-watered lagoons on undulating double- or even triple-humped footbridges, with one pair leading to and from a tiny island, and another one connecting with Kamehameha Avenue and the seafront. A moving memorial, dedicated to all victims of Big Island *tsunamis*, consists of two low black lava ridges which shield a central tiled design.

Banyan Drive

The hotels of Banyan Drive are reviewed on p.104 onwards, and marked on the map on p.106.

Green, semi-rural **Banyan Drive**, a mile east of downtown Hilo not far from the airport, has become the prime hotel district for the city since being spared by the most recent *tsunamis*. In the opinion of the mortgage companies, that was just luck; there's no great reason to suppose it would be spared again.

It's an attractive area, graced by long curving rows of the eponymous giant drooping banyan trees. Incredibly, these magnificent specimens are just sixty years old, planted in the 1930s by the celebrities after whom they are named – Franklin Roosevelt, Babe Ruth, King George V and Cecil B De Mille among others.

The best place for a peaceful stroll among the trees is **Liliuokalani Gardens**, an ornamental Japanese park built to honour Japanese migrants to Hawaii. A slender footbridge stretches out to **Coconut Island**, now just a green speck on the edge of the bay but once, as Mokuola ("healing island"), the site of a *pu'uhonua* or "place of refuge", like that at Hōnaunau on the other side of the island (see p.67). There was also a *luakini,* or temple of human sacrifice, where human offerings were killed by having a huge stone dropped on their chests while lying bound to a rock.

A small covered market area next to the quayside on Lihiwai Street, just off Kamehameha Avenue, is the site each morning (except Sun) of the **Suisan Fish Auction.** Now something of a ritual for early-rising tourists, you have to arrive around 7am to be sure of seeing anything – a stall nearby sells coffee. *Suisan* is a

---

HILO'S GARDENS

Hilo is renowned for its spectacular tropical **gardens,** which include commercial orchid farms, public parks and scientific research facilities. Probably the best combination of a wide range of plants in a scenic setting is the **Hawaii Tropical Botanical Garden,** a few miles up the Hāmākua coast, off Hwy 19 (see p.115). However, within the city confines there are several alternative options, of which the following are just a selection:

Hilo Arboretum
Mon–Fri 7.45am–4.30pm; admission free.
Almost twenty acres of publicly-owned woodlands, at the intersection of Kilauea Avenue and Kawili Street, just over a mile from downtown and Banyan Drive. This is one of Hilo's most peaceful spots, as it's primarily a research establishment, planted from the 1920s onwards and intended to include specimens of all the trees that currently grow anywhere in Hawaii. Trails are virtually non-existent and labels few and far between, but the overgrown lawns present no challenge to walkers.

Hilo Tropical Gardens and Gallery
1477 Kalaniana'ole Ave; daily 9am–4.30pm; admission $3, under-12s free; ☎935-4957.
Just south of Onekahakaha Beach Park on the *makai* side of the highway, not actually beside the sea but laid out among the tidepools. Two acres of colourful gardens, packed with orchids and heliconia, plus a gift store, ice creams and free coffee.

Mauna Loa Macadamia Nut Factory
daily 9am–5pm; admission free; ☎966-8612.
A couple of miles east of Hwy-11, three miles out of Hilo towards the volcanoes. Basically a factory tour with a handful of free nuts, but the setting is reasonably attractive and the orchards pleasant enough, if rather monotonous.

Nani Mau Gardens
421 Makakila St; daily 8am–5pm; admission $5, $2.50 children 13–19, under-12s free; ☎959-3541.
Formal, landscaped commercial gardens, on the east side of Hwy-11 towards the volcanoes, between the three- and four-mile markers. The gardens can be explored on foot or, for an extra $3, on a narrated tram tour. The main business, however, is as a midday stop for tour parties; a copious daily lunch buffet is served 10.30am–1.30pm, while Sunday's spread, out in the gardens, is more of a brunch and served 10am–1pm.

The Panaewa Rainforest Zoo and the Nani Mau Gardens are marked on the Puna map on p.134.

large operation – you may spot their refrigerated plant and fleet of trucks if you head south past the port – and fishing vessels from all over the island come here to sell their catch. Most of the trays are packed with glistening tuna, jammed together in an undignified mass, but you can also see red snapper, parrotfish, squid, ripped-up multi-coloured reef fish speared by scuba divers, and the occasional unfortunate shark. Though it's a hectic and lively spectacle, there's no dramatic shouting to round off the display; the auction consists of buyers inspecting the shiny rows of fish, labelled according to their weight and who caught them, and writing down their bids.

Panaewa Rainforest Zoo

The zoo is open daily except Christmas Day and New Year's Day 9am–4pm; admission free; ☎959-7224.

One of Hilo's least-known attractions, but worth a stop on the way towards the volcanoes, is the **Panaewa Rainforest Zoo**. Having originated in 1969 as a children's zoo at Onekahakaha Beach Park (see opposite), it relocated a few years later to the fringes of the rainforest, well away from the bustle of the city. Said to be the only rainforest zoo in the US, it holds a relatively small menagerie of animals, few of which are all that unusual; the main pleasure of a visit is the chance to roam for an hour or two beneath the canopy of tropical vegetation. Coming south from Hilo on Hwy-11, you turn right just after mile marker 4, along the signed turning a short way beyond Stainback Highway.

On weekdays you may find you're the rarest species of all, and that the animals will go out of their way to have a closer look at you. Walkways through the dense, steamy undergrowth lead past various enclaves holding a pigmy hippo (with giant-sized teeth), a Shetland pony, an ominously rotund American alligator, iguanas from south America, giant land turtles from the Seychelles, and wide-eyed lemurs and bushy-tailed colobuses from Madagascar. Several impressive and colourful peacocks wander the grounds at will, displaying their wares to all and sundry, while rare Hawaiian owls and hawks are confined in rusty cages. The largest, lushest enclosure holds Bengal tigers, though the vegetation is so thick that you may well not spot any unless you're prepared for a long wait by their watering hole. Plans are underway to build an on-site research centre to house a colony of endangered orang-utans from Borneo.

Beaches

If you're not bothered by sharks or pollution, you could in theory swim out among the canoes and fishing boats from the **Hilo Bayfront Park**, across the highway from downtown Hilo. This was said to be one of the finest black-sand beaches in all the islands, before the construction of the breakwater in 1908 and the dredging of the harbour in 1913. Now it's a pleasant place for a picnic, but the only spot nearby where you might be tempted by a swim is at Coconut Island, off Banyan Drive (see above).

The Merrie Monarch Festival

Since 1963, the city of Hilo has celebrated the week-long **Merrie Monarch** *hula* festival during the third week of each April. The centre-piece is a royal parade down the main street, in honour of the "Merrie Monarch" himself, King David Kalākaua. He was largely responsible for the revival of *hula* following decades of disapproval from the missionaries, when at the time of his coronation in February 1883 he staged a performance of women dancers and male drummers on the lawns of Honolululu's 'Iolani Palace.

Male and female performers from *hula halau* (schools) from the five principal islands compete for awards in both ancient and modern styles of *hula*. Performances take place at the **Kanaka'ole Stadium**, named after Auntie Edith Kanaka'ole, one of the Big Island's best-loved twentieth-century *kumuhulas* (*hula* teachers).

Schedules of events are available from the *Merrie Monarch* office at 400 Hualani St, Hilo (☎935-9168); tickets go on sale each year on January 1 but sell out almost immediately. For more information on *hula*, see p.186.

All Hilo's designated **beach parks** lie southeast of downtown, facing Mauna Kea across the bay and reached by following Kalaniana'ole Avenue from its starting point just beyond Banyan Drive. As few have any sand to speak of, consisting instead of shallow pools in the black lava at the ocean margin, usually backed by small grass clearings ringed with coconut palms, they tend to attract local families rather than tourists, and so are particularly crowded on weekends.

Probably the best spot for family groups is **Onekahakaha Beach Park**, a mile and a half down Kalaniana'ole Avenue. Here a solid breakwater of boulders creates a safe, calm lagoon for children to swim, while the spacious lawns alongside are good for picnics. The open ocean beyond the breakwater can, however, be extremely dangerous, while fifty yards or so back from the sea the park has a sizeable population of homeless living in makeshift shelters.

Leleiwi Beach Park, a couple of miles farther along, is a little more exposed, with no sandy beach and some dangerous currents. Away from the open sea, the lagoon is so supremely still and tranquil as to appeal primarily to anglers, who stand in quiet contemplation almost entirely undisturbed by bathers.

Just beyond Leleiwi, four miles from downtown, Kalaniana'ole Avenue comes to a dead end at **Richardson Ocean Park**, where a tiny black-sand beach among the coconut groves is very popular with families with young children. Some venture out to play in the surf as it sweeps into the bay roughly fifty yards out, beyond the snorkellers who explore the rock pools. Behind the sea wall there's a larger "beach" area – more of a sandpit, really – while the adjacent gardens are laid out around some ancient fish ponds, with a few explanatory labels.

Kalaniana'ole Avenue is lined with blue signs indicating the "Evacuation Route" in the event of another tsunami – not surprisingly, the idea is to get away from the sea as fast as possible.

Restaurants

Hilo offers the most interesting assortment of **restaurants** on the Big Island; many have been here for a long time, and have more at stake in satisfying their customers than some of the fly-by-night Kona-side joints.

The closest Hilo comes to having a lū'au is the Sunday evening buffet at the Queen's Court.

Downtown is at its busiest during the working week, however, and with relatively few visitors around you may be surprised quite how quiet things are on weekends. If you're looking for crowds, you're probably better off spending the evening somewhere along **Banyan Drive**.

As for **fast food**, a wide selection of outlets can be found at malls such as the Prince Kuhio Plaza (*KFC*, *Pizza Ala Slice*, *Woolworth* and half a dozen others) and the Puainako Town Center (*McDonald's*, *Pizza Hut*, *Taco Bell*, *Subway's*); both *KFC* and *McDonald's* have downtown restaurants as well.

Bears Coffee, 110 Keawe St; ☎935-0708.
Hilo's coolest breakfast hang-out, one block back from the ocean in the heart of downtown. All kinds of delicious coffees are available – *espressos*, *capuccinos*, *lattés*, you name it. Also bakery goodies and freshly squeezed juices, as well as a menu of cooked specials such as souffléd eggs on muffin with spinach for around $3. Lunch consists of $5 sandwiches, salads, and mostly Mexican specialities. Open Mon–Fri 7am–5pm, Sat 8am–4pm.

Boomers, *Spencer Health & Fitness Center*, 197 Keawe St.
Clean, modern, deli-style café in downtown health club. Breakfast specials cost $4–6, a pasta lunch from around $3 and burgers and sandwiches, plus Pad Thai noodles or Thai fried rice, both served with chicken or tofu are around the $6 mark.

There's another Café Pesto at Kawaihae Harbor: see p.84.

Café Pesto, S. Hata Building, 130 Kamehameha Ave; ☎969-6640.
Large, very light and modern Pacific-influenced Italian restaurant, facing the ocean at the southern end of downtown Hilo. For a substantial snack, the lunchtime sandwiches, such as the Japanese eggplant *Sandalwood* or the shrimp *Milolii*, are excellent value. There's a wide selection of pizzas, but the real highlights are the calzones, folded pizza parcels with tasty and inventive fillings such as the "East-West" with Japanese eggplant and artichokes, or the South Kohala, stuffed with lime-marinated fresh fish. In the evening you can also get seared, broiled or sautéed fresh fish at market prices and a paella with lobster and hot calabrese sausage for $17. Open Mon–Thurs & Sun 11am–9pm, Fri & Sat 11am–10pm.

Fuji Restaurant, *Hilo Hotel*, 142 Kinoole St; ☎961-3733.
Simple but well-prepared Asian cuisine served in a light, airy Japanese-style hotel dining-room with a small *lanai*, a couple of blocks up from the sea in downtown Hilo. For lunch, choose from broad *udon* noodles in broth, or *donburi* meals of rice and soup for around $7. Dinner options, all around the $10 mark, include chicken, pork and beef dishes served with rice, noodles, or potato salad, all kinds of broiled, grilled or deep-fried fish or a mixed *tempura* with shrimp. Closed Mon.

Harringtons, 135 Kalaniana'ole Ave; ☎961-3733.
Popular and relatively informal dinner-only restaurant which is all too easy to miss. It's a mile or so out of downtown, looking out over the peaceful waters of Reeds Bay from a low, unassuming, reddish-brown timber building on the *makai* side of Kalaniana'ole Avenue as it sets off south from Banyan Drive towards the beach parks. Appetizers include steamed clams and *escargots en casserole* at around $8, or an inexpensive seafood chowder. Main courses all cost in the region of $16–20 and include various steaks and prime ribs, along

with some excellent seafood, such as *scallops chardonnay* with brie, *calamari meunière*, Cajun prawns and a seafood brochette. Dinner is served from 5.30pm daily; live performances of "Contemporary Hawaiian" music Wed–Sat.

Ken's House of Pancakes, 1730 Kamehameha Ave; ☎935-8711.
A much-loved Hilo landmark, very near the intersection of Banyan Drive and Kamehameha Ave; open 24 hours for snacks, sandwiches, and, above all, pancakes galore.

KK Tei's, 1550 Kamehameha Ave; ☎961-3733.
Popular and successful Japanese restaurant on the *mauka* side of Kamehameha Avenue just short of Banyan Drive. Dinner specials start at $10, or try the Deluxe Seafood Tempura for $20. A bar in the adjacent building serves *pupus* and has karaoke every evening. Lunch served Mon–Fri only 11am–1.30pm, dinner daily from 5pm.

Lehua's Bay City Bar & Grill, 90 Kamehameha Ave; ☎935-8055.
Very central downtown restaurant, with huge plate-glass windows looking out to sea from the south corner of Waianuenue Avenue. For lunch there's a choice of sandwiches, burgers, salads and pasta specials, all costing $7–9, but the evening menu is varied in the extreme. The range of inexpensive Spanish-style *tapas* snacks, such as anchovies and black olives on French bread or Jalapeno peppers stuffed with cream cheese, extends to include Asian and Japanese specialities like Thai coconut shrimp or *sashimi*. From 9pm onwards on Fri and Sat, there's normally live music of some description. Open for breakfast, lunch and dinner Mon–Sat and dinner only on Sun.

All these restaurants are marked on the maps on p.101 or p.106.

Miwa, Hilo Shopping Center, 1261 Kilauea Ave; ☎961-4454.
An unexpected gem; traditional Japanese cuisine and ambience in an unassuming mall, a mile or so southeast of downtown along Kilauea. Full *sushi* bar, with individual rolls starting under $5 and plates at around $10, plus a full menu of mostly seafood appetizers and main courses, which are best value on the wide range of combination dinners. Open Mon–Sat 11am–10pm, Sun 5–9pm.

Nihon Cultural Center, 123 Lihiwai St; ☎969-1133.
Just off Banyan Drive between the Suisan Fish Auction and Liliuokalani Gardens, this Japanese restaurant has exquisite fresh fish and magnificent views. Lunch specials cost under $10; reservations are required for dinner, when full meals starting at $15 are served until 9pm, and the *sushi* bar remains open until 10pm. Open daily for all meals.

Pescatore, 235 Keawe St; ☎969-9090.
Formal Italian dining, in a vivid pastel-yellow building opposite the HVB downtown. Lunchtime pasta specials cost $7–10 while, for dinner, pricier meat and pasta dishes, such as the anchovy-rich *pasta puttanesca*, are served. Try the delicious *cioppino classico*, a *bouillabaisse*-style stew of lobster, mussels, scallops and clams, with garlic bread. Open daily for lunch and dinner.

Queen's Court, *Hilo Hawaiian Hotel*, 71 Banyan Drive; ☎935-9361.
The huge dining room of this luxury hotel enjoys panoramic views of Hilo Bay and Mauna Kea, and makes a perfect setting for top-quality nightly buffets. During the week you can choose from a selection of American and Pacific-Rim dishes; on Friday and Saturday there's a fine array of seafood delicacies for $21. On Sunday evenings, typical *lū'au* dishes are served and Sunday's champagne brunch is a very reasonable $17.

Reubens, 336 Kamehameha Ave; ☎961-2552.
Mexican restaurant just south of *Café Pesto*, offering the same dishes as at the *Reubens* in Kailua (see p.53), all served at tables draped with the Mexican flag. Main courses cost $8–9 in the evening, or $5 at lunchtime. Open Mon–Sat until 9pm.

Roussel's, 60 Keawe St; ☎935-5111.
Simple but very classy French Creole restaurant in downtown Hilo; its lack of views helps maintain the illusion of being tucked away in a New Orleans backstreet. Lunch dishes, served Mon–Fri only, hover around the $7 mark

Shopping

Although **downtown Hilo** is an enjoyable district to walk around, few of its stores are worth going out of your way for. Those that there are are mainly concentrated along sea-facing Kamehameha Avenue, with assorted outlets selling clothes, T-shirts, souvenirs and fairly undistinguished "crafts". Much the best times for a stroll are Wednesday and Saturday mornings, to coincide with the **market** on Mamo Street (see p.105).

Most locals do their shopping at the various **malls**, of which **Prince Kuhio Plaza**, just south of the airport on Hwy-11, is the most extensive. As well as *Sears*, *Liberty House* and *Woolworth* department stores, it has its own movie theatre (☎959-4955), two bookstores – *The Book Galleries* and *Waldenbooks* – and two music stores, *Da Wreckx* and *JR's Music*. **Banyan Drive** has a very limited selection of convenience stores.

and include soup, various salads, shrimp creole and vegetable gumbo. The dinner menu, served every evening, features many of the same items at around double the price; other options include Cajun prime rib, a seafood medley and a Chateaubriand Grillé.

Ting Hao Seafood Restaurant, *Hawaii Naniloa Hotel*, 93 Banyan Drive; ☎969-3333.
Simply furnished ground-floor Chinese restaurant in grand seafront hotel, specializing in well-prepared seafood dishes such as mussels in sesame or black bean sauce, various scallop delights and ginger lobster or crab for a pricey $25. Chicken and other meats are also served, but note that most of the vegetable dishes, such as eggplant in garlic, seem to contain a little pork.

Uncle Billy's, *Hilo Bay Hotel*, 87 Banyan Drive; ☎961-5818.
Themed Polynesian restaurant, aimed at providing tourists with value for money and a fun time. Most of the menu consists of steak and breaded fish dishes for $9–12, but the $14 seafood platter and the $16 lamb cutlet are excellent. Free nightly performances of Hawaiian music and *hula* dancing, often presided over by the beaming Uncle Billy himself, and certainly featuring members of his extensive family. Open daily for breakfast and dinner only.

The Hāmākua Coast

The **Hāmākua coast** extends for fifty ravishing, colourful miles north and then west from Hilo up to Waipiʻo Valley. Drenched by the Pacific rains that tumble down Mauna Kea, its farms once fuelled the economy of the Big Island. Now agri-business has all but pulled out – the last sugar mill along the coast closed in the fall of 1994 – and no one knows quite what might take its place.

For most of this stretch of shoreline, the Belt Road (Hwy-19) follows the original route of the sugar-company railroad, which used to carry local produce to ships waiting in Hilo and other smaller harbours. The highway seldom rises or falls; instead it clings to the hillsides, crossing a succession of ravines on slender bridges. Damage to the bridges in the 1946 *tsunami* put the railroad out of business, but they were repaired enough to carry the road instead.

The drive is neither difficult nor particularly tortuous, but it's so beautiful that you may find it impossible to exceed the posted

minimum speed of 40mph. Each of the little bridges offers its own
tantalizing glimpse of the verdant scenery – sometimes close to the
ocean but high above, sometimes winding farther in to follow the
contours of the gorges and passing babbling streams and waterfalls.

At first, the fields are crammed into narrow stream-carved
"gulches" and relatively few places offer the chance to stop and
enjoy the views. The two most popular off-road sight-seeing spots
are the **Hawaii Tropical Botanical Garden**, just a few miles north
of Hilo, and the impressive **Akaka Falls**, another ten miles on,
where a short loop trail through the rainforest offers a rare view of
the interior. Otherwise, if you just want to pause and take a few
photos along the way, look out for the bridge just north of mile-
marker 18 (and south of Nīnole), where you can watch the
Waihaumalo River crash into the sea amid dramatic orange-
blossomed trees and giant fanning palms, and the deeply indented
Maulua Gorge at mile-marker 22.

Farther north, beyond **Laupāhoehoe**, the land spreads out and
there's room for larger plantations. The Belt Road veers inland
towards Waimea just before the old-fashioned sugar town of
Honoka'a, but keeping on another eight miles on dead-end Hwy
240 brings you out at one of the most unforgettable viewpoints on
all the islands – the **Waipi'o Valley overlook**.

Pepe'ekeo Scenic Drive

The small side road that drops down towards the sea four miles
north of Hilo, then curves around another four miles or so to rejoin
Hwy-19 at Pepe'ekeo, is officially designated the **PEPE'EKEO
SCENIC DRIVE**, a worthwhile if brief detour from the Belt Road.
Until the highway came through, this was yet another part of the
Old Māmalahoa Highway that once encircled the island (see p.91).
That explains why the trouble was taken to plant its most
impressive stretch – a superb avenue of overhanging Alexandra
palms, originally imported from Queensland Australia but
established here for at least a century. They make their appearance
just beyond a delightful gorge that bursts with African tulip trees.

Few visitors make it to the end of the Scenic Drive without
indulging in a daydream or two about the various real-estate parcels
on sale on its *makai* side; even if you could afford the asking price
for a piece of land, the restrictions on development ensure that you
couldn't do much with it once you'd bought it.

Hawaii Tropical Botanical Garden

Set in one of the greenest, prettiest bays of the Hāmākua coast, the
non-profit-making **Hawaii Tropical Botanical Garden** is the Big
Island's premier showcase for tropical trees, orchids and flowering
plants. This labour of love has been created by Californian retiree
Dan Lutkenhouse since 1978, who has gathered specimens from as
far afield as Brazil, Malaysia, Madagascar and Guatemala, alongside

endemic Hawaiian species, and garnished the collection with a few flamingoes and macaws. It's a major stop on the tour-bus circuit, with crowds and prices to match, but still comes closer than anywhere to matching the popular conception of what a tropical rainforest should look like.

The Registration Office is a mile or so down the Scenic Drive as you approach from Hilo. Having parked here and bought your ticket, join one of the regular shuttle-bus trips down the steep road to the garden itself. Insect repellent, drinking water and umbrellas are available at the drop-off point. Allow an hour in the garden itself, plus around half an hour to coincide with the buses.

The botanical gardens are open daily 8.30am–5.30pm; first shuttle 8.50am, last 4.30pm; $12, children under 16 free; ☎964-5233.

A signposted self-guided trail runs along narrow gravel walkways, occasionally interspersed with large wooden stairways, and starts by leading to the ocean. At three little inlets in Onomea Bay you can enjoy fine views of the verdant shoreline; the largest, Turtle Bay, has a small black-sand beach, but at none of them are visitors allowed to leave the paths and approach the water.

The first plant you'll notice is the red-leafed *obake*, which with its lurid white or yellow "prong" is something of an island trademark. Most species are labelled, in a heady succession of gingers, bromeliads, dramatic orange and yellow heliconia, coconut palms with their writhing worm-like roots, and *hala*, or pandanus trees, whose roots serve as stilts that seem to lift the trunk off the ground.

Once you head back into the valley from the sea, a spur trail leads up beyond a waterfall to a huge Cook pine – not in fact a true pine, but a Polynesian species brought to Hawaii from New Caledonia by Captain Cook. The tree is surrounded by spectacular heliconia and vast spreading "travellers' trees" – so named because they are said always to hold a little water at the base of their leaves – as well as indigenous species. A taller waterfall, on the innermost wall of the valley, can be seen at the end of the "palm jungle" of Alexandra palms. Follow the Onomea stream down from here and you're swiftly back at the sea and the shuttle pick-up point.

Isabella Bird described Onomea Bay as having a picturesque "native village" in the 1870s; a few years later it had become a fully fledged harbour serving the Hāmākua sugar plantations. The area has recently been the subject of controversy, with Hawaiian campaigners claiming that they have been illegally denied access to the shoreline, and that the processes of landscaping and planting may well have destroyed historic sites. Despite that, the garden has recently acquired around twenty more acres and now encompasses the whole of the bay; plans are afoot to open a new visitor centre just across the northern ridge.

Akaka Falls

Three or four miles up the slopes of Mauna Kea from the Belt Road, and a total of fifteen miles out of Hilo, **Akaka Falls** is one of the most photogenic sights on the Big Island. Though not the highest waterfall on the island, its setting is unrivalled – a sheer drop through a chasm overrun by tropical vegetation and orchids. An easy and highly enjoyable mile-long paved trail leads visitors through a dense "jungle" and past other falls, culminating at a viewpoint looking upstream to Akaka itself. You don't get close to the riverbed, let alone the falls; the only dangers to contend with are the steamy heat and persistent mosquitoes.

The trail starts from a parking lot which is reached by following a straightforward series of signs off the highway, through Hōnomu (see below) and up Hwy-220 via a small belt of meadowland. A narrow staircase leads down from the edge of the parking lot, plunging you into dense tropical foliage, with thickets of bamboo soaring from the gorge below to meet high above your head. Few of the plants that line the route are native to Hawaii, and the whole forest is a battleground of yellow, purple and pink blossoms. Among the most lurid are the fiery red "lobster-claw" heliconia and that colourful relative of the banana, the bird of paradise, bedecked either in orange and blue, or white. Tread carefully, as the trail can be slippery with fallen leaves and petals.

Shortly after you cross a narrow stream, the overhead canopy opens up and you reach an overlook facing across another gorge to **Kapuna Falls**. Slightly retracing your steps, you then follow the path up to your right. Alongside stand mighty trees festooned with thick green mosses, fern and creepers, with all kinds of parasitic plants erupting from their branches and trunks. To the left of the path, a vast banyan drips with tendrils; hundreds have rooted themselves and it's impossible to tell which was the original trunk.

Immediately across the next bluff, you get your first view of Akaka Falls itself, foaming through a narrow channel to plunge around 450 feet down a mossy cliff face and disappear in a cloud of spray into the pool below. After leaving the viewing area, you re-cross the stream at a higher point, where a small waterfall bubbles beneath another overhanging bamboo grove.

Hōnomu

Were it not for the steady flow of visitors making their way to and from Akaka Falls, tiny HŌNOMU, on the *mauka* side of Hwy 19, a dozen miles north of Hilo, would probably have been swallowed up by the rainforest by now. As it is, three or four timber-built cafés and diners along its one false-front street compete to provide tourists with budget lunches and a couple of galleries and antique stores sell a routine selection of crafts and souvenirs. To sample the flavour of the place, the best stop is *Ishigo's General Store*, an authentic plantation store which has been run by the same family since 1910.

Kolekole Beach Park

Having cascaded over Akaka Falls, Kolekole stream reaches the ocean a mile or so north of Hōnomu, at the only sizeable seafront park between Hilo and Laupāhoehoe. Look out for a small turning on the left of the highway, just before a tall, narrow bridge.

The road down to **Kolekole Beach Park**, lush even by Hāmākua standards, doubles back to end at the foot of the bridge struts, far below the highway. On both sides, the gorge is thick green, half-swallowing the rusting tin-roofed pavilions of the park. There's no beach, however, and while local youths thrill to ride the breakers back into the mouth of the river, lesser mortals should be wary of submitting themselves to the high surf that lies just a few yards out beyond the rounded black boulders of the shoreline.

Laupāhoehoe

For most of the length of the Hāmākua coast, the shoreline cliffs are too abrupt to leave room for settlements by the sea. Hence the significance of **LAUPĀHOEHOE**, twelve miles up the coast from Kolekole, where a flow of lava extrudes into the ocean to create a flat, fertile promontory (*lau* means leaf, and *pāhoehoe* is smooth lava).

As the best canoe landing between Hilo and Waipiʻo, Laupāhoehoe has long been home to a small community; the location has its perils, however. On April 1, 1946, a ferocious *tsunami* destroyed the village school that stood at the tip of the headland, killing 24 teachers and children. All boats and canoes in the vicinity were wrecked by waves up to thirty feet high, which delayed rescue attempts by several hours. Both school and village were subsequently relocated to the top of the cliffs, an area that is itself prone to frequent landslides.

Twenty-five miles north of Hilo, the approach road to Laupāhoehoe drops down from Hwy-19 to the sea. Once it rounds the first tight corner, you're confronted by a stunning view of the green coastal cliffs, dripping with vegetation, as they stretch away to the south. After rain, countless small waterfalls cascade from crevices in the rock.

The Wreck Of The Hornet

It was at Laupāhoehoe, on June 15, 1866, that the appalling ordeal of fifteen shipwrecked sailors finally ended. Left to drift across the open Pacific in a badly damaged longboat after their clipper ship, *Hornet*, caught fire and sank, they somehow survived 43 days and four thousand miles, drinking a few drops of rainwater each day and eating whatever fish and seabirds they could capture with their bare hands, as well as even their own boots and clothes. When they were finally washed ashore, as the young Mark Twain reported, *"a crowd of natives (who are the very incarnation of generosity, unselfishness and hospitality) were around the strangers dumping bananas, melons, taro, poi – anything and everything they could scrape together that could be eaten – on the ground by the cartload; and if Mr. Jones, of the station, had not hurried down with his stewards, they would soon have killed the starving men with kindness"*.

The narrow road winds down past the Jodo Mission, a temple built by Japanese immigrants in 1899, and arrives at a flat spit of land at the bottom of the cliffs. Most of the space here is taken up by a large lawn, fringed with tall coconut palms that have an alarming tendency to shed their fruit in high winds. A number of seafront parking lots are squeezed in before the forbidding black-lava coastline and its pounding surf, where swimming is definitely not advisable. To the right is the small boat launching ramp of Laupāhoehoe Harbor, which is so dangerous that it's usually sealed off from public access, while round to the left an open-sided beach pavilion tends to be the preserve of locals around sunset.

Practicalities

The last of the Hāmākua sugar mills having finally closed, Laupāhoehoe is facing an uncertain future. A fair few people still live along the various back roads in the district, but there's no town for visitors to explore, and no accommodation is currently available.

However, up above Hwy-19, near mile-post 24 but reached via a loop road that starts nearer mile-post 26, the *Local Café* (☎962-6669) is an extremely friendly converted general store and soda fountain, run by Canadian Charles Pelladeau and his wife Judi as a traditional small-town diner. The menu runs the entire gamut from breakfast omelettes, through jumbo sandwiches, burgers both meat-packed and vegetarian, stir fries, meat loafs and deep-pan pizzas in all sizes, plus malted milk shakes, ice cream and apple and blueberry pies. The *Café* is open from 10am until late daily, except on Sunday when it closes at 1pm after a pancake brunch, and most of the customers who stumble upon it seem to end up staying for a couple of hours to talk story.

Kalōpā Native Forest State Park and Recreation Area

The final opportunity to investigate the upland slopes of Mauna Kea comes a couple of miles south of Honoka'a, where the **Kalōpā Native Forest State Park and Recreation Area** is reached by turning *mauka* off Hwy-19 and following a series of signs for just over a mile.

The reserve covers 615 acres, including the deep and dramatic Hanaipoe Gulch which holds its greatest concentration of indigenous vegetation. The gorge is pristine because animals find it impossible to graze on its steep sides, and it's similarly very difficult for humans to gain access. The trails that lead there are very muddy and overgrown and the rangers positively discourage casual visitors from attempting the hike.

Instead, you're advised to follow the Native Forest Nature Trail, a loop of less than a mile starting from the State Park parking lot and winding through variegated woodlands. Most of what you see is planted rather than natural, but the trail still provides an interesting introduction to the native flora of the Big Island. It's a peaceful stroll rather than a spectacular one, and in places can be quite hard to follow. By the end of the trail you'll probably be able to spot the difference between the giant *ohia* and *kopiko* trees, be familiar with ferns such as the *hapu'u* and the *nianiau* and be appalled by the evil ways of the aggressive strawberry guava plant. The *io* (Hawaiian hawk) and the tiny but melodious *elepaio* make their nests in this area, though you may see nothing larger than voracious mosquitoes.

See p.182 for an account of how wild pigs were introduced into the Big Island.

Local wild-pig hunters tend to be active in the reserve, especially on weekends; their role in keeping down the pig population is one of the factors that helps the forest survive.

The park has a small, free tent-only **campground**, alongside an arboretum of native plants, as well as four eight-bunk cabins, each with bath, bed linen and blankets, and sharing the use of a central kitchen and communal area. The cabins are let for a maximum of five nights, and cost $12 per night for two people, $20 for four, and $28 for eight. Either reserve on the spot by finding the caretaker before 4pm, or call ☎933-4200 in Hilo during business hours.

Honoka'a

The largest and most characterful of the Hāmākua towns is rough-and-tumble **HONOKA'A**, forty miles north of Hilo where the Belt Road curves west to run across the island for the twelve miles to Waimea (see p.85). Consisting largely of a row of quaint timber-framed stores, set on the wooden boardwalks that run along either side of Mamane Street, it stands a couple of miles back from the ocean, surrounded by rolling meadows that are alive with flowers.

Just over two thousand people live in Honoka'a, whose economy has depended since 1873 on a mill belonging to the *Hāmākua Sugar Company*. Although that finally shut down in 1994, this is one of several Big Island communities to have been spruced up and revitalized by federal funding, and its historic downtown district makes it an appealing port of call for visitors passing through en route to or from Waipi'o Valley.

The Tanimoto family also built the Aloha Theater; see p.60.

The most conspicuous landmark along Mamane Street is the Art-Deco **Honoka'a People's Theater**, built as a movie theatre in 1930 by the Tanimoto family. Restored and repainted over the last decade, it is now in use once again for occasional movie performances and musical evenings, still using the projectors and popcorn machine it acquired in the 1940s. In December 1994 it hosted the first, successful Honoka'a Music Festival, where Hawaiian bands and singers performed. It is hoped that this will become an annual event to add to Honoka'a's regular western week, featuring rodeo, which takes place each May.

If you're lucky enough to find it open – afternoons are a better bet than mornings, but that's as far as regular hours go – a visit to octagenarian James Rice's **Hawaiian Shop** is the most memorable experience Honoka'a has to offer. At first glance it looks like a typical junk shop – and it holds its fair share of ordinary, locally produced, crafts and souvenirs – but many of the artefacts piled high on all sides, crammed at random into crates and poking out from beneath layers of old newspaper, are genuine anthropological museum pieces. The place is heaving with Buddhas, bottles, Aladdin's lamps, stuffed hog's heads, carved-lava Hawaiian deities and packing cases that appear to hold swathed mummies, but most importantly idols, fertility symbols and masks from Papua New Guinea. Although the prices are not cheap – the simplest mask costs around $70 – this is stuff you're unlikely ever to see anywhere else. Mr Rice assures his customers that its manufacturers would be only too happy to "eat your ass" if they knew you had one of their masks. After that, the town's handful of other antique and junk stores, a couple of hundred yards up the road to Hilo, pall by comparison.

A steep road drops straight down towards the sea from the centre of Honoka'a. As yet, despite the closure of the sugar mill that blocks the way, you can't get right to the ocean. However, very near the bottom, the **Macadamia Nut Factory** (daily 9am–6pm; free; ☎775-7201) is, for no very good reason, a stop on many bus tours of the Big Island. It basically consists of a gift shop, selling cookies, coffees and the oleaginous nuts themselves. A window runs along the interior wall, enabling you to see into the factory and affording an insight into the mundane world of mac-nut preparation.

Practicalities

The only **accommodation** available in central Honoka'a is the *Hotel Honoka'a Club*, on Mamane Street at the Hilo end of town (PO Box 247, Honoka'a HI 96727; ☎775-0678; ②). Having begun life as a simple boarding house serving the sugar plantations, it now offers $15 hostel beds, as well as private rooms and has a cocktail bar with superb views down the hill to the ocean. The restaurant was closed for renovation at the time of writing, but plans are afoot to reopen it along with a mini-museum and information centre. Two miles out of Honoka'a towards Waipi'o, the *Waipi'o Wayside B&B* (PO Box 840, Honoka'a, HI 96727; ☎775-0275; ③–④) has five themed rooms in an attractive old plantation house.

Much the best place to **eat** in Honoka'a is *Jolene's Kau Kau Korner* (Mon–Fri 10am–8pm, Sat 10am–3pm; ☎775-9498), next to the intersection of Lehua and Mamane streets in the centre of town. Basically a clean, attractive Hawaiian-style diner, it has a well-earned reputation for serving top-quality local food in a friendly atmosphere. A lunchtime burger, stir-fry or other Chinese dish will set you back around $5; in the evening, various plates of chicken or fish, a tasty seafood platter of breaded fish and shellfish or a steak cost around the $10 mark. If you're looking for something a little lighter, the main alternatives are the *Mamane Street Bakery Café*

The Hāmākua Coast

If you enjoy the Hawaiian Shop, you'll probably also like the Kamuela Museum in Waimea; see p.87.

next door, for its breads, sandwiches, chocolate-filled croissants and coffee, or *Mateo's Pizza* opposite, which sells pizza by the slice.

Waipi'o Valley

Beyond Honoka'a, Mamane Street continues north as Hwy-240, to come to an abrupt end after nine miles at the edge of **WAIPI'O VALLEY**. The southernmost of a succession of deeply indented sheer-walled valleys stretching away up the coast to Pololū (see p.96), Waipi'o is the only one accessible by road. It's as close as the Big Island gets to the classic South Seas image of an isolated and self-sufficient valley, sparkling with waterfalls, dense with fruit trees and laced by footpaths leading down to the sea. More dramatic examples of this kind of scenery abound on older islands such as Kauai, but as the Big Island is the newest in the chain, only here on the flanks of Kohala, its oldest volcano, has rainwater had the necessary aeons to gouge out such spectacular chasms.

Between the high walls, the floor of the valley is surprisingly broad, filled with the rich silt carried down from the Kohala slopes by the meandering Waipi'o Stream (also known as Wailoa Stream). Visitors unfamiliar with Hawaii might not appreciate quite how unusual such large areas of prime agricultural land are in the islands. This was probably the leading *taro*-farming valley of the entire archipelago; its produce alone could feed the whole population of the island in times of famine.

The valley is now far more overgrown than it was in its heyday, inhabited by just a few farmers who squelch their way across paddy-like *taro* fields (known as *lo'i*) that have been described as having the consistency of a "semi-jelled chocolate pudding". Some locals also harvest the ferns served as "Waipi'o greens" in restaurants.

Only a small proportion of the steady trickle of visitors who admire the view from the Waipi'o overlook make their way down into the valley itself. It's a very strenuous hike, so most people join a motorized or horseback tour (see p.125 for details). Facilities at the bottom are minimal; there's nowhere to eat and only a very restricted choice of accommodation. However, it's a magical, irresistible spot, and one that deserves to figure on even the most hurried Big Island itinerary.

The history of Waipi'o

Wai being Hawaiian for water, and *pi'o* meaning a loop, bow, or thing bent on itself, Waipi'o Valley was named "curving water" to describe the sinuous course of the Waipi'o Stream as it winds its way across the valley floor. This beautiful and enormously productive location occupies a crucial place in the history of the Big Island, and to this day it retains a great cultural significance.

Legend and fact are inextricably interwoven in Hawaiian history, and accurate dates are almost impossible to determine. However, the

> **The Legacy of a Hawaiian Man**
>
> Musician Eddie Kamae's recent film *Legacy of a Hawaiian Man* is a
> moving evocation of the traditional culture of Waipi'o. It tells the story of
> Sam Li'a, a fiddler and songwriter who died in 1975, having lived in
> Waipi'o for most of his 94 years. He was a living link with the days when
> groups of serenading musicians would wander through the valley and the
> island as a whole playing for families and small groups of workers in the
> sugar fields; his songs eulogized the beauties of its landscapes and people.

Hawaiian word for "law", *kanawai*, literally means the equal sharing
of water, and the system to which it refers is said to have been
instigated in Waipi'o during the eleventh century by the *ali'i* (chief)
'Umi-a-Liloa. The first ruler to unite the entire Big Island, he lived
here as a *taro* farmer and was responsible for the development of its
highly complex network of irrigation channels. Many remain in use to
this day. 'Umi also had his nastier side, as one of the first major
practitioners of large-scale human sacrifice. Victims, such as his rival
high chief and half-brother Hakua-a-Liloa, were baked in an *imu* pit
and their remains placed on the altar of Waipio's Moa'ula Heiau.

Both 'Umi and Hakua were the sons of the previous chief, Liloa.
'Umi was the product of a secret liaison, and raised near
Laupāhoehoe in obscurity. As an adult, he revealed himself to his
father in Waipi'o by swimming across the stream and climbing the
walls of his stockade – an offence that would have been punishable
by death had he not been able to prove his birthright.

Another Waipi'o legend states that a pit at the mouth of the
valley (now ploughed over) marked the entrance to the underworld
known as Kapaaheo, the Hawaiian equivalent of the Greek Hades.
This insubstantial and barren wasteland was populated by famished
ghosts gnawing on lizards and butterflies; dead souls could
occasionally be seen making their way to it at night, in stately
processions along the Old Māmalahoa Highway (see p.91).

Waipi'o was also the boyhood home of Kamehameha the Great,
another future chief brought up in secrecy for his own protection. In
adulthood his warriors fought Kahekili of Oahu just offshore in the
inconclusive but bloody "Battle of the Red-Mouthed Gun" of 1791,
in which for the first time Hawaiian fleets were equipped with
cannons, operated by foreign gunners.

All sorts of estimates have been made of the population of
Waipi'o in different eras. In Kamehameha's day, during the 1760s,
there may have been as many as 7500 inhabitants; within a century
that was down to more like two thousand, but you'll probably still
meet people brought up in the valley who can point out overgrown
spots where Catholic, Protestant and Congregational churches, and
a Chinese temple were thriving as recently as the 1930s.

However, large-scale settlement of Waipi'o came to an end after
the *tsunami* of April 1 1946, which scoured the valley from end to

end. No one died, but few felt much inclination to rebuild their devastated homes. The busiest Waipiʻo has been since then was during the 1960s, when it was used by the Peace Corps to train volunteers heading to work in Asia.

These days, sixty percent of the land is owned by one landlord – the Bishop Estate – which leases it to private farmers. So far, all threats to "develop" Waipiʻo have come to nothing – tourists, and golfers in particular, don't want to put up with the rain. However, plans have been approved for a smallish luxury resort a couple of miles away near Kukuihaele, *mauka* of the highway.

Exploring the Valley

If you simply want to say you've seen Waipiʻo, the view from the overlook is more comprehensive than any you get down below. Assuming that you've driven here, you'll be obliged in any case to leave your vehicle at the top. A few yards down from the parking lot, a pavilion stands in a small grassy area on the very lip of the cliff, about 900 feet above the sea. Spreading away to your left is the green floor of Waipiʻo, with terraced fields but barely a building in sight as it reaches back towards misty Kohala mountain. As you look straight up the coast, across the beach at the mouth of the valley, you should be able to make out three distinct headlands. The first is etched with the zigzagging trail that climbs up towards Waimanu Valley (see p.126); thanks to a landslide, it reaches right to the edge of the *pali*. The second is Laupāhoehoe Iki, while Kauhola, beyond that, is on the far side of Pololū. Unless you're the hardiest of hikers or kayakers, or take a flight-seeing tour, you'll never see the hidden valleys that lie in between. On clear days, the island of Maui is visible in the far distance.

A rough paved track heads down the side of the *pali* from the parking lot, but don't try to drive it yourself. Without four-wheel-drive it's suicidal – as the rusting relics in the undergrowth at the foot of the slope attest – and even if you do have 4WD it's dangerous unless you know exactly what you're doing.

That leaves you with the choice of either taking a tour – see oposite – or **walking** down. It only takes about fifteen minutes to reach the floor, and the return trip doesn't necessarily take all that much longer, but the 25 percent gradient makes for some heavy going. It's so steep that even standing still, bracing yourself against the slope, can be exhausting, and the presence of mosquitoes won't add to your enjoyment.

One thing the tour operators don't usually mention is that they're no longer allowed to take visitors to the seashore. On foot, however, you're free to make your own way there. To do so, double back as soon as you come to the yellow warning sign at the bottom of the slope, onto what swiftly becomes a muddy lane. Don't stray off this path; the *taro* fields to either side are strictly private.

It takes about five minutes, the last of them through a fine avenue of ironwood trees, to reach the very flat **beach** of grey sand, fronted by small black lava boulders that have been well buffeted by the waves. You may have heard stories about the black-sand beaches of Hawaii, but whatever people say this isn't one of them. The sand here is simply silt washed down the mountainside, whereas a true black-sand beach is absolutely jet black, and composed of tiny glass-like fragments of freshly spewn lava. The wide mouth of Waipi'o Stream cuts the beach in two; usually it's not too difficult to wade across, but you shouldn't attempt it if the water is any deeper than your thighs. Neither should you drink it, as it's liable to carry diseases from wild animals in the hills. Surfers and boogie-boarders while away days on end playing in the white breakers, but it's no place for a casual dip.

If instead of heading for the beach you keep going at the foot of the slope, as the tours do, towards the back of Waipi'o, you soon come within sight of the 1200-foot **Hi'ilawe waterfall**, with the parallel but slimmer Nani cascade plummeting to its left. Both feed Waipi'o Stream as it emerges into the heart of the valley. The waterfall is farther away than it looks; walking to its base takes an hour and a half and involves scrambling up a channel of giant boulders. This spot was once the site of Nāpo'opo'o, Waipio's main village, which was said to have had several thousand inhabitants.

A disused century-old trail runs across Hi'ilawe, halfway up, following the line of the aqueducts and tunnels that formerly carried water to the sugar farms. The square building to the left of the falls, conspicuous for its mirrored panelling, is also empty. It was built as a restaurant in the 1960s, but local protests at the developers' ever more grandiose plans, which included installing a cable-car ride to the top of the falls, led to the project being abandoned.

Waipi'o Tours
Organized tours around the valley floor (available in horse-drawn wagons, on horseback and in four-wheel-drive vans) all drive visitors down the access road, thus avoiding the hike down. They also offer the opportunity to learn more about the valley from local people; many of the guides were either born or live in Waipi'o, and are eager to share stories of the old days. However, exactly what each operator is and isn't allowed to do is somewhat controversial, and regulations tend to change from year to year. The beach is off limits and the waterfalls are too remote, so most tours consist of anecdotal rambles through the *taro* fields and along the riverbank.

The *Waipi'o Valley Shuttle*, which runs ninety-minute **van trips** from the overlook, is based at the *Waipi'o Valley Art Works* in Kukuihaele, a mile from the end of the road (see p.127). They prefer you to call ahead to reserve a trip, but there's normally a driver hanging around the parking lot waiting to fill up his vehicle (Mon–Sat 8am–4pm; $31 per person; ☎775-7121).

Hiking Beyond Waipiʻo

The moment you arrive at Waipiʻo Overlook and look across to the trail that climbs the far wall of the valley, you'll probably start wondering what lies **beyond Waipiʻo**. Very few people ever find out – it's one of the most difficult hikes in all Hawaii, way beyond what it's possible to achieve in a single day. In addition, the trail only continues as far as **Waimanu Valley**, eleven miles away. The four more valleys before Pololū (see p.97) are inaccessible from this side; a trail from Pololū in theory gets to two of them, but that too is an extremely demanding undertaking.

Because it involves wading through at least two deep fast-flowing streams, the trail to Waimanu is only passable in summer, between May and October. Only consider setting off from Waipiʻo if you're equipped with a camping permit (see below) and everything necessary for a backcountry expedition – most notably, a rainproof tent and clothing and some kind of water purification system.

Start by heading slightly inland from the far end of Waipiʻo beach, and you'll soon pick up the uphill path. For most of the way, it passes through thick woodlands, so there are virtually no views of either sea or valley. The trail doesn't drop to sea level again until Waimanu, but climbs up and down through what feels like an endless succession of gullies.

Waimanu itself is a sort of miniature Waipiʻo, with even more waterfalls. It too was once densely populated by *taro*-farmers and only abandoned after the *tsunami* of 1946. The beach itself is made up of large boulders, which means that not only is it not safe for swimming, you can hardly even walk along it.

The main **campground** is on far side of Waimanu stream. **Camping** is free, but limited to nine sites, and you can only stay a maximum of three nights. Free permits are issued by the *Dept of Forestry* in Hilo (1643 Kilauea Ave, Hilo HI 96720; ☎933-4221).

Local experts say that the easiest way to get to Waimanu and beyond is not by hiking at all, but by **kayak**. Naturally, only experienced kayakers should attempt such an expedition.

Waipiʻo Valley Wagon Tours takes groups of up to twelve people on two-hour **covered-wagon excursions** from the foot of the cliff (Mon–Sat, up to four tours daily; $37 per person; ☎775-9518). **Horseback expeditions** along the stream and the unpaved lanes on the far side, costing around $70 for a couple of hours, are conducted by *Waipiʻo Naʻalapa Trail Rides* (Mon–Sat; ☎775-0419) and the *Hawaii Resorts Transportation Company* (☎775-7291), whose tours can be booked through most of the Kona-side resorts.

Finally, if you've hiked down and are too tired to face hiking back up, tour vehicles on their way out are usually prepared to carry an extra passenger or two, for a negotiable fee.

Accommodation

Waipiʻo Valley doesn't have a restaurant or café to feed visitors, but it is possible to spend the night down in the valley itself. As well as two **hotels**, both tiny but at opposite ends of the spectrum, there's free **camping**, by permit, near the beach.

A small tin-roofed bungalow among the banana trees in the heart of the valley, around ten minutes' walk from the bottom of the cliff, is known variously as *Tom Araki's Hotel* or the *No-Name Hotel* (c/o Sueño Araki, 25 Malama Place, Hilo, HI 96720; ☎775-0368; ①). Its five simple bedrooms have no electricity – they're lit by kerosene lamps – but share the use of a kitchen equipped with a gas stove, where guests prepare their own food. The octogenarian Tom Araki himself keeps a watchful eye over proceedings.

The *Waipi'o Tree House*, deeper in the valley in full view of a pair of magnificent waterfalls, (PO Box 5086, Honoka'a, HI 96727; ☎ and fax 775-7160; ⑦) is a genuine tree house, perched 35 feet up a monkey-pod tree. It's as comfortable as the situation allows, with electricity, running water and cooking facilities; the sheer strangeness and the superb setting make it worth the $175 per night asking price. Less adventurous guests can stay in the *Hale*, a cottage in the grounds, for the same rate. Both operate a two-night minimum. Owner Linda Beech meets her guests by arrangement at the valley overlook and ferries them to the *Tree House* from there.

Permission for free tent **camping** in the woodlands adjacent to the beach, on the near side of the stream only, is granted by the *Bishop Estate* (PO Box 495, Pa'auilo HI 96776; ☎776-1104). With enough warning, they'll send a permit through the post; otherwise call in at their offices near the *Pa'auilo Store* in **Pa'auilo**, six miles east of Honoka'a. They plan to introduce a system of numbered sites to control numbers more effectively, but camping is expected to remain free of charge.

Kukuihaele

The village of **KUKUIHAELE**, on a looping spur road off Hwy-240, less than a mile short of the Waipi'o overlook, is the nearest community of any size to the valley. Its name, which means "travelling light", is a reference to the lights carried by the ghostly nocturnal processions of the dead heading for the underworld below Waipi'o (see p.123).

As well as the *Waipi'o Valley Art Works* (☎775-0958), the appealing crafts store and snack bar that serves as the base for the *Waipi'o Valley Shuttle*, it's home to a delightful little B&B, *Hale Kukui* (PO Box 5044, Kukuihaele, HI 96727; ☎775-7130; ④). Set in lush gardens high above the ocean, the cottage where you stay, stands a couple of hundred yards off the loop road as you head towards Waipi'o. Accommodation is in either a one-bedroom studio or a two-room unit.

The Saddle Road

From a glance at the map, the **SADDLE ROAD** looks the quickest route from one side of the Big Island to the other. What no map can

The Saddle Road

convey, however, is quite how high and remote it is, involving a long slow haul to an altitude of well over 6000 feet in order to cross the "saddle" of land that lies between **Mauna Kea** to the north and **Mauna Loa** to the south. The fifty-mile stretch from Hilo to the point where it re-joins the Belt Road – six miles south of Waimea; and more than thirty northeast of Kailua – is one of the bleakest stretches of road imaginable, utterly unlike anything you'd expect to encounter in the middle of the Pacific Ocean.

Even if the Saddle Road is not much use as a short cut, driving it makes an enjoyable adventure in its own right. Despite the road's elevation, it passes a long way below the summits of the two mountains, so you probably won't see the snowcaps, but there's still some memorable scenery along the way. The trouble is, all the car-rental chains **forbid** drivers to take their vehicles along the Saddle Road, on pain of forfeiting your insurance cover and all rights to emergency rescue if you get into difficulties. The only way round this is to rent a four-wheel-drive vehicle from a company such as *Harper's* (☎969-1478; see p.17).

The rental-car ban is imposed for several reasons. First of all, the road is not perfectly surfaced all the way and narrows to a single lane nineteen miles out of Hilo. In addition, there are military bases in the high stretches and you may encounter large convoys; the weather is often atrocious, so visibility can be very bad; and finally, what's probably the main factor, there are no facilities of any kind for the entire 85 miles from Hilo to Kailua – no gas stations, no stores, no snack bars, nothing. Having said that, the road is not in particularly bad condition and even when it's single-track there's always plenty of room for cars to pass on the shoulder. If you do choose to risk it, take it slowly, and be sure to allow time to complete your journey in daylight.

Leaving Hilo, along first Waianuenue Avenue and then Kaūmana Drive, the Saddle Road seems to go on climbing forever, straight from the ocean. Beyond the lush suburbs with their tropical gardens, it heads up into the clouds, winding through a moist and misty heathland of spindly trees, then undulating across bare lava fields, until with any luck it emerges into the sun, on what feels like a wide grassy plain between Mauna Loa and Mauna Kea.

Gradually the road curves to the north, circling Mauna Kea and bringing Hualālai into view as well. Various plans have been put forward over the years to cut a more direct course down to Kailua, and save perhaps twenty miles on the total distance; so far the presence of environmentally or archeologically important sites have prevented them from materializing.

Mauna Kea

For the moment, **MAUNA KEA** is at 13,796 feet the highest mountain in the entire Pacific, let alone in Hawaii. Being extinct, however, and therefore already eroding away, it's steadily losing ground to its still-active rival Mauna Loa, 25 miles southwest. Nonetheless its height and isolation, two thousand miles from the nearest landmass, make Mauna Kea one of the very best sites for **astronomical observatories** on earth. Its summit is an other-worldly place, not just because of the surreal ring of high-tech telescopes trained out into the universe, but because it's so devoid of life, with naked hillocks composed of weird multi-coloured minerals. A spur road ascends to the summit from the Saddle Road, though its last seven miles are restricted to four-wheel-drive vehicles only, and the observatories do not welcome casual visitors.

The ancient Hawaiians named Mauna Kea the "white mountain" because it is capped by snow for over half the year. That didn't deter them from climbing right to the top, however. Like Mauna Loa, Mauna Kea is a shield volcano, so most of its slope is very gentle; but it differs from its neighbour in having been here during the last Ice Age, which means it was the only spot in the central Pacific to be covered by **glaciers**. The ice had the effect of rapidly chilling its molten lava, and hardening it to create the best basalt in the islands. Incredibly, there's an ancient **adze quarry** 12,400 feet up the mountain. Dating as far back as 1100 AD, it was probably the major source of the stone which was used for all the islanders' basic tools, and especially prized for hollowing out canoes.

For an account of how Hawaii's volcanoes were formed, see p.140.

Ellison Onizuka Visitor Center

The turn-off to the summit of Mauna Kea comes at mile-marker 28 on the Saddle Road. At first the road passes through grazing land, covered with springy wiry grass although devoid of trees. Most of it is open cattle range – a broad swathe of this flank of Mauna Kea, just like the northern side, belongs to the Parker Ranch (see p.88). The road surface is good for the nine miles to the **Ellison Onizuka Visitor Center**. In theory this is the place to find out about more about the observatories – call ahead to see if they're planning any of their occasional guided tours. However, there's no guarantee that it will be open at the posted hours, which are Mon–Fri 1–5pm, Sat & Sun 8am–5pm (☎961-2180); in any case, the centre's disappointingly small.

The views from this point, 9000 feet up, are downright eerie, and make it worth coming even if you don't head on to the summit. Bizarre reddish cinder cones and other volcanic protrusions seem to float in and out of the mists that swathe the grasslands; in the afternoon, the clouds usually obscure Hilo and the coast altogether.

The Summit of Mauna Kea

The road on from the visitor centre is kept in reasonable condition – the astronomers who work at the top have to commute this way – but it's only safe to attempt it in a four-wheel-drive vehicle. In anything else, you'd quickly burn out your brakes coming down.

The Saddle Road

A few operators arrange guided tours to the summit of Mauna Kea by appointment; contact the Waipi'o Valley Shuttle *(☎775-7121),* Paradise Safaris *(☎322-2336), or, by far the cheapest,* Arnott's Lodge *in Hilo (☎969-7097).*

If you're feeling energetic, it's possible to **hike** up, though you should first acclimatize yourself to the altitude for at least an hour at the visitor centre. When you do set off, you're letting yourself in for six miles of exposed road and 4000 feet of climbing, before you finally get a glimpse of the summit.

The great white golf balls of the **observatories** dwarf the rusty red and gold cones of ash dotted across the mountain side. All this land is under the control of the University of Hawaii, who have so far leased around ten separate sites where national and international consortiums strive to outdo each other by building bigger and better telescopes. The University of California's W M Keck Observatory opened in 1992 boasting the largest telescope in the world, but *Mitsubishi* will soon surpass it with the giant **Subaru Observatory** – named for the Japanese name of the Pleiades, or "Seven Sisters", not the car company.

Just below the summit, Mauna Kea holds one last surprise – **Lake Wai'au**, a permanent lake set in a cinder cone 13,020 feet above sea level. Out of misguided bravura, some visitors swim in its frozen waters, which are replenished by thawing permafrost. It makes more sense to wander over to the brass plaque by the shore that marks where the ashes of Ikua Purdy, the 1903 world Rodeo champion, were scattered. From time to time, he and his fellow Parker-Ranch cowboys (see p.89) would come all the way up here when roping wild horses.

Mauna Kea State Park

Once past the summit approach road, the Saddle Road starts to head slightly north, and views begin to open up of the whole Kona coast. Very near mile-marker 35, a short, but very tiring, two-mile hike in **MAUNA KEA STATE PARK** can bring you to superb views of the island's three largest volcanoes.

Once you've parked in the main lot, head past the assortment of wooden cabins, and follow a jeep track straight back towards what you can see of Mauna Kea. Having first made your way as far as three pale-blue water towers, continue along the track until just before you reach an older, rustier, tower farther back.

So far the trail has all been flat, but now a footpath leads upwards to the right, straight up a small-looking mound. The next few hundred yards are extraordinarily, chest-thumpingly, steep; you're doing well to take fifty short steps without pausing to catch your breath. Climbing across a loose surface of powdery brown dust, you pass a wide range of brittle high-altitude plants, including dessicated shrubs and a few native silverswords. Though far below the top of Mauna Kea, the crest of the mound makes a perfect if windy vantage point for views of the entire deceptively gentle slope of Mauna Loa across the saddle, Hualālai away to the east, and the sprawling army camp closer at hand down below.

Chapter 4

The South Coast: Volcano Country

othing you've ever seen could prepare you for the south coast of the Big Island, where the most active volcanoes on the planet are still at work building the youngest and largest member of the Hawaiian chain. In this extraordinary, exhilarating landscape, the earth itself ebbs and flows, prey to the changing moods of **Mauna Loa** and **Kīlauea**. Houses, roads, beaches and even towns are liable to stop existing at any moment, and as rivers of molten rock steam their way into the ocean they create a new coastline by the day.

Tourists have been marvelling at this spectacle since the early nineteenth century. Mauna Loa and Kīlauea now constitute the **Hawaii Volcanoes National Park**, which is perhaps America's most dramatic national park. Quite apart from the two volcanoes, it ranges from arctic tundra and sulphurous desert to lowland rainforest and remote Pacific beaches.

The park overlaps the districts of **Puna** to the east and **Ka'ū** to the south and west. Many visitors don't bother to leave the highway as they pass through – and neither region has the facilities, the sights or even the inclination to lure people off it. Puna, on the windward side, clings to the most pristine stretches of rainforest in the state, but they remain so unspoilt largely because they're not accessible to casual visitors. Especially around the self-consciously outlaw town of **Pāhoa**, Puna is dominated by latterday hippies and back-to-the-landers, but it does have a few photogenic beaches. Most of **Ka'ū**, lying downwind of the acrid volcanic fumes, is much less fertile. Nonetheless, it may well have been home to the first Polynesian settlers and remains one of the last bastions of anything approaching the traditional Hawaiian way of life.

The **southern coastline** is now very sparsely populated; the villages that once stood along its central section were abandoned around 150 years ago, following a succession of devastating *tsunami*. Although ancient Hawaiians, who identified volcanic

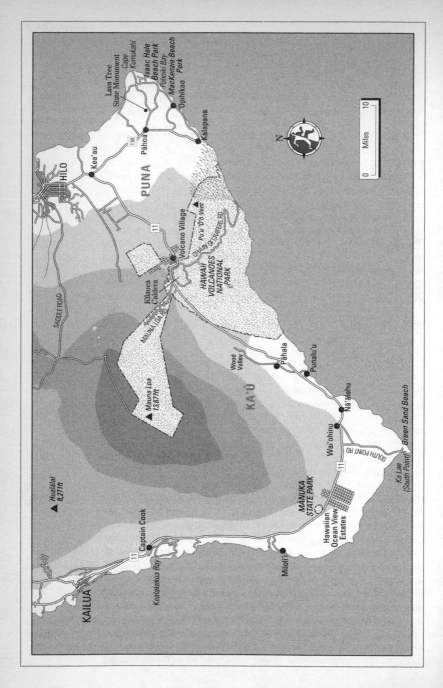

Accommodation price codes

Prices have been graded with the symbols below, according to the quoted
rate for the least expensive double room for most of the year, not
including state taxes of 10.17 percent (see p.20 for a fuller explanation).

①	up to $30	④	$75–100	⑦	$170–225
②	$30–50	⑤	$100–130	⑧	$225–300
③	$50–75	⑥	$130–170	⑨	over $300

activity with the goddess **Pele**, saw the power of the volcanoes as
something to respect rather than to fear, they took care to live
well away from potentially eruptive vents. For no rational reason,
settlement in this century has been concentrated in the "rift zone"
of Kīlauea, and several towns have paid the ultimate penalty of
being destroyed by lava. In addition, the underground upheavals
make the region extremely prone to earthquakes; in 1960 the
entire south coast dropped by three feet, and campers in
backcountry sites were washed out to sea after another major
landslide in 1975.

Among the casualties of the latest eruptions have been several
of the **black-sand beaches** for which southern Hawaii used to be
famous. The one at **Kalapana** finally disappeared in 1990, and a
beautiful newcomer at **Kamoamoa** lasted for just five years before
being swallowed up in 1992. In fact, a true black-sand beach – and
they really are jet black – rarely survives for long. Most are
produced literally overnight, when red-hot liquid rock explodes on
contact with the cool ocean and millions of shards of shiny glass are
washed ashore. Gradually the sea washes away this "sand" and
without another eruption the beach soon disappears. Currently the
best example is at **Punaluʻu** in Kaʻū – and there's even a **green-sand
beach** not far away, near South Point.

Puna

Tourists are not the only ones with a tendency to neglect the district
of PUNA, which takes up the southeastern corner of the Big Island.
The county government too seems to see it as a land apart, a quirky
enclave that doesn't quite fit in with the rest of the island. In the
1960s and 1970s, large portions of the region were re-zoned for
residential development, but it still lacks the infrastructure that you
– and the twenty thousand people who now live here – would
expect. The volcanoes haven't helped matters either, incinerating
newly built homes and cutting the coastal road to leave poor, traffic-
ridden **Keaʻau** as the only point of access to the whole region.

Although the eleven-mile stretch of oceanfront highway that still
survives makes an attractive drive, there's no great reason to spend
more than a couple of hours in Puna. Stop for a restaurant lunch in

Pāhoa, perhaps, or try one of its hippy cafés, but don't expect to go swimming from any of the beaches. If you're on your way to the national park, save your volcano-watching for there; lava trails from Kīlauea are visible throughout Puna, but nowhere are they as dramatic or accessible as in the park.

Puna has long had the reputation of being the Big Island's main centre for the illegal cultivation of **marijuana** (*pakololo*, "crazy weed"). Recent police crackdowns have put paid to most large-scale projects, but if you ever get the feeling of being made unwelcome as you explore the backwoods areas, the chances are that you're close to some clandestine activity.

Kea'au

Little more than three miles beyond the city limits of Hilo, the town of **KEA'AU** lies just south of Hwy-11 as it climbs towards the volcanoes. Its two main roles are as a dormitory for Hilo's labour force and as the gateway to the rest of Puna. As a result, the intersection of Hwys 11 and 130 is the scene of huge jams during the morning and evening rush hours.

Kea'au consists of little more than the large parking lot for the **Kea'au Shopping Center**. This low-key wooden shopping mall holds the *Sure-Save* supermarket, as well as its funkier rival *Kea'au Natural Foods*, a laundromat, a raucous sports bar and two small Asian fast-food diners, *Lunch at Miu's* and the *New Seoul Bar-B-Q*.

Pāhoa

With its false-front stores and rudimentary timber boardwalks, tiny **PĀHOA**, a dozen miles southwest of Kea'au down Hwy-130, is a distinctive blend of Wild-West cowboy town and Shangri La. Life here moves so slowly that it hasn't quite kept up with the rest of America and the streets seem to be filled with refugees from the Sixties – even if most of them were born a decade or two later. Just as incongruous are the occasional groups of *aloha*-shirted tourists, who watch the locals with the same bemusement as the coach parties that flocked to San Francisco to see the world's first hippies.

The only building of any size in Pāhoa is the venerable **Akebono Theater**, which celebrated its 77th anniversary in December 1994. Vice-President Al Gore and State Governor Cayetano, who sent their congratulations, were possibly unaware of the theatre's one-day conversion on March 2, 1994 into the *Holy Smoke Café* – part of the ongoing local campaign for the repeal of the marijuana laws, spearheaded by Dwight Kondo of the *Hawaiian Hemp Co*. His store, fifty yards away on the boardwalk, sells hemp (*cannabis sativa*) products of all kinds, as well as textiles from China and paintings and is crammed with leaflets and brochures. The parking lot in front of the theatre is the scene of a lively Sunday-morning flea market.

Practicalities

Pāhoa's, and Puna's, only **hotel** is the centrally located, old-style *Village Inn* (PO Box 1987, Pāhoa HI 96778; ☎965-6444; ②), at the corner of the *Akebono Theater* parking lot. Double rooms, themed to honour such personalities as Mark Twain, Robert Louis Stevenson and Princess Kaiulani, are arranged around a ramshackle courtyard which is shared with neighbouring buildings and backs onto the rainforest.

At the bottom end of the village, a short way beyond the boardwalk, the *Godmother* (☎965-5055) is Pāhoa's most upmarket **restaurant**, though still inexpensive by island standards. Specializing in Italian cuisine, it's open for all meals daily, with indoor seating and a spacious wooden *lanai*. Breakfast options include a good-value eggs benedict, while at lunch burgers, sandwiches and pasta are served. Prices for pasta dishes rise to around $9 in the evening. More adventurous alternatives in town include *Naung Mai Thai Kitchen* (☎965-8186), a small pink-painted diner on the boardwalk. For both lunch and dinner they serve the same delicious Thai menu, with *tom yum* soup for $6–10 in vegetarian or seafood versions, and a wide range of red, green, and yellow curries with eggplants in coconut milk for around $8.

If you want to check out Pāhoa's barefoot, tie-dyed denizens, try such hang-outs as the *Café Makana*, *Lanai Coffee* and the *Huna Ohana*.

Lava Tree State Monument

Lava Tree Monument is open daily dawn–dusk; free.

Set back in the rainforest just off Hwy-132, almost three miles out of Pāhoa, **LAVA TREE STATE MONUMENT** preserves the petrified record of a double catastrophe that took place more than two hundred years ago. First there was a fast-flowing lava stream, that destroyed the underbrush and lapped against the ʻōʻhia trees of the forest, clinging to their trunks and cooling as it met resistance. Then came an earthquake, which opened fissures in the ground into

---

The Puna Geothermal Venture

If you were responsible for trying to reduce the cost of generating electricity in Hawaii, you might well find it frustrating to be confronted every day by the apparently limitless power of the volcanoes. What's hard to accept for many people in Puna, however, is that anyone would be prepared to take the risk of trying to harness that power, let alone in a populated area.

The **Puna Geothermal Venture** (PGV), based just outside Pāhoa at Pohoiki, is an attempt to do just that, by means of a power plant standing above 3000-feet-deep wells. Superheated water is pumped to the surface and used to turn electrical turbines, and then fluids and steam alike are returned back underground.

To its promoters, this is a clean, renewable source of energy; to protesters, who have included *Greenpeace* and assorted rock stars, it's an appalling desecration. Native Hawaiian campaigners say that the very concept of geothermal development is offensive to Pele and even the US Fish and Wildlife Service argue that the construction of access roads and facilities causes irreparable environmental damage to the Wao Kele O Puna rainforest.

Local residents blame emissions from the plant for symptoms such as nausea, migraine, sore throats, chronic colds and severe fatigue. Following a big blow-out in June 1991 – when toxic steam blasted into the air for 31 hours – and another leak in February 1993, locals have been suing the PGV in large numbers. State and county authorities tend to dismiss such claims as being "psychogenic", the general tone according to one resident being that they're just "smoking too much pot".

It was possible for a while to tour the plant yourself. However, the visitor centre, just beyond Lava Tree State Monument, has long since given up the unequal struggle and never opens any more.

---

which the liquid rock quickly drained. That left the landscape scattered with upright columns of lava, hollow inside where the trees themselves had burned away.

It takes around half an hour to walk the level, paved trail that now loops around the best preserved specimens. With the exception of the mosquitoes, this is a tame and relatively clear section of rainforest, echoing to the sound of multi-coloured birds. The lava trees themselves look like black termite mounds or old candle drippings. On top of some of the tallest ones, new trees have somehow managed to root themselves. While this landscape is undoubtedly unusual and striking, if your time is limited, it's best to push on to the main attractions of the national park.

The Puna Coast

Hwy-130 continues for another eight miles from Pāhoa before its luck finally runs out, a few hundred yards up from the sea. A thick layer of shiny black lava, unceremoniously dumped by Kīlauea in 1988, brings the road to an abrupt halt close to mile-marker 21. Some trees are still visible beyond, and new plant growth is starting to appear, but barely a trace survives of the extensive **Royal Gardens** residential area that once stood here.

Almost all the village of **Kalapana**, down below, has also been destroyed, though the timber-framed **Star of the Sea** church was hauled up the slopes to safety and now stands forlorn by the roadside half a mile before the end of the highway.

Fortunately it's still possible to join up with the **coast road** at this point. Hwy-137 reaches the ocean slightly to the east of where the **Kaimū black-sand beach** used to be. Until it was obliterated in 1990, this was one of the most photographed beauty spots on the Big Island. Only the adjacent restaurant, formerly used by round-island bus tours and now seldom open, was spared by the lava, although some of the coconut palms from the beach were rescued and airlifted to the *Hilton Waikoloa* hotel in Kohala (see p.74).

Driving east along Hwy-137 takes you through a quick-fire landscape that varies from one minute to the next, depending on the age of the lava flow you're crossing. In places the undergrowth thins out to bare black rock, but most of the route is dripping with tropical technicolour vegetation. From time to time you get glimpses of the ocean and successive palm-bedecked headlands, but there are no access points to the coast in the seven miles before 'Opihikao. As you approach this tiny community, the road becomes a tunnel burrowing its way beneath a dense canopy of trees, which provides the setting for the *Kalani Honua Culture Center and Retreat* (PO Box 4500 Pahoa HI 96778; ☎965-7828 or 1-800/800-6886; ③). Part New Age teaching centre, with courses in yoga and the like, and part B&B, the *Kalani Honua* offers an idyllic situation, if not especially luxurious

The Kalani Honua organizes a hula festival each April to tie in with Hilo's Merrie Monarch event (see p.111).

accommodation, for long-stay visitors, and has a small restaurant and cafe open to all.

Just outside 'Opihikao, **Mackenzie State Recreation Area** is a large-level picnic ground in a grove of ironwoods on the oceanfront cliffs, where the earth underfoot is crisp with shed needles. Access to the seashore here is all but impossible; high surf scoops inexorably at the shallow cliff faces, hollowing them out to the extent that even walking to the edge is foolhardy. This tranquil forest glade is popular with locals, though tourists may feel it's not quite "Hawaiian" enough to be worth a stop.

Another two miles beyond, **Isaac Hale Beach Park**, just north of the junction with a minor road from Pāhoa, finally lets you get down to the sea. Set in **Pohoiki Bay**, with its small beach of variegated black and white pebbles, overhanging green vegetation and high surf, the park is popular with surfers, anglers and picnickers, though it's not a place for family bathing or for anyone inexperienced in the ways of the rough Hawaiian seas. A small boat ramp, protected by an army-built breakwater, is used by local vessels; surfers occasionally hitch rides out into the breakers.

As a paved road, Hwy-137 comes to an end four miles on from Pohoiki Bay, where it meets Hwy-132 from Pāhoa. To reach this spot, you pass over the site of **Kapoho**, yet another town swallowed up by the lava, this time in January 1960. A dirt road east from the intersection leads for just over a mile to the rudimentary lighthouse at **Cape Kumukahi**, which is not open to visitors. Much of the land in this area is entirely new, though at the edge of the vegetated zone you may spot an old Japanese cemetery and a *heiau* platform.

Hawaii Volcanoes National Park

Park open 24 hours daily, 365 days a year; $5 per vehicle, $3 for cyclists, motorcyclists and hikers (admission valid for seven consecutive days). The annual Hawaii Volcanoes Pass costs $15 and system-wide national parks passes (see p.32) are also valid; 24-hour eruption information line ☎967-7977; visitor centre ☎967-7311.

The raw power of an active volcano is not something that can be tamed and labelled to suit those who like their scenery to stay still and their sight-seeing to run to schedule. **HAWAII VOLCANOES NATIONAL PARK** may well be the most dynamic, unpredictable place you'll ever visit, and it's one where normal rules just don't seem to apply. What you see, and how long it takes to see it, is beyond all human control. **Kīlauea**, at the heart of the park, is often known as the "drive-in volcano"; it's said to be the only volcano in the world where news of a fresh eruption brings people flocking *towards* the lava flows. Only very rarely does the lava claim lives, but much of the excitement of coming here undeniably stems from the ever-present whiff of danger.

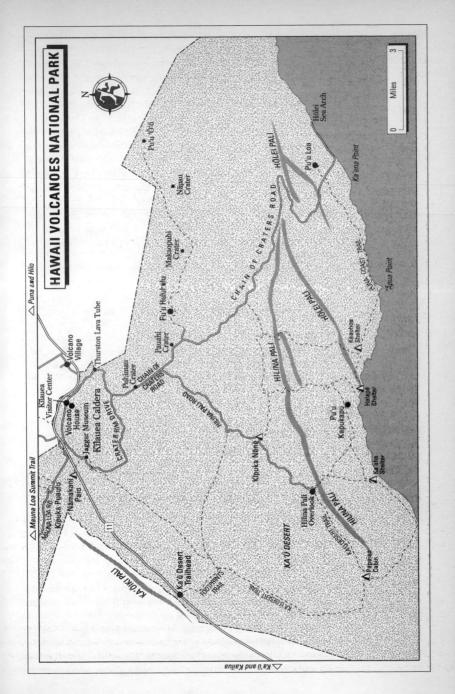

HAWAII VOLCANOES NATIONAL PARK

N

Miles
0   3

△ Puna and Hilo

Hōlei
Sea Arch

Puʻu ʻŌʻō

Kaʻena Point

Nāpau
Crater

Apua Point

Makaopuhi
Crater

PUNA COAST TRAIL

Puʻu Loa

CHAIN OF CRATERS ROAD

Puʻu Huluhulu

HŌLEI PALI

Pauahi
Crater

Keauhou
Shelter

Thurston Lava Tube

Volcano
Village

Puliliau
Crater

HILINA PALI

Kīlauea
Visitor Center

CHAIN OF
CRATERS
ROAD

Halapē
Shelter

Volcano
House

HILINA PALI ROAD

Kīlauea
Caldera

Jaggar Museum

Puʻu
Kapukapu

CRATER RIM DRIVE

Kīpuka Nēnē

Kaʻaha
Shelter

△ Mauna Loa Summit Trail

Namakani
Paio

Kīpuka Puaulu

HILINA PALI

MAUNA LOA RD

Hilina Pali
Overlook

KAʻŪ DESERT

KAʻŪ DESERT TRAIL

11

Kaʻū Desert
Trailhead

Pepeiao
Cabin

KAʻŪ DESERT TRAIL

CRATER TRAIL

KAʻŪ DESERT TRAIL

KAʻŪ OIKI PALI

▽ Kaʻū and Kailua

**Hawaii
Volcanoes
National
Park**

The park entrance is roughly a hundred miles southeast of Kona, thirty miles southwest of Hilo, and ten miles (as the crow flies) from the ocean. Driving from the west of the island takes at least two hours, and the last thirty miles or so is spent gradually ascending through the kind of barren lava landscape that will already be familiar from the Kona airport region. The road from Hilo, on the other hand, climbs more steeply through thick, wet rainforest.

Unexpectedly, you arrive at the park headquarters, beside the caldera (summit crater) of Kīlauea, with no real sense of being on top of a mountain. That's because Kīlauea, at only four thousand feet high, is a mere pimple on the flanks of **Mauna Loa,** which despite its deceptively gentle incline stands almost ten thousand feet taller. Furthermore, for all its trails and overlooks, the crater area is a long way from the park's most compelling attraction. Somewhere down the side of the mountain, there's a non-stop eruption of molten lava that has been bursting out of the ground and cascading down to the sea since 1983 (see p.156).

In total, the irregular boundaries of the national park take in 377 square miles. At the start of this century, it only occupied the Kīlauea Caldera area. Now it incorporates the summit craters and most of the eruption-prone rift zones of both volcanoes, an area that is largely desert but includes scattered pockets of rainforest and even one or two beaches. Although the most recent flows have been beyond the official boundaries of the park, its rangers control public access to the danger spots. From being a solely geological park, its brief has expanded to cover responsibility for preserving the vestiges of pre-contact occupation in the region and protecting indigenous wildlife such as the Hawaiian goose, the *nēnē*.

Western visitors to the volcanoes have tended to see them as purely destructive, while the ancient Hawaiians, whose islands would never have existed without the volcanoes, were much more aware of their generative role, embodied in the goddess **Pele**. It may take longer to create than it does to destroy, but fresh lava is rich in nutrients, and life soon regenerates on the new land. On a single visit to the park, it's impossible to appreciate the sheer rapidity of change. What's a crackling, flaming, unstoppable river of molten lava one day may well be a busy hiking trail the next; come back twenty years later and you could find a rich, living forest.

The Shield Volcanoes of Hawaii

For an explanation of the difference between ʻāʻā and pāhoehoe lava, see p.145.

According to the classic popular image, a volcano is a cone-shaped mountain, with a neat round crater at the top that's filled with bubbling lava and spouts columns of liquid fire.

Hawaiian volcanoes aren't like that. Although you may be lured to the park by photos of pillars of incandescent lava, you're unlikely to see any such event. These are **shield volcanoes**, which grow slowly and steadily rather than violently, adding layer upon layer as lava seeps out of fissures and vents all along the "rift zones" that cover their sides. The effect is to create a long low profile, said by geologists to resemble a warrior's shield laid on the ground.

Mauna Loa and Kīlauea are simply the latest in the series of volcanoes responsible for creating the entire Hawaiian chain. Like all the rest, they are thought to have been fuelled by a "hot spot" in the earth's crust, way below the sea floor, which has been channelling magma upwards for seventy million years. As the continental plates drift northwestwards, at the rate of around three inches per year, that magma has found its way to the surface in one volcano after another. Each island in turn has been created by the same process, clawing its way up from the depths, emerging above the waves and then ceasing to grow as its volcanoes become ever further removed from the life-giving source. In time, erosion by rain and sea wears away the rock, sculpting the fabulous formations seen at their most dramatic on Kauai, and eventually the ocean washes over it once more, perhaps leaving a ring of coral – an atoll – to bear witness. Though Kauai is the oldest Hawaiian island of any size, the oldest of all are by now 3500 miles away, mere specks in what's known as the Emperor chain, off the coast of Japan.

Look at the gentle slope of **Mauna Loa**, project that gradient down through almost 20,000 feet of ocean, and you'll see why its Hawaiian name, "long mountain", is so appropriate. It's the most massive single object on earth; its summit is at 13,677 feet very slightly lower than Mauna Kea (13,796 feet), but its volume of 10,000 cubic miles makes it a hundred times larger than Washington's Mount Rainier. It took two million years for Mauna Loa to swell from the bed of the Pacific into the air, and for another million years it has continued to climb. In the last 150 years, the world's highest active volcano has erupted every three or four years – in a single hour in 1984, it let forth enough lava to pave a highway from Honolulu to New York. Geologists predict that every spot on its surface will receive at least one more coating of fresh lava before the fires die down.

However, only around once a century does Mauna Loa erupt simultaneously with Kīlauea, and of late it's the younger upstart – literally "much spewing" – that has been grabbing the attention, having been in a record-breaking continuous state of eruption since 1983. Although fed by a separate conduit from the fires below, Kīlauea emerged as a lump on the side of Mauna Loa, so you can hardly tell it's a separate mountain. Its lava tends to flow consistently in the same direction, down towards the ocean. Between 1983 and 1995, it added well over 500 acres of new land to a nine-mile stretch of the Puna coastline.

Meanwhile the next volcano is on its way. Scientists are already monitoring the submarine "seamount" of **Lō'ihi**, 20 miles southeast of the Ka'ū coast. Were you to stay for three thousand years, you might see it poke its head out for the first time. One day it too may seem no more than a blemish on the vast bulk of Mauna Loa; or it may be destined to overrun its older sisters altogether.

Planning a visit

Few people allow anything like enough time to see the Hawaii Volcanoes Park properly. In just a day trip you'd be hard pushed to drive the two main roads, let alone hike any of the trails. Worse still, you'll probably miss the most spectacular experience of all – watching the eruption after dark.

Much the best option is to **spend the night** nearby, either in the park itself, at the *Volcano House* hotel (see p.144), at the campgrounds (p.146 and p.154) or in a B&B in the village of Volcano (p.160). Failing that, at least base yourself in Hilo, 30 miles away, rather than distant Kona.

Although the best way to explore the park is in your own vehicle, it is possible to at least get there by **public bus** from Hilo. On Monday to Friday only, the *Mass Transportation Agency* (see p.102; ☎935-8241) runs a service that leaves Hilo's Mooheau Bus Terminal at 2.40pm and calls at both Volcano village and the park visitor centre around an hour later. The return ride is in the morning, leaving the visitor centre at 8.10am. Buses continue beyond the park as far as Ocean View (see p.167), but not all the way to Kailua. Alternatively, you could opt for an organized **bus tour** (some are listed on p.18), but generally these are not a good idea. They'll show you Kīlauea Caldera from above, but are unlikely to give you the flexibility to approach the eruption.

Hawaii
Volcanoes
National
Park

Broadly speaking, visiting the park involves some combination of three principal elements. First of all, there's the eleven-mile loop tour around Kīlauea Caldera from the visitor centre, on **Crater Rim Drive**; secondly, you may choose to **hike** into or near the caldera, from one or more points along the way; and finally comes the fifty-mile round trip down the **Chain of Craters Road** to the ocean, ending at the site of the current eruption. If you have the time, two further areas are open to exploration. Getting right to the **summit of Mauna Loa** involves a four-day hike, but it's possible to drive the first 3000 feet of the route to gain a different perspective on the region, while the **Ka'ū desert** away to the west offers more trails into a harshly beautiful moonscape.

Inevitably, what you do will depend on conditions on the day you arrive. The active lava flow might be right there at the end of the road, it might be an hour's hike away, it might be somewhere else entirely or it might have stopped altogether. If it *is* flowing, then seeing it should be your top priority; why linger over photos in a museum when you can see the real thing?

For details of helicopter tours of the park, see p.9.

Crater Rim Drive and the park headquarters

The **entrance** to Hawaii Volcanoes National Park is just off Hwy-11, the Belt Road, about a mile west of the village of **Volcano** (see p.160). If you're coming from the Kona side of the island you can visit the park without ever passing through Volcano, though as it holds the only gas station in the neighbourhood you may well have to. Within a few yards of the park's main gate, before you get a sight of the volcano, you find the **Visitor Center** immediately ahead of you to the right. From this point **Crater Rim Drive** takes eleven miles to loop around the summit crater ("caldera") of Kīlauea – for safety reasons, not always within sight of the edge.

Looking from a distance like a large oval of predominantly grey lava, roughly three miles long by two miles wide, **Kīlauea Caldera** is ringed on two sides by a steep *pali*, around 400 feet high. On those sides, and in places down below the wall as well, patches of rainforest have succeeded in dodging the fires; off to the south and east, however, the cliff dwindles to almost nothing, and strong-smelling sulphur drifts across the plains to ensure that nothing living can find a foothold. It's possible to walk right to the edge of what has long been the main centre of activity within the caldera, **Halema'uma'u Crater**, either from a parking lot on Crater Rim Drive or all the way across from *Volcano House*, on a trail that passes over the site of the last eruption in 1982.

The major hiking trails in the caldera area are described in a separate section, starting on p.148.

*The visitor
center is open
daily
7.45am–5pm;
☎967-7311.*

Kīlauea Visitor Center

Although the sprawling **KĪLAUEA VISITOR CENTER** does not overlook the crater of Kīlauea, it's well worth calling in as soon as you arrive, to pick up the latest information on the state of the eruption as well as advice on hiking trails (if you plan to camp in the backcountry, you must register here; see p.157). The centre has a bookstore and a small museum and provides lots of excellent free literature about the park. Every hour, on the hour, between 9am and 4pm, it shows a ten-minute video, packed with footage of eruptions, although in terms of explaining the geology of the volcanoes, the **Jaggar Museum** (see opposite) does a better job. Frequent lectures explain aspects of local geology, botany and environmental issues; at 7pm on most Tuesdays, the centre reopens for a popular series of talks entitled *After Dark in the Park.*

Volcano House

PO Box 53, Hawaii Volcanoes National Park, HI 96718; ☎967-7321; fax 967-8429; ④–⑤.

Pride of place on the lip of Kīlauea Caldera as you enter the park belongs to the *Volcano House* hotel, which has in various incarnations stood near this spot since 1846. When Mark Twain was a guest, in 1866, it was a neat little four-roomed thatched cottage; now it consists of two separate motel-style buildings, the main one of which stretches for well over a hundred yards just a few feet back from the abyss. The **Crater Rim Trail** squeezes its way along the edge, commanding views over the edge of the *pali*, beyond the rainforest below and across the caldera. Halema'uma'u Crater should be visible, three miles out, but the chances are that clouds and/or sulphurous mist will be obscuring Mauna Loa on the far side.

During the day, *Volcano House* fills up with day-trippers, attracted in part by the hurried and rather poor-quality $11 lunch buffet. At night, however, it reverts to something like its old self, its timbers warmed by the fire in the hearth that has burned continuously in one *Volcano House* after another since 1877 (and managed to destroy one version). The dining room is much better in the evening, serving conventional pasta and meat dishes in formal surroundings, with main courses costing around $18.

The **guest rooms** are simple and slightly faded, and not all of those in the main building face the volcano; the twelve which don't, plus ten more in the *Ohia Wing*, are significantly cheaper.

In addition, the *Volcano House* management is responsible for renting the **cabins** in the Nāmakani Paio campground (see p.146). Under the name of *Hawaiian Outdoors Tours*, it also plans to organize escorted hikes into the backcountry, including overnight camping expeditions to the beaches below Hilina Pali (see p.157); contact the hotel reception for further details.

Volcano Art Center

Set a little way back from the road, just beyond the visitor centre, the **Volcano Art Center** is a non-profit-making gallery and crafts store which sells the work of local artists in varying media. The building itself, the original 1877 *Volcano House*, is interesting to wander around. Prices are slightly higher than elsewhere, but so is the standard of the artwork on offer.

Sulphur Banks and Steam Vents

The first two stops on the Crater Rim Drive, on opposite sides of the road a few hundred yards and a mile respectively beyond the visitor centre, are natural phenomena with the self-explanatory names of **Sulphur Banks** and **Steam Vents**. Both these unspectacular spots are characterized by white fumes emerging from cracks in the ground to drift across open meadows; the difference is that the Sulphur Banks stink to high heaven, while the vapour from the Steam Vents is, once it condenses, in theory pure enough to drink.

Jaggar Museum

A little less than three miles from the visitor centre, and sited here for the good reason that it has the clearest, highest view of the caldera, is the fascinating **THOMAS A JAGGAR MUSEUM**. Its primary aim is to illustrate in simple terms the work of the adjacent **Hawaiian Volcano Observatory**, which is not open to the public. Videos show previous eruptions and large panel displays illustrate Hawaiian mythology and historical observations by travellers.

This is the place to get the distinction clear in your mind between the kinds of lava known as *'ā'ā* and *pāhoehoe* (which are among the very few Hawaiian words to have been adopted into other languages, used as they are by geologists throughout the world). Chemically the two forms are exactly the same, but they differ due to the temperature at which they are ejected from the volcano. Hotter, runnier *pāhoehoe* is wrinkled and ropy, like the sludgy skin of custard pushed with your finger but still with a sandpaper finish; cooler *'ā'ā* does not flow so much as spatter, creating a sharp, jagged clinker. Other volcanic by-products on display in the museum include what's known as **Pele's hair** – very fine filaments that really do look like hair, although they're made of glass – and the shiny droplets called **Pele's tears**.

Outside, a viewing area looks down into Kīlauea, and Halema'uma'u Crater in particular, which is 360 feet deep at this point. By now you're on the fringes of the Ka'ū Desert, so there are no trees to block the view. The trade winds have for millennia blown the noxious emissions from the crater southwest, so despite receiving large quantities of rainfall the land supports no growth.

The Volcano Art Center is open daily 9am–5pm; ☎ *967-8222.*

The Jaggar museum is open daily 8.30am–5pm; ☎ *867-7643.*

Controlling The Flow

When ancient Hawaiians found their homes threatened by approaching lava, they usually attempted to propitiate Pele with offerings (see p.151), but if in the end they had to move away they were not greatly inconvenienced. Unlike their modern counterparts, they did not own the land on which they lived, and could simply rebuild elsewhere. They could also load their possessions into canoes and paddle out of harm's way.

A full-scale emergency in Puna today would be very different, with hundreds of vehicles attempting to flee along the one road out, which might be rendered impassable at any moment. What's more, anyone unfortunate enough to lose a home may face economic ruin.

That sort of scenario loomed in the mind of Thomas Jaggar, when he founded the **Hawaiian Volcano Observatory** in 1911. Its Latin motto, *ne plus haustae aut obratae urbes*, means "no more swallowed up or buried cities", and one of its main goals was to understand the behaviour of the volcanoes enough to control them.

In both 1935 and 1942, when Hilo appeared to be under threat from eruptions of Mauna Loa, attempts were made to **bomb** the lava flow. Angled walls have also been constructed at strategic points on the slopes, in the hope of channelling the stream away from specific targets. A military installation high on Mauna Loa seems to have been spared as a result, though a similar scheme in the Kapoho district (see p.138) could not prevent the town's destruction.

These days the emphasis is much more on prediction than containment; the emergency services are briefed to stop fires but not to try to divert the flow. Only partly is that out of respect for Pele – more important is the fear of **litigation**. Directing lava away from one site might have the effect of "aiming" it at another; aggrieved homeowners who lost their property could then blame the authorities responsible.

Nāmakani Paio

*There's
another, more
remote
campground at
Kīpuka Nēnē,
off the Chain of
Craters Road;
see p.154.*

A ten-minute walk from the Jaggar Museum parking lot, away from the caldera, brings you to the only **campground** in the main area of the park, **NĀMAKANI PAIO**. It's actually just across the Belt Road, so if you're driving to it you don't enter the park proper. The pleasant wooded sites are **free** and available on a first-come, first-served basis for maximum stays of seven nights (in any one year).

Basic **cabins**, sharing use of the campground's rest rooms and showers, can be rented through the *Volcano House* (see p.144; ☎967-7321; ②). Each holds one double bed and two bunk beds, and has a picnic table and barbecue area (bring your own fuel). Bed linen is provided, though as there's no heating you'll be glad of a sleeping bag or extra blanket.

Halema'uma'u Crater

Although Kīlauea is extremely active it's very unusual for eruptions to take place up here at the summit. Since 1980, it's happened only twice, both times for less than a day. When they do occur, such eruptions can create smaller distinct craters within the caldera; the most conspicuous of these, the **HALEMAʻUMAʻU CRATER**, is the next stop on the drive, just over a mile from the museum.

Although you can see the crater from the roadside parking lot, you'll get a much clearer idea of it if you're prepared to walk a couple of hundred yards across the caldera floor. The trail is very clearly marked and there's a handrail for some of the way, but with gusts of white mist spouting from crevices in the rock on all sides you still feel as if you're taking your life in your hands.

The overlook, looking down into a steaming abyss heavy with the stench of white and yellow sulphur, may well be where your courage deserts you. As you approach the rim it's very easy to see where sections of the wall have collapsed, as well as the yawning cracks where they will do so in future. In the 1830s, Halemaʻumaʻu was described as a dome rising out of the lava field; when Mark Twain saw it in 1866 it was a "heaving sea of molten fire", with walls a thousand feet high. Since a huge explosion in 1924, however, it's been shallower and quieter and is now a circular depression that drops around 400 feet below the rest of the caldera.

If this walk whets your appetite, you might be tempted to brave the entire three-mile length of the **Halemaʻumaʻu Trail**, right across the caldera from *Volcano House* (see p.148).

Keanakākoʻi and Puʻu Puaʻi

From time to time, the route of the Crater Rim Drive has had to be redrawn, as fresh lava paves over the road and a new layer of tarmac is in turn laid down on top of the lava. The stretch immediately to the east of Halemaʻumaʻu was cut in two in 1982, and now passes in between the sites of two recent eruptions.

Until it was filled almost to the brim by new outpourings, **KEANAKĀKOʻI CRATER**, south of the road, was the site of an ancient adze quarry, a source of the hard stone used by Hawaiians to make tools and weapons. PUʻU PUAʻI, farther along, is a bare rust-coloured cinder cone thrown up in 1959 and accessible along the Devastation Trail (see p.153).

Thurston Lava Tube

Once past the Chain of Craters turn-off (see p.153), Crater Rim Drive plunges back into dense rainforest. This much less intimidating landscape is the location of the only short walk attempted by most tour groups, into the **THURSTON LAVA TUBE**.

As soon as you cross the road from the parking lot, a mile or so short of the visitor centre, you're faced by a large natural basin bursting with huge *ʻōhiʻa* trees. Down beneath it is the tube itself, which was created when the surface of a lava stream hardened on exposure to the air and the lava below was able to keep flowing 28 miles to the sea with only a slight loss of temperature. When the lava eventually drained away, it left behind a damp, empty tunnel, an artificially lit portion of which is now open to the public. If you've ever travelled on a subway system, the basic concept and appearance will be familiar.

It takes less than ten minutes to walk to and through the tube, which is remarkable only for the smoothness of its walls and its conveniently flat natural floor. Occasionally roots from the gigantic ferns that grow up above have worked their way through cracks in the rock to dangle from the ceiling, while outside, the native red-billed *'i'iwi* bird can always be heard, if not seen.

Hiking in Kīlauea Caldera

As trying to lay a road across the unstable surface of the caldera itself would be ludicrous even by the standards of this topsy-turvy park, the only way to experience the crater floor is by hiking.

The only safe trails are those named and maintained by the park service and shown on their free hand-outs; venturing off these would be suicidal. To embark on even the most popular trails requires an act of faith verging on the superstitious: they're no more than ill-defined footpaths across the bare, steaming lava, guided only by makeshift rock cairns (known as *ahus*). Frequent cracks reveal a crust that is on average around four inches thick, although considering the many layers piled up beneath you that's not as alarming as it may sound. As a rule, the geologists estimate that the molten lava here is two miles down.

There's no need to register for any of the caldera hikes. You must do so however if you're heading into the backcountry: see p.144.

The caldera is not a place for agoraphobics; you can't assume that anyone will be following a trail at the same time as you, so it's up to you to find your way and cope with the occasional burst of fear. Only two people in two centuries have been killed by eruptions, both of them photographers in search of the perfect shot. However, more mundane accidents happen frequently, and trying to hike at night is a very bad idea.

The longest trail in the caldera area is the **Crater Rim Trail**, at 11.6 miles. It's not described in detail here because it so closely parallels the Crater Rim Drive, though it generally runs nearer the edge than the road. It is an exciting, dramatic walk and a level and easy one too, but it shows you very little that you can't see from a car. All the trails in this section start from or cross the Crater Rim Trail, however, so you're likely to walk at least a short section of it.

The Halemaʻumaʻu and Byron Ledge trails

Two separate hiking trails – the **Halemaʻumaʻu** and the **Byron Ledge** – cross the main floor of Kīlauea Caldera. However, as they meet each other twice and you will presumably need to hike back to your starting point, it makes sense to combine the two into one single round trip, of roughly seven miles and around four hours.

The obvious place to start is along the Crater Rim Trail from *Volcano House*. Heading northwest (away from the park entrance), the path drops slightly for a hundred yards, until a signpost points

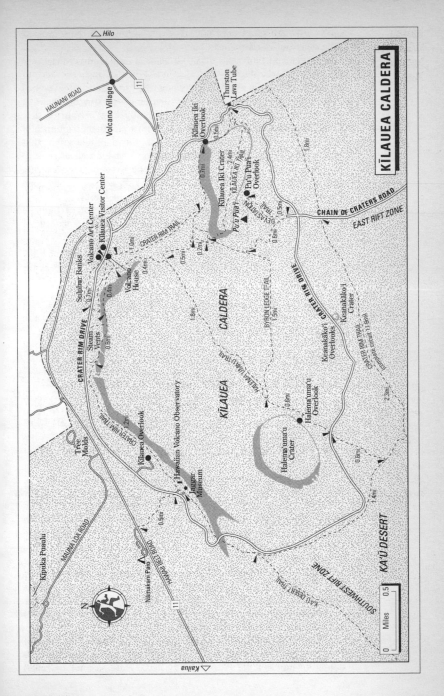

KĪLAUEA CALDERA

to the left down the **HALEMAʻUMAʻU TRAIL**. From there, a clear easy walkway descends through thick **rainforest**, with the bright orange heliconia growing to either side interspersed with delicate white-blossomed shrubs and green *hāpuʻu* ferns, capable of growing 40 feet high. Except when the odd helicopter passes overhead, the only sounds are the chatter of the tiny bright birds that flit through the canopy and the steady drip of rain or dew falling from the highest branches. Every now and then, a glimpse of the steam vents on the crater floor far ahead reminds you that you're now inside an active volcano. Soon a sheer wall of rock to your left marks the abrupt fault line of the outermost crater rim. Less than half a mile down, from a small rain shelter, views open out across a small gorge filled with gently stirring jungle.

Not far beyond are the massive rock slides left by an earthquake measuring 6.7 on the Richter scale, in November 1983; a cascade of giant cubic boulders tumbled down the cliff face and they now reach to the very edge of the path. Thereafter the vegetation rapidly thins out, and you soon find yourself at the edge of the vast black expanse of the **crater floor**. The trail from here on is nothing like as distinct as you might expect. At first the passage of worn feet is clear enough, but before long you're gingerly picking your way from cairn to crude cairn, the schoolyard game of not treading on the cracks taking on a real urgency when you think of the lake of molten lava somewhere beneath your feet. The state of the trail depends on the age of the flow at each precise spot. Different vintages overlap in absurd profusion, and from time to time it becomes a jumble of torn, cracked and uplifted slabs of rock.

For at least half an hour you cross a plain where tiny ferns seem to have taken root in every fissure, creating a green lattice-work of fault lines. Here and there *ʻōhelo* bushes, with the dew-glistening red berries sacred to Pele, have established themselves. Then the ground begins to rise again, the cairns become harder to pick out against the general chaos, and wisps of sulphurous steam gust across the path with ever-greater regularity.

In due course you're confronted by what appears to be a low ridge of sharp, rough hills, like the battlements of some medieval castle, with no indication of what lies behind. A single clear footpath leads up to a gap; through that gap, a similar landscape to the one you've just crossed opens up once again. If you don't know what a **spatter cone** is yet, turn around; on this side the walls of most of the castellated hillocks are hollow, exposing fiery red interiors. They were created by the eruption of April 1982, when hikers in this lonely spot had to be evacuated immediately before a 19-hour onslaught. As you look back through the gap, the Jaggar Museum is perfectly framed high on the crater rim.

This spot is clearly marked as the intersection of the Halemaʻumaʻu and Byron Ledge trails, which head on together for a couple of hundred yards to the very lip of **Halemaʻumaʻu Crater**.

You can reach the overlook much more easily, via the short trail from the Crater Rim Drive; that walk, and the actual crater, is described on p.147. If you can arrange to be picked up at the parking lot, you can end your hike here. Alternatively, double back and take your choice as to your return route.

Pele: the Volcano Goddess

Every visitor to Hawaii Volcanoes National Park soon hears the name of Pele, the "volcano goddess" of the ancient Hawaiians. The daughter of Haumea the Earth Mother and Wākea the Sky father, she is said to have first set foot in the Hawaiian chain on Kauai. Pursued by her vengeful older sister, the goddess of the sea, she travelled from island to island and finally made her home in the pit of Kīlauea. As well as manifesting herself as molten lava, she appeared sometimes as a young woman, sometimes as an elderly crone. Small acts of charity to her human forms could spare the giver a terrible fate when she returned as fire.

Imbued as they are with poetry, legend, history and symbolism, it's impossible now to appreciate all that the tales of Pele meant to those who once recounted them by the distant glow of Kīlauea. Certainly these were a people who studied the volcanoes carefully; specific places appear in the chants describing Pele's progress through the archipelago in the exact order of age agreed by modern experts. However, the destructive power of the volcanoes was just one small aspect of the goddess; she was also associated with the *hula*, with fertility and with creation in general.

Talk of Hawaiian religion as a single system of belief ignores the fact that different groups once worshipped different gods. The god Kū, to whom human sacrifices were made in the *luakinis* (see p.180), was probably only the chosen deity of the warrior elite; Pele may have been far more central to the lives of many, possibly most, of the islanders. She seems to have been a Polynesian deity whose worship first became prominent in Hawaii around the thirteenth century. That may be because, together with Kū, she was brought to the islands by the wave of migrants who arrived at that time from Tahiti, or it may be that that was when Kīlauea entered the period of high activity that still continues today.

The earliest Christian missionaries to the Big Island were disconcerted to find that even after the *kapu* was broken and the old ways supposedly abandoned – see p.173 – belief in Pele endured. They made great play of an incident in 1824, when Queen Kapi'olani, a recent convert to Christianity, defied the goddess by descending into the caldera (probably on what's now known as the Byron Ledge), reading aloud from her Bible, eating the *kapu* red *'ōhelo* berries and throwing their stones into the pit. Rather less fuss was made in 1881, when an eight-month flow from Mauna Loa had reached within a mile of central Hilo, Christian prayer meetings had elicited no response and Princess Ruth Ke'elikōlani was called in from Oahu to help. Under the sceptical gaze of journalists and missionaries, she chanted to Pele at the edge of the molten rock and offered her red silk handkerchiefs and brandy. By the next morning, the flow had ceased. Well into this century, inhabitants of Puna and Ka'ū brought up in the old traditions would state that their families were directly descended from Pele and that, in a sense, each individual *was* Pele.

If you decide to head back along the **BYRON LEDGE TRAIL**, you'll find it considerably easier to follow, with a shorter distance across the crater floor; the walk to the edge of the crater from the junction of the two trails takes around half an hour. This trail is more even underfoot, although once or twice it requires you to step across narrow (roughly nine inches) but alarmingly impenetrable cracks in the ground, including one with a small tree in it.

The ascent up to **Byron Ledge** (named after the cousin of the poet, who came here in 1825) is quite precipitous. The surface of the path is a sort of unstable gravel – made of the same sharp shards of black glass as a new "black sand" beach – and occasionally the scree slope plunges away below your feet. It can be very vertiginous; from this close, the black crater floor is so huge and featureless that the brain can't really take it in, and it feels like a sheer wall rising up against you, or a bottomless pit. The rainforest at the top is gloomier and less lush than on the Halema'uma'u Trail.

At one point along the ledge, you pass a spur trail that leads within a couple of minutes to the Kīlauea Iki trail (see below). Sticking to the Byron Ledge trail involves dropping right back down to cross a small segment of the caldera floor, in order to rejoin the Halema'uma'u Trail back to *Volcano House*, at the spot where it reaches the basin.

The Kīlauea Iki Trail

Just east of Kīlauea Caldera proper, but still within the Crater Rim Drive, the subsidiary crater of **KĪLAUEA IKI** (literally "little Kīlauea") took on its current shape during a gigantic eruption in 1959. Prodigious quantities of lava, exploding in a vertical column that reached a record height of 1900 feet, raised the crater floor by around 350 feet; a few hundred feet below the surface, some of it is still thought to be red hot. Though Kīlauea Iki may not have quite the same sense of scale as the main caldera, it offers a similar and in some ways even more spectacular assortment of terrain, which can be explored along the two-hour, four-mile **KĪLAUEA IKI TRAIL**.

The trail is most easily done as an anti-clockwise hike from the parking lot at the **Thurston Lava Tube** (see p.147), a mile south of the visitor centre. Start by following the Crater Rim Trail for about a mile, as it circles close to the lip of the gulf. At a three-way junction with the spur that leads to Byron Ledge (see above), signs point left to the Kīlauea Iki Trail proper. At this point the rainforest becomes especially dense, with ultra-dark oily green leaves, startled wild game birds running along the path ahead and songbirds overhead.

Soon you begin to get views of the far wall of Kīlauea Iki, tinged with pastel greens and yellows against the general darkness, with Mauna Loa visible in the distance on clear days. Views of the crater floor thus far have made it appear smooth, but after a half-mile or so the path drops abruptly down steep steps cut into the rock to reach a jagged primeval mess of tumbled *'a'ā* lava. From the edge you follow the line of cairns for a few hundred yards before arriving at the vent where the 1959 eruption took place. This sudden gaping maw in the hillside, filled like an hourglass with fine reddish-orange sand, is seen across an open scar in the lava; a barrier makes it clear that you should approach no closer.

The trail then descends slightly to a much more even but no less alarming expanse of undulating *pāhoehoe*, punctuated by white- and yellow-stained cracks that ooze stinking plumes of white vapour. You have to step across the odd fissure and, once again, it takes an act of faith to follow the scattered cairns that mark the way; it's easy to stray from the path and to succumb to a moment of panic at the thought that you're a mile from safety in a vague plain of swirling mists and splintered lava. Eventually, however, you pass through a final chaos of rocks into the dripping dank bosom of the rainforest. The path then zigzags back up to the rim; the gradient is never steep, but it's a fair walk and can get pretty muddy.

Devastation Trail
Much of the lighter debris from the 1959 Kīlauea Iki eruption (see above) was blown clear of the crater itself, then carried by the wind to pile up as a **cinder cone** near its southwestern edge. This is **Pu'u Pua'i**, which can be reached along the half-mile **DEVASTATION TRAIL** between two parking lots on Crater Rim Drive (see p.147).

If you set out from the Devastation parking area, opposite the beginning of Chain of Craters Road, you start by following the old route of Crater Rim Drive, which was severed at this point by the eruption. A paved pathway snakes from the end of the parking lot through low light pink undergrowth – a favourite haunt of the park's population of *nēnē* geese. Most of what you see is new growth, though a few older trees survived partial submersion in ash by developing "aerial roots" some way up their trunks. Pu'u Puai itself is just a heap of reddish ash, while the land around it is utterly barren, scattered with bleached branches.

Chain of Craters Road
CHAIN OF CRATERS ROAD winds down to the ocean from the south side of Crater Rim Drive, sweeping around a succession of cones and vents in an empty landscape where only the occasional dead white tree trunk or flowering shrub pokes up. From high on the hillside the lava flows look like streams of black tarmac, joining in an ever-widening highway down to the endless blue Pacific. Long **hiking trails** and the minor **Hilina Pali Road** lead to sites of geological and historic interest all the way down, but the real reason you're likely to head this way is to see what may be at the end – the ongoing **eruption** of Kīlauea.

Chain of Craters Road used to run all the way to Puna, then loop back up to the highway. The scale of the damage since 1983 has been too great to repair, however, so now it's a dead end and getting shorter year by year. One by one the landmarks along its seafront stretch – such as **Waha'ula Heiau**, another temple which claimed to be where human sacrifice was introduced to Hawaii, and the gorgeous black sand beach at **Kamoamoa**, whose short existence lasted only from 1988 until 1992 – have been destroyed and before long the road may not follow the shoreline at all.

Check current conditions at the visitor centre when you arrive and make sure you have enough fuel. The end of the road is a fifty-mile round trip from the park entrance, and there are no facilities of any kind along the way.

Hilina Pali Road

Four miles down Chain of Craters Road, a sign to the right points out a detour along **HILINA PALI ROAD**. This crosses the bleak Ka'ū Desert for nine miles, to reach an overlook above the main 1200-foot drop of **Hilina Pali**. *Pali* is the Hawaiian word for cliff; you may be used to hearing it applied to the lush razorback hills of the Hāmākua coast, but Hilina is much starker and rawer than that, being the huge wall left behind when a piece of the island dropped into the sea. The views are immense, but desolate in the extreme. Infrequent clusters of battered palms in the distance show the locations of former coastal villages; the hillock of Pu'u Kapukapu, near the shore to the southeast, however, obscures the most popular of the park's backcountry campgrounds, at Halapē.

Halfway along the road, you come to **Kīpuka Nēnē**, a clump of forest that holds one of the park's two fully equipped drive-in **campgrounds**. Like Nāmakani Paio (see p.146), it's free and available on a first-come, first-served basis for up to seven nights in any one year. However, as one of the very few breeding grounds used by *nēnē* geese, it's usually closed during the November–March breeding season, to allow the birds a little privacy.

Hiking in this area is never less than gruelling, involving extended periods of walking across barren, exposed and baking hot lava flats. If you want to get to the shoreline, it makes much more sense to hike the **Puna Coast Trail**, described on p.157, than to oblige yourself to climb up and down the *pali* as well. However, real gluttons for punishment have a choice of two trails to the sea from the overlook. Both the **Hilina Pali** and **Ka'aha** trails start by zigzagging down the cliff along the same very steep and poorly maintained footpath; the Ka'aha leads for just under four miles to **Ka'aha Shelter** (see p.158), while the Hilina Pali covers the eight miles to the **Halapē Shelter**, joining the **Halapē Trail** from Kīpuka Nēnē. In addition, you can even walk to the Hilina Pali overlook from the Jaggar Museum, along the eighteen-mile **Ka'ū Desert Trail** (the "Footprints" section of which is detailed on p.159).

Mauna Ulu Trail and Pu'u Huluhulu

Another three miles along the Chain of Craters Road beyond the Hilina Pali turn-off, a small approach road on the left leads to the start of the **MAUNA ULU TRAIL**. A couple of miles along, this becomes the **Nāpau Trail**, then runs for ten miles to the open **Pu'u 'Ō'ō** vent, far out along Kīlauea's East Rift Zone – the culprit responsible for most of the lava flows since 1983. Only with expert guidance and *very* up-to-date information should you consider attempting to walk the whole way, however. You must register if you plan to use the basic **campground** at Nāpau Crater, three miles short of the end, and the trail beyond there is almost certain to be closed. As of April 1995, Pu'u 'Ō'ō was extremely unstable, with gaping holes splitting open its sides to release floods of liquid rock.

Most hikers content themselves with the three-mile round trip through pockets of forest and patches of lava to **Pu'u Huluhulu**, an ancient cinder cone that has somehow escaped inundation for several millenia. It owes its name (*huluhulu* means "very hairy") to the dense coating of unspoiled, old-growth rainforest that surrounds it as a result. Following the footpath to the top of this small mound enables you to peer into its inaccessible hollow interior, filled with primeval-looking green ferns and darting birds. The sensation of being in a real-life "Lost World" is enhanced by the wasteland visible all around. Views to the south are dominated by the miniature shield volcano of **Mauna Ulu**, created between 1971 and 1974 and already home to native trees and shrubs like the *'ōhi'a* and *'ōhelo*.

Pu'u Loa Petroglyphs

Ten miles beyond Mauna Ulu, and just after its descent of the 1000-foot Hōlei Pali, Chain of Craters Road passes within a mile of the most extensive field of **petroglyphs** – ancient rock carvings – on the Big Island.

The level trail east to **PU'U LOA** ends at a circular raised boardwalk. Most of the petroglyphs visible from here are no more than crude holes in the lava, the kind you might make by rotating a coin against a brick. They only inspire any wonder if you're aware that each one was probably carved to hold the umbilical cord of a new-born infant, carried here at a time when this spot was even more remote than it is today. *Pu'u loa* means long hill, and by extension "long life", so this was considered a lucky spot for the traditional ceremony.

The real purpose of the boardwalk is not to display the most elaborate petroglyphs, but to discourage you from exploring further, for fear that you might damage such irreplaceable works of art as the images of pre-contact **surfers**, said to lie somewhere in the area.

Hōlei Sea Arch

At the time of writing, Chain of Craters Road came to an end just beyond mile-marker 20, with the small parking lot near **HŌLEI SEA**

ARCH used as a turn-around point for all vehicles. Less than two miles survive of its previous eleven-mile shoreline route to Kalapana, and at its current rate it may soon not reach the coast at all.

Until recently, few visitors bothered to pause at the sea arch, which is simply a natural hole in a seafront headland. Now it's the only named feature left in what was once a very scenic area. From the parking lot, near the sea, you cross a few yards of sparsely grassed lava before seeing to your right a chunky pillar of basalt blocks, tenuously connected to the rest of the island by the top slab. The thudding of the waves against the cliffs makes the ground reverberate beneath your feet – clear evidence of the fragility of this coastline, most of which is too dangerous to approach, and no encouragement at all to linger.

Approaching the eruption

It's impossible to do more than generalize as to what might lie beyond the end of Chain of Craters Road. Granted that the eruption is still continuing, somewhere high on the hillside one or more fissures in the earth will be spilling out large quantities of molten lava, which then sets off towards the ocean. En route it may or may not have to pour over fault scarps, and its surface may or may not harden to create an underground stream like the one preserved as the Thurston Lava Tube (see p.147). You will probably only be able to view the lava itself if the nearest active flow pushing its way down the flanks of Kīlauea has reached a point you can walk to from the road; if it is flowing directly into the ocean, which is easy to spot because the contact produces great plumes of steam; or if it is crossing or flowing along the road itself.

You can find out if any of these scenarios apply by calling the park's 24-hour Volcano Update line (☎967-7977); the Kīlauea visitor centre (☎967-7311) can offer more detailed advice. Considering the dangers involved, you might expect to be told to keep away; instead you're enthusiastically encouraged to come and see for yourself. The park service maintains a wooden information shack (on wheels, for obvious reasons) at the end of the road, where they hand out alarming leaflets explaining that new lava is unstable and may collapse at any time, and that it's best to avoid clouds of hydrochloric acid. When safety permits, rangers lead **guided hikes** to the site of the eruption. A daily schedule is posted at the visitor centre; as a rule they start in the early afternoon, in order to be sure of getting back to the road before nightfall.

Walking across flaky, crumbling, new lava is an extraordinary experience. Every surface is like sandpaper, a fall can shred your skin and even far from the apparent centre of activity the ground can be too hot to touch. Heavy rain dries off without penetrating your clothing. The sight of liquid rock oozing towards you, swirling with phlegmy gobbets and destroying all it touches; the crackle as it crunches across previous layers of lava; the sudden flash as a dried-out tree bursts into flame; all leave you with a disconcerting sense of the land itself as a living, moving organism.

The most dangerous situation occurs when lava flows directly into the **ocean**, and there's a risk of inhaling toxic fumes that contain not only acids but even tiny particles of glass. In addition, new land is extremely unstable; it may be no more a thin layer of solidified lava resting on seawater and thus liable to collapse at any moment. Swirling mists can make it hard to keep your bearings and also mean that only occasionally do you see the actual lava.

After dark, the orange glow of the eruption becomes even more apparent. Pinpoint incandescent lights become visible all across the slopes and leave the mountain looking like the proverbial city on a hill. Without official sanction or approval, and heedless of the immense risks, many visitors stay out all night to marvel at the glowing orange rivers of molten rock. If you try it, be sure to carry a flashlight for the walk back across the treacherous lava.

Puna Coast Trail

Although it's roughly a mile up from the sea, the Pu'u Loa parking lot (see p.155) is also the point at which the **PUNA COAST TRAIL** sets off west, away from the eruption area, towards the coastal campgrounds at **Keauhou** and **Halapē**.

Also known as the **Puna Ka'ū Trail**, this is a long and very challenging hike, and only worth attempting if you have several days to spare. It would be possible to get to 'Āpua Point and back in a single day, but that's a long way short of the more interesting spots along the trail and in itself not a very rewarding thirteen-mile round trip. If you plan to camp out, you must register at the visitor centre in Kīlauea. This area is prone to landslides and *tsunamis* and if there has to be an emergency evacuation your chances of survival won't be helped if no one knows you're here. Collected rainwater is available at the shelters, but you should carry plenty more yourself to cope with the effects of walking in the baking heat.

From Chain of Craters Road, the trail makes its indistinct way across a patchwork of lava flows, the new ones glistening in the sun and crunchy underfoot and older ones worn and smooth. Rock cairns help to plot a course in the vaguer patches and, here and there, coarse weeds have managed to establish themselves. Roughly four miles along, you finally reach the low seafront cliffs, which you then follow for a couple more miles to **'Āpua Point**. From a distance it's a welcome flash of green against the relentless greys and blacks of the lava; when you arrive it turns out to have just a few coconut palms emerging from a tangled carpet of the ivy-like native *naupaka* shrub.

With no water, shelter or other facilities at 'Āpua, you either have to turn back to the road, or continue along the coast. Heading west, you're faced by the massive fault scarp of Hilina Pali looming

Hawaii
Volcanoes
National
Park

ever larger inland. As well as releasing cascades of rock and even lava towards the ocean, landslides like those that created the *pali* also produce *tsunamis* that rush in to flood the coastal plains – a "double whammy" that means little is left standing along this stretch of the shoreline. Both the **Keauhou** and **Halapē** campgrounds, three and five miles respectively from 'Āpua, remain visibly scarred by the battering they received in November 1975 (when two campers lost their lives at Halapē). However, the park service has been replanting coconut palms to restore their lost beauty, and Halapē especially still has the feel of a little oasis beside the Pacific. So many campers trek out to enjoy the shady grove around its tiny white-sand beach that the whole area is unfortunately swarming with insects; at both Halapē and Keauhou you're likely to get a better night's sleep in your own tent than in the ant- and cockroach-infested cabins. Snorkelling in the tidal pools is excellent, but the open sea can be very dangerous. In theory these are nesting grounds for sea turtles, though the regulations against disturbing them seem to be a case of too little, too late and hardly any seem to land here any more.

There is another oceanfront campground, at **Ka'aha**, but to get there from Halapē involves following a very difficult six-mile hike up and along the top of a lesser *pali*. You can also climb down, with equal effort, from Hilina Pali Road (see p.154). Either way, it too is riddled with insects and even more dangerous for swimming.

Mauna Loa

If you're interested in seeing a bit more of **MAUNA LOA**, as opposed to Kīlauea, leave the caldera area by the main entrance and head west for a couple of miles. The third turning on the right, **Mauna Loa Road**, winds up towards the summit from there, although it stops a long way short and only very rarely allows you views either up the mountain or down towards Kīlauea and the sea.

Kīpuka Puaulu

The great majority of those who come along the Mauna Loa Road drive less than a mile of its fourteen-mile length, to visit the enchanting little forest sanctuary of **KĪPUKA PUAULU**. Often known as the "bird park", this enclave makes a complete contrast with the raw landscape elsewhere in the national park. In Hawaiian, a *kīpuka* is a small patch of land that has by chance been left untouched by lava, and thus forms a sort of natural island. Kīpuka Puaulu holds some of the best-preserved rainforest in the volcanoes region and serves as a sanctuary for rare native birds such as the *'elepaio* fly-catcher and the *'amakahi* honey-creeper.

A woodland stroll around the two-mile loop path takes you past some huge old *koa* trees and through sun-dappled clearings, with birds audible on all sides. Unless you have a lot of patience – and binoculars – you may not manage to see more than the odd flash of colour. Your best bet is to walk slowly and quietly and hope to surprise a group on the ground.

The Mauna Loa Summit Trail
Beyond Kīpuka Puaulu, Mauna Loa Road climbs through thick woodland virtually all the way to the end, crossing just one stray lava flow. Its width varies between one and two lanes and, here and there, thick tree roots have pushed up from beneath the tarmac, but it's drivable if not exactly quick. The surrounding tree-cover gradually changes from tropical to high-altitude before the road finally stops in a small clearing something over 6000 feet up.

The parking lot here is the trailhead for the **MAUNA LOA SUMMIT TRAIL**. As the very explicit signs in the small pavilion explain, this is no trail to attempt on a whim. The summit is a gradual but exhausting 19 miles farther on across bleak, barren lava, with a round trip usually taking four days. There's no shelter along the way except for two crude cabins – check with the Park service, with whom you must register anyway, to see whether they are stocked with water. Hypothermia is a very real threat, as the higher slopes are prone to abominable weather conditions. If you make it to the top, you're confronted by the **Moku'āweoweo Caldera**, similar in size to Kīlauea's, which last erupted in 1984.

The Ka'ū Desert
All the land in the national park that lies to the south and west of Kīlauea Caldera is officially known as the **KA'Ū DESERT**. By the conventional definition of a desert, it should therefore receive no rain; in fact it receives almost as much as the rainforest to the east, but here it falls as a natural acid rain, laden with chemicals from Kīlauea. Only a few dessicated plants ever managed to adapt to this uncompromising landscape, and most of those have in the last century been eaten away by ravenous wild goats.

Walking the eighteen-mile **Ka'ū Desert Trail** can bring you into close contact with this region if you so desire; there's one overnight shelter on its great curve from the Jaggar Museum down to Hilina Pali Road (see p.154). For a short taste, the **Footprints Trail** leads to the site of a curious incident in Big Island history.

The Footprints Trail
Ten miles west of the park entrance on the Belt Road, an inconspicuous roadside halt marks the start of the **FOOTPRINTS TRAIL**, which leads due south for just under a mile across rough 'a'ā lava. A small shelter at what might seem like a random spot covers a bunch of vague depressions in the rock, which popular legend says are human footprints. Whether or not you agree, the factual basis for the legend is bizarre.

Hawaii
Volcanoes
National
Park

*Keoua himself
met a no less
dramatic end:
see p.82.*

In 1790, Keōua, a rival of Kamehameha, was returning to his own kingdom of Ka'ū after two major battles in Puna. As his armies, complete with attendant women and children, traversed this stretch of desert, he divided them into three separate groups. The first group got safely across; then Kīlauea erupted, and the third group found the members of the second strewn across the pathway. All were dead, poisoned by a cloud of gas from the volcano. The legend goes that their footprints in the falling ash solidified and can still be seen, alternately protected and exposed as sand blows across the desert.

Volcano Village

Unless you stay in *Volcano House* (p.144) or the park-service campgrounds (p.146 and 154), the village of **VOLCANO** offers the only **accommodation** in the vicinity of the park. Though it's just a mile or so east of the park entrance, towards Hilo, it would be easy to drive straight past it without realizing it's there. The main street runs parallel to the highway, on the *mauka* (uphill) side, but well hidden by a roadside fringe of trees. Along it you'll find nothing much of interest other than a small post office, a couple of general stores and the only gas station for miles.

Mauka and **makai**

Remember *mauka* means away from the sea and towards the mountain, and *makai* means away from the mountain and towards the sea.

Volcano Village accommodation

The strange thing about staying in Volcano is that there's nothing to suggest you're anywhere near an active volcano – only *Volcano House* in the park can offer crater views. Instead, the village's crop of small-scale **bed and breakfast** places are tucked away in odd little corners of a dense rainforest. Property owners wage a constant war against both rain and insects, but the compensations are the beautiful gardens, and the sheer tranquility.

Carson's Volcano Cottage, PO Box 503, Volcano HI 96785; ☎967-7683 or 1-800/845-LAVA (US); ④.
A very friendly, romantic little place, on Sixth Street south of the highway. There's one en-suite room in the owners' house and a private cottage in the garden, plus an open-air jacuzzi. They also offer two separate rental cottages.

Chalet Kilauea, PO Box 998, Volcano HI 96785; ☎967-7786 or 1-800/937-7786 (US); fax 987-8660; ④–⑦.
Plush, lavishly furnished B&B, set well north of the highway on Wright Road, with individual rooms in the main house and separate cottages, including a "tree house" in the grounds. The owners also run the *Volcano Accommodations* agency, so if they don't have room themselves, they may able to find you a place elsewhere.

Hale Kilauea, PO Box 28, Volcano HI 96785; ☎967-7591; ③–⑤.
A small cluster of buildings north of the main street, with simple rooms in the central lodge and a restored plantation cottage nearby. The furnishings are

functional, rather than antique, which helps to keep the prices down; and the owner, a long-time local resident, is a mine of information on the area.

Hale Ohia, PO Box 758, Volcano HI 96785; ☎967-7986 or 1-800/455-3803; fax 967-8610; ④–⑤.
Accommodation ranging from studio apartments to a three-bedroom cottage, in small well-maintained buildings scattered across the neat lawns of a former private estate, just south of the highway across from the centre of the village.

Kilauea Lodge, PO Box 116, Volcano HI 96785; ☎967-7366; fax 967-7367; ④.
Former YMCA on the main street, converted into an upmarket and very comfortable 12-bedroom B&B. Accommodation is in secluded chalets and cottages dotted across the grounds, all of which have private baths. The central lodge building holds unquestionably the finest restaurant in the area – see below.

My Island, PO Box 100, Volcano HI 96785; ☎967-7216; fax 967-7719; ③.
Several different grades of accommodation in individual properties set amid dense tropical vegetation. The friendly owner, author and island expert Gordon Morse, lives in the central lodge; guests can use his library as well as a communal TV lounge.

Hawaii
Volcanoes
National
Park

Eating in the Volcano area

The choice of restaurants in the neighbourhood of the national park is very limited. Apart from *Volcano House* (see p.144), there are only two real alternatives for a full meal.

Up a side road two miles west of the park entrance (towards Kona), the restaurant at the *Volcano Golf & Country Club* (☎967-7331) serves a conventional menu of steaks, fish and salad at around $10 for a main course. Its large picture windows look out across unlikely but boring meadows and there's no atmosphere; however, the food's not bad.

Much the better option is the large dining room, equipped with rich wooden furnishings and warmed by an open fire, at *Kilauea Lodge* in the heart of Volcano village (☎967-7366; see above). It's open for dinner nightly, though non-residents should reserve well in advance. You can choose from a full range of strong-flavoured European-style meat and game dishes, plus house specialities such as *Prawns Mauna Loa* (Gulf prawns sautéed in a cream and brandy sauce) or *Seafood Mauna Kea* (seafood and mushrooms on pasta). Most main courses cost under $20.

If you're just looking for an inexpensive day-time snack, the *Ali'i Bakery and Drive-In* (☎967-7103), near the post office in Volcano village, serves cooked breakfasts as well as burgers, sandwiches, plate lunches or *saimin* (noodle soup).

Ka'ū

The district of **KA'Ū** occupies the southern tip of the Big Island, which is also the southernmost point of the United States. Stretching for roughly 50 miles along the southern side of the immense west flank of the "long mountain", Mauna Loa, it ranges from the bleak Ka'ū Desert area, now included in Volcanoes National Park, via fertile, well-watered hillsides, to the windswept promontory of **South Point** itself.

Still one of the most fiercely traditional areas in the whole state, Ka'ū was a separate kingdom right up to the moment of European contact. Its last independent ruler was **Keōua**, the arch rival of Kamehameha the Great, some of whose warriors met a bizarre end in the Ka'ū Desert (see p.160) and who was himself killed during the dedication of Pu'ukohola Heiau (see p.82).

The population today is very sparse, and is likely to get sparser when the sugar mill at **Pāhala**, the last working mill on the island, succumbs to pressure and closes. All the towns in the area are absolutely tiny; on the map the grid of streets at **Hawaiian Ocean View Estates** (usually abbreviated to H.O.V.E.) may look impressive, but this twenty-year-old residential development remains barely occupied, due to a lack of employment in the region.

One recent attempt to revitalize the local economy was a vigorously promoted plan to build a commercial **spaceport** at Pālima Point, just three miles outside the national park, to launch satellites and the Space Shuttle. That would supposedly have created ten thousand jobs, but the concept of positioning such a facility on the *tsunami*-battered slopes of an active volcano attracted so much derision that it now seems to have been quietly abandoned. The spaceport was due to be named after the late *Challenger* astronaut and local hero Ellison Onizuka, who came from Ka'ū, until enterprising journalists uncovered remarks he made before his death opposing the plan.

Although it has a handful of accommodation options, few people spend more than a day exploring Ka'ū. Access to the sea is limited throughout the region, as the highway curves around the ridge of Mauna Loa roughly ten miles up from the shoreline. The two most obvious stops are **South Point**, to admire the crashing waves and perhaps hike to **Green Sand Beach,** and **Punalu'u**, which since the demise of Kalapana boasts the island's finest **black sand beach**.

As you pass through Ka'ū, look out for the strange eroded cinder cones that dot the landscape. Some of these craters are so steep-sided as to have been forever inaccessible to man or beast, and paleobotanists are intrigued by the pre-contact vegetation that is thought to survive within.

Pāhala and Wood Valley

As the vegetation reasserts itself after the bleakness of the Ka'ū Desert, 23 miles west of the national park entrance, the little town of PĀHALA stands just *mauka* of the highway. Apart from its tall-chimneyed sugar mill, a gas station and a small shopping mall, there's nothing to catch the eye in the village, but a drive back up into the hills to the northwest takes you through some appealing agricultural scenery. Just when you think the road is about to peter out altogether, it enters a grove of huge eucalyptus trees and you find yourself confronted by one of the Big Island's most unexpected buildings: on top of a hill, and announced by streamers of coloured prayer flags, stands a brightly-painted **Tibetan temple**.

Originally built by Japanese sugar labourers, the **Wood Valley temple** (or Nechung Drayang Ling) was rededicated by the Dalai Lama in 1980 and now serves as a retreat for Tibetan Buddhists from around the world (PO Box 250, Pāhala HI 96777; ☎928-8539; ①/②). Priority is given to religious groups, but when space is available travellers are welcome to stay in the simple dormitory accommodation or private rooms.

Punalu'u

Five miles beyond Pāhala, at the point where the highway drops back down to sea level, **PUNALU'U** has been flattened by *tsunamis* so often that it's given up trying to be a town any more. A single road loops from the highway to the ocean and back, running briefly along what is now the only sizeable **black sand beach** on the island.

Black sand is a finite resource, as it's only created by molten lava exploding on contact with the sea, and at any one spot that happens very rarely. Even those beaches that aren't destroyed by new lava – such as the ones at Kalapana (p.137) and Kamoamoa (p.133) – usually erode away within a few years. Each time the coastline of Punalu'u Bay gets redrawn, however, its black sand washes in again, and piles up to create a new beach. At the moment it's irresistibly beautiful, a crescent of jet-black crystals surrounding a turquoise bay and framed by a fine stand of coconut palms.

On the north side of the bay, you can make out the remains of an old concrete **pier**. Until a century ago tourists used to disembark from their ships at Punalu'u for the ride up to the volcanoes by horse; later it became the terminus of a short railroad from Pāhala and was used for shipping sugar. In 1942, by which time it had fallen into disuse, the military destroyed it as a potential landing site for Japanese invaders.

Swimming in these rough waters is almost always out of the question, but many people come to Punalu'u to **camp**. Hawksbill turtles drag themselves ashore on the main beach at night, so camping on the sand is forbidden, but there's a very pleasant campground tucked into the rolling meadows of Punalu'u Beach Park, immediately to the south. Permits can be bought from Hilo, at the Department of Parks and Recreation ($1 per day; ☎961-83411). Further pockets of black sand are scattered in the adjacent inlets.

The very grand-looking complex of buildings behind the palms in the centre of the beach, facing the sea across its own private lagoon, holds a restaurant that has been closed ever since the Gulf

War downturn in tourism. The only **accommodation** currently available in the vicinity is in the *Colony One at SeaMountain* condo complex, a few hundred yards from the beach on the southern segment of the loop road (PO Box 70, Pahala HI 96777; ☎928-8301 or 1-800/488-8301; fax 928-8008; ④–⑥). A two-night minimum stay applies to all its well-equipped studio or one- or two-bedroom apartments, arrayed along what looks like a typical suburban residential street. Alongside it, but a separate entity, is the *SeaMountain* **golf course** (☎928-6222), where the $25 green fees are among the lowest on the island. The "sea mountain" of the name, incidentally, refers to the growing underwater volcano of Lō'ihi, here just 20 miles offshore (see p.141).

Nā'ālehu

You can't miss NĀ'ĀLEHU as you drive through Ka'ū. Eight miles south of Punalu'u, it lines each side of the highway for around half a mile, though the town doesn't stretch very far away from the central ribbon. By way of persuading drivers to stop, Nā'ālehu has managed to hang very little on the peg of being "America's southernmost town". **Whittington Beach Park**, a couple of miles outside it to the north is not so much a beach as a picnic ground, and the only reason to call in at Nā'ālehu is for a quick lunch.

The failure of the short-lived *Southernmost Vegetarian Café* leaves the town with just three basic **restaurants**. The *Nā'ālehu Coffee Shop* (Mon–Sat 6.30am–3pm & 5–8pm; ☎929-7238) is a short distance down a side road *makai* of what you might call the centre of town. A simple diner-style place, with a gift shop and walls festooned with astronaut memorabilia, it serves sandwiches, and cooked dishes such as liver and onions or *teriyaki* steak. *Tabbada's Drive-In* (☎929-8022), a little farther east on the main road, is a very basic dining counter and takeaway, open daily from 7am until 9pm. Its tasty good-value plate lunches include a shrimp and chicken combo, and a killer blueberry milkshake. Finally, the *Nā'ālehu Fruit Stand* (☎929-9009) is basically a general store (keeping ordinary store hours), which also sells sandwiches and drinks as well as lots of fresh island fruit.

Wai'ohinu

After climbing away from the sea for two miles, west of Nā'ālehu, the highway makes a sweeping curve around the small settlement of WAI'OHINU. There were a dozen houses here when Mark Twain passed through in 1866, and barely more than that today; the place's one claim to fame is that Twain supposedly planted a monkeypod tree here, but even that has now been dead for forty years. There's a really pretty little chapel, however, the white-and-green clapboard **Kauahā'ao Church** dating from 1841. Nearby, is the basic but reasonable *Shirikawa Motel* (PO Box 467, Nā'ālehu

South Point Road

As you circle the southern extremity of the Big Island on the Belt
Road, you're too far up from the ocean to see where the island
comes to an end. It is possible, however, to drive right down to the
tip along the eleven-mile **SOUTH POINT ROAD**, which leaves the
highway six miles west of Wai'ohinu.

Car rental agencies forbid drivers from heading to South Point
because vehicle damage is more likely on poor road surfaces, and
providing emergency recovery is inconvenient. Like the similarly
proscribed Saddle Road (see p.127), however, it's not a difficult or
dangerous drive. Most of the way it's a single-lane paved road, with
enough room to either side for vehicles to pass comfortably.

The road heads almost exactly due south, passing at first through
green cattle-ranching country. As it starts to drop, the landscape
takes on a weatherbeaten look, with pale grass billowing and the trees
bent double by the trade winds. It comes as no surprise to encounter
the giant propellors of the **Kamoa wind farm**, though you're unlikely
to see many of them turning; the winds have proven too gusty and
violent for the farm to be a commercial success.

Ka Lae

After ten miles, 100 yards beyond a sign announcing the entrance to
the **KA LAE NATIONAL HISTORIC LANDMARK DISTRICT**, the
road forks. The right fork ends a mile later at a red-gravel parking
lot, perched above a thirty-foot cliff where you will usually find local
people fishing over the edge. Ladders drop down the cliff face to
fishing boats bobbing at a small mooring below, and there are
winches to help the fishermen hoist their catch to the top.

Walk a couple of minutes south and you come to **Ka Lae**, or
South Point, where you can reflect that everyone in the United
States is to the north of you and the vast majority of them are in
considerably less danger of being blown to Antarctica. The earliest
colonizers of Hawaii battled against these same winds to reach this
spot long before the Pilgrims crossed the Atlantic, and in doing so
travelled a far greater distance from their homes in the distant
South Seas. Abundant bone fish-hooks found in the area are among
the oldest artefacts unearthed in Hawaii, dating as far back as the
third century AD. At the newly restored **Kalalea Heiau**, at the very
tip, offerings wrapped in *ti* leaves are still left by native Hawaiians.
Beyond that is a ledge of black lava, steadily pounded by high surf.

The deep waters immediately offshore were renowned by the
Hawaiians for two reasons. One was that they held vast quantities of
fish, the other that they are prey to such fierce currents that it can
take days on end for human- or sail-powered boats to negotiate the

cape. An old legend tells of a king of Ka'ū who became deeply unpopular after stealing fish from fishermen and forcing his people to build heavy-walled fish ponds for his benefit. He was finally abandoned by his warriors after he plundered a fleet of canoes near Ka Lae, and stole so much fish that his own canoe began to founder. The currents swept him away to a lonely death.

Among the rocks at the headland, you can still see holes drilled for use as **canoe moorings**. In ancient times, fishermen would tie their canoes to these loops by long cords, enabling themselves to fish in the turbulent waters without having to fight the sea.

Looking inland, you can follow the grey outline of Mauna Loa in the distance; on a cloudless day, you might even make out its snow-capped peak, which must have amazed the first Polynesians who landed here. Nearer at hand, across a foam-flecked sea to the northwest, is the stark shoreline cinder cone of **Pu'u Waimānalo**.

Green Sand Beach

The one thing that has to be said about **GREEN SAND BEACH**, a couple of miles northeast of Ka Lae, is that it doesn't live up to its name. It is a beach, and it is green-ish in a rusty olive sort of way, but if you're expecting a dazzling stretch of green sand backed by a coconut grove you'll be disappointed. The only real reason to venture there is if you feel like a bracing, four-mile, oceanfront hike, with a mild natural curiosity at the end of it. Without extravagant expectations, and on a rain-free day, it's worth the effort.

If you want to try it, go back to the junction on South Point Road a mile short of Ka Lae, and drive down the left fork as far as you can go, which is a turn-around point just beyond some military housing. If conditions are dry enough, you might continue down to the boat landing below on any of the many rutted mud tracks that criss-cross each other down the slope. However, you'd have to have a very high-clearance four-wheel-drive vehicle to follow the two-mile track from there to the beach.

Apart from one or two heavily rutted sections, the walk itself is very easy, although on the way out you can expect to be pushing into a stiff trade-winds breeze. For most of the route you cross rolling pastel-green meadows – an oddly pastoral landscape considering the mighty surf pummelling at the lava rocks alongside.

There's no mistaking your destination, which comes into sight after something more than a mile – the obviously crumbling **Pu'u O Mahana** cinder cone that forms the only significant bump on the general line of the coast. As you approach you can see that half the cone has eroded away, and the resultant loose powder has slipped down the cliffs to form a long sloping beach. You can see all there is to see from up above, but with care it's possible to scramble down to the seashore and examine handfuls of the "green sand". Close inspection reveals shiny green-tinged crystals of various sizes – this is in fact a mineral called **olivine**, which once formed part of a lava

flow. Green Sand Beach is, however, much too exposed for Ka'ū
swimming – or even walking too close to the sea.

Hawaiian Ocean View Estates

West of South Point Road, there are no more places to get down to
the sea in the twelve miles before the Belt Road reaches South
Kona. The road does however run past a few isolated buildings and
communities, where you can get a snack or fill up with fuel.

For amazingly long views from its blue *lanai*, it's fun to stop for
a meal or drink at the *South Point Bar & Restaurant*, raised above
the highway at the 76-mile marker (Mon–Sat noon–8pm, Sun lunch
only; ☎929-9343). They try out a different menu every month and
occasionally offer live entertainment as well, but don't bank on
anything more exotic than burgers, grilled chicken or a steak.

A little farther on, you enter the residential zone of **HAWAIIAN
OCEAN VIEW ESTATES**, known also as "Ocean View" or
"H.O.V.E.". This area was designated for development by the county
during the 1960s as a purely speculative venture. Intricate grids of
hypothetical roads were planned, and in some instances home sites
were sold that were no more than patches of bare, jagged, *'ā'ā* lava.
Only a tiny proportion of the lots have been built on and many of
the roads still don't exist. Unless the plans to develop a mega-resort
at Pōhue Bay, a currently inaccessible white-sand beach directly
below Ocean View, ever get off the drawing board, there's little
prospect of the area acquiring a substantial population.

The centre of Ocean View consists of two small malls to either
side of the highway. The *makai* one has a *Texaco* gas station and
the fast-food *Ohana Drive-Inn* (☎929-9679), while the *mauka* one
is home to a slightly more upmarket Italian joint, *Santangelo's
Pizzaria* (☎929-9677). Just off the highway a couple of hundred
yards farther north is the *Kau Drive-Inn* (☎929-9291), set in
colourful gardens, where the take-out counter serves breakfast for
$4.50 and basic plate lunches (burgers, sandwiches, *saimin*) that
can be eaten on a large shady *lanai*.

The only place to stay nearby is the three-roomed *South Point
B&B*, on the eastern fringes of Ocean View, off the highway on the
mauka side (92-1408 Donola Drive, Donola HI 96704; ☎929-
7466; ③).

Manukā State Park

Ka'ū comes to an end half a dozen miles west of Ocean View, as you
finally cross the long ridge of Mauna Loa. The fundamental land
division for the ancient Hawaiians was the *ahupua'a*, a wedge that
stretched from the coastline up to the mountains (see p.178). Those
ahupua'a that lay on the borders of two major regions were
especially significant, and regarded as royal property. The
ahupua'a between Ka'ū and Kona, known as **MANUKĀ**, remains

set aside to this day, as the **Manukā Natural Area Reserve** – at 25,000 acres the largest natural reserve in the state.

Only a small segment of the reserve is open to the public, however – **Manukā State Park**, three miles west of the centre of Ocean View on the *mauka* side of the highway. From its leafy roadside parking lot, equipped with a picnic pavilion, rest rooms, benches and rolling lawns, the one-hour, two-mile **Manuka Nature Trail** leads into peaceful woodlands. Almost all the terrain is *'ā'ā* lava, and although there's no great climb the path can be very rough underfoot. Humans aren't the only ones who find it hard to cross lava flows, so pigs and exotic plants alike are relatively scarce, which is why areas such as this remain havens for well-adapted native plants. One of the main features of long-established native species tends to be that they've lost unnecessary defences against predators; thus you'll see a mint with no smell and a nettle with no sting. The only dramatic feature is a collapsed lava pit, whose sides are too steep to permit access to wild pigs (see p.182), and which gathers enough moisture to feed plants such as the *'ie 'ie* vine that normally only grow in much wetter areas.

Free maps, available at the trailhead, explain how the vegetation varies according to the age of the lava flow. Some of the ground is new and barren, and some is around two thousand years old, but those areas that date back four thousand years have managed to develop a thick coating of topsoil.

Around eight miles beyond Manukā, as the road heads due north towards Kailua, you come to the turn-off down to **Miloli'i Beach** – see p.69.

The Contexts

A Brief History

The story of the Big Island of Hawaii is inextricably interwoven with that of the archipelago which now bears its name. The largest of the islands played a crucial role in the development of Hawaiian culture; it may well have been the first island to be settled by humans, it was the scene of the death of Captain Cook and the birthplace of the only ruler ever to conquer the whole archipelago, Kamehameha the Great. After his death, however, the seat of power passed irreversibly to the island of Oahu. For the last two centuries, the fate of the Hawaiian islands has been largely determined by economic and political events in the rest of the world, and the Big Island has been at the mercy of events and changes in Honolulu.

The Age of Migrations

Until less than two thousand years ago, the Big Island remained an unknown speck in the vast Pacific, populated by the mutated descendants of the few organisms that had been carried here by wind or wave (see p.181). Carbon dating of fishhooks and artefacts found at Ka Lae (South Point) suggests that Hawaii's earliest human settlers arrived during the second or third centuries AD. Except perhaps for their first chance landfall, they came equipped to colonize, carrying goats, dogs, pigs, coconut palms, bananas and sugar cane among other essentials.

These first inhabitants were **Polynesians**, probably from the Marquesas Islands in the South Seas. Their ancestors had spread from the shores of Asia to inhabit Indonesia and the Solomon Islands around 30,000 years ago. Such migrations, across coastal waters shallower than they are today, would for the most part have involved hopping from island to island without having to cross the open ocean. There then followed a 25,000-year hiatus, while the techniques were acquired to make it possible to venture farther (see p.184). Just over three thousand years ago, the voyagers reached Fiji; they then spread via Tahiti to populate the entire "Polynesian Triangle", extending from Easter Island in the east to Hawaii in the north and finally down to New Zealand (which they called Aotea Roa) in the south.

Successive waves of settlers came to Hawaii at widely spaced intervals. There was one influx in the eighth century, another four or five hundred years later, and none after that, until the arrival of the Europeans. One early group of Hawaiians figures in legends as the *menehune*, hairy elves or leprechauns who worked by night and hid by day. It seems likely that this is, in fact, a corruption of the word *manhune*. The original Polynesian people of Tahiti, the *manhune* were displaced first from their homeland, then from Hawaii itself by warriors from the leeward Tahitian island of Raiatea. Rather than literally being dwarfs as the legend suggests, they were probably treated as social inferiors by their conquerors, and became the lowest caste in Hawaiian society. For a full account of the daily life, traditions and culture of the ancient Hawaiians see p.178.

The Coming of the Foreigners

No Western ship is known to have chanced upon Hawaii before **Captain Cook** in January 1778; the first European to sail across the Pacific, the Portuguese Ferdinand Magellan, did so without seeing a single island. It is however sometimes suggested that Spanish mariners were shipwrecked here during the sixteenth century, which might explain the similarity of the feather headdresses of Hawaiian warriors to

Spanish soldiers' helmets, and account for the fact that the Hawaiians were already familiar with iron. There are also much earlier legends of inter-island wars for the possession of a mighty Excalibur-style iron sword, which may have been washed accidentally from medieval Japan.

When Cook first encountered Hawaii, he sailed past the Big Island before stumbling upon the western shores of Kauai, on his way to the north Pacific, in search of the illusory Northwest Passage. When he returned a year later, he skirted Maui and cruised the coast of the Big Island for almost seven weeks before anchoring in Kealakekua Bay. Just a few weeks later he was killed; for more on the events leading to his death and the legends surrounding it, see p.64.

Cook's ships carried news of the existence of the "Sandwich Islands" to the rest of the world (the Russians were the first to hear, thanks to a halt for provisions on the Siberian coast). Hawaii swiftly became a port of call for all traders crossing the ocean, especially for ships carrying furs from the Pacific Northwest to China.

Kamehameha the Great

For a few brief years the Hawaiians remained masters of their own destiny, with the major beneficiary of the change in circumstances being the astute young warrior **Kamehameha** on the Big Island. Although he remains the greatest Hawaiian hero, to some extent Kamehameha played into the hands of the newcomers, who flocked to the islands from all over the world. His conquest of the entire archipelago, with their help, and his creation of a single Hawaiian kingdom, greatly simplified the manoeuvres that enabled the outsiders to achieve first economic, and eventually political, domination over the islands.

The future Kamehameha the Great was born in northern Kohala in 1758. Both his mother Kekuiapoiwa and father Keōuau were of royal blood, though it's not clear whether they were niece and nephew of the then ruler of the Big Island, Alapa'i, or of the ruler of Maui. In any event, Alapa'i felt sufficiently threatened by the birth of this potential rival that the infant Kamehameha was whisked away, to be brought up in secret in Waipi'o Valley.

By the time Kamehameha grew to adulthood, Kalaniopu'u had become high chief of the island. Kamehameha proved himself a valuable warrior on the king's behalf, helping to defeat insurrections in Ka'ū and Puna, and was

present on the waterfront during the death of Captain Cook. When Kalaniopu'u died in 1782, and his son Kiwalao inherited his position, civil war broke out almost immediately. Kiwalao was killed in a battle at Moku'ōhai, and Kamehameha took control of the Kona, Kohala and Hāmākua regions; but Kiwalao's brother **Keōua** survived, and established his own powerbase in Ka'ū.

For more than a decade a three-way struggle for domination raged back and forth between Kamehameha, Keōua and Kahekili, the ruler of Maui and Oahu. It looked for a while as if Kahekili might be the man to unite all the islands, but his hopes of capturing the Big Island were dashed by the "Battle of the Red-Mouthed Gun" off Waipi'o Valley in 1791, when for the first time Hawaiian fleets were equipped with cannons, operated by foreign gunners. The long campaign against Keōua (many of whose warriors were wiped out by an eruption of Kīlauea: see p.160), finally came to an end at the dedication of the great *heiau* at Pu'ukoholā, the last of the *luakinis*, when Keōua himself was the chief sacrifice.

As sole ruler of the Big Island, Kamehameha went on to reconquer first Maui, Lanai and Molokai, then Oahu, and finally to exact tribute from Kauai; he even considered the possibility of launching expeditions against other Pacific islands. So eager was he to obtain military assistance from the Europeans that he briefly ceded the Big Island to Great Britain, though this was never made formal.

Although European governments piously forbade their representatives to exchange arms with the islanders, freelance traders had no such scruples. Kamehameha's most important foreign advisers, John Young and Isaac Davis (see p.84), acted in their own interests, and led by example, personally gunning down enemy warriors in droves. In addition, practical skills of all kinds were introduced to the islands, by European artesans such as blacksmiths, carpenters and stonemasons.

For some time Kamehameha had his capital in the fledgeling port of Lahaina on Maui, but by the time he died in 1819, he had returned to live in a palace on the Kona Coast of the Big Island.

The End of the Old Order

Kamehameha's successor, his son Liholiho, was a weak figure who was dominated by the regent **Queen Ka'ahumanu**. As a woman, she was excluded from the *luakini heiaus* that were the real centre of political power, so she set out to bring down the priesthood. Liholiho was plied with drink and cajoled into dining with the women at a public banquet; that simple act brought about the end of the *kapu* system (see p.180), and precipitated a civil war in which the upholders of the ancient religion were eventually defeated in a battle near Hōnaunau. Altars and idols at *heiaus* throughout Hawaii were overthrown and destroyed.

Hawaii found itself thrown into moral anarchy at the very moment when the first Puritan **missionaries** arrived from New England. Inspired by the pious death of Henry 'Opukaha'ia, a converted *kahuna* priest from Hikiau Heiau (see p.48), they were determined to turn the islands into the Promised Land. Ka'ahumanu did not exactly jump at the chance to replace the old priests with a new bunch of interfering moralizers, but they were eventually given permission to land. Their wholehearted capitalism and harsh strictures on the easy-going Hawaiian lifestyle might have been calculated to compound the chaos, as they set about obliging Hawaiian women to cover unseemly flesh in billowing *mu'umu'u* "Mother Hubbard" dresses; condemning the *hula* as lascivious and obscene; and discouraging surfing as a waste of time, liable to promote gambling and lewdness.

In general, the missionaries concentrated their attentions on the ruling class, the *ali'i*, believing that they would bring the commoners to the fold in their wake – hence the mistrust of the charismatic evangelist Titus Coan, whose populist "Revivals" had great success in the Hilo region during the 1830s. At first great tensions manifested themselves between missionaries and the new breed of foreign entrepreneurs; these were to disappear as their offspring intermarried, acquired land and formed the backbone of the emerging middle class.

The Foreigners Take Control

For ordinary Hawaiians, the sudden advent of capitalism was devastating. Any notion of Hawaiian self-sufficiency was abandoned at the expense of selling out the islands' resources for cash returns. The most extreme example of that was perhaps the earliest, the **sandalwood** trade.

Sandalwood: the first sell-out
Sandalwood logs were first picked up from Hawaii by a passing ship in 1791, scattered among a consignment of fuel. Traders had been searching for years for a commodity they could sell to the Chinese in return for tea to meet English demand. Once it was realized that the Chinese would pay enormous prices for the fragrant wood – the scent of a bowl of sandalwood chips lasts for up to fifty years – the race was on. Kamehameha had a monopoly on the trade until his death, but thereafter individual chiefs out for their own profit forced all the commoners under their sway to abandon *taro*-farming and fishing and become wage slaves. The wood was sold in units known as piculs, which weighed just over 133 pounds. "Picul pits", the exact size and shape of a ship's hold, were dug in the hills and filled with logs; men, women, and children then carried the wood down to the sea on their naked backs. Each picul sold for one cent in Hawaii and 34 cents in China; most of the profits went to New England merchants. By the end of the 1820s, the forests were almost entirely denuded and the traditional Hawaiian agricultural system had collapsed.

Whaling
The first whaling ships arrived in Hawaii in 1820, the same year as the missionaries – and had an equally dramatic impact. With the ports of Japan closed to outsiders, Hawaii swiftly became the centre of the industry. Any Pacific port would have seemed a godsend to the whalers, who were away from New England for three years at a time, and paid so badly that most were either fugitives or plain mad. Hawaii was such a paradise that up to fifty percent of each crew would desert, to be replaced by Hawaiian *sailamokus*, born seafarers eager to see the world.

Whaling centred on the burgeoning ports of Honolulu on Oahu, and Lahaina on Maui, but it had huge implications for all the islands (and even brought Hawaii's first tourists). Provisioning the whaling ships became the main focus of activity on the Big Island, most conspicuously in the rapid growth of the **Parker Ranch**. The Hispanic cowboys imported to work there, known as *paniolos* (a corruption of *españoles*), were among the first of the many ethnic groups to make their homes on the Big Island.

By now the centre of power had moved, for good, away from the Big Island to Oahu. From the very first, Westerners had recognized Pearl Harbor as the finest deep-water harbour in the Pacific; the Hawaiians had never needed such conditions, and Honolulu had been the tiniest of villages in ancient times.

The Great *Mahele*

By 1844, foreign-born fortune-seekers dominated the Hawaiian government. Fourteen of King Kamehameha III's closest advisers were white, including his three most important ministers. The various foreign powers jostled for position; it is easy to forget now that it wasn't inevitable that the islands would become American, and that it was only in the 1840s that New Zealand was taken by the English and Tahiti by the French.

The most important obstacle to the advance of the foreigners was that they could not legally own land. In the old Hawaii there was no private land; all was held in trust by the chief, who apportioned it to individuals at his continued pleasure only. After a misunderstanding with the British consul almost resulted in the islands' permanent cession to Britain, the king was requested to "clarify" the situation. A land commission was set up, under the direction of a missionary, and its deliberations resulted in 1848 in the **Great Mahele**, or "Division of Lands". In theory all the land was parcelled out to native Hawaiians only, with sixty percent going to the crown and the government, 39 percent to just over two hundred chiefs, and less than one percent to eleven thousand commoners. Claiming and keeping the land involved complex legal procedures, and required expenditures that many Hawaiians, paid in kind not in cash, were unable to meet. In any case, within two years the *haole* (non-Hawaiians) too were able to buy and sell land. The jibe that the missionaries "came to Hawaii to do good – and they done good" stems from the speed with which they amassed vast acreages; their children became Hawaii's wealthiest and most powerful class.

Many Hawaiians were denied access to the lands they had traditionally worked, arrested for vagrancy, and used as forced labour on the construction of roads and ports for the new landowners. Meanwhile, a simultaneous water-grab took place, with new white-owned plantations diverting water for their thirsty foreign crops from the Hawaiian farmers downstream.

The Sugar Industry and the US Civil War

At the height of the whaling boom, many newly rich entrepreneurs began to put their money into **sugar**. It swiftly became clear that this was an industry where large-scale operators were much the most efficient and profitable, and by 1847 the field had narrowed to five main players. These **Big Five** were *Hackfield & Co* (later to become Amfac), *C Brewer & Co, Theo Davies Co, Castle & Cooke* (later Dole) and *Alexander & Baldwin*. Thereafter, they worked in close cooperation with each other, united by common interests and, often, family ties.

Hawaii was poised to take advantage when the Civil War broke out, and the markets of the northern US began to cast about for an alternative source of sugar to the Confederate South. The consequent boom in the Hawaiian sugar industry, and the ever-increasing integration of Hawaii into the American economic mainstream, was the major single factor in the eventual loss of Hawaiian sovereignty.

Hawaii's first sugar plantation was started in 1835 in Koloa on Kauai, while the Big Island's first sugar mill opened in Kohala in 1863, followed by plantations all along the Hāmākua coast. The ethnic mixture of modern Hawaii is largely the product of the search for labourers prepared to submit to the draconian conditions on the plantations. Once the Hawaiians had demonstrated their unwillingness to knuckle under, agents of the Hawaiian Sugar Planters Association scoured the world in search of peasants eager to find new lives.

Members of each ethnic group got their start on the plantations and then left to find more congenial employment or start their own businesses. First came the **Chinese**, recruited with a $10 inducement in Hong Kong, shipped over for free, and then signed to five-year contracts at $6 or less per month. The **Portuguese** followed, brought from Madeira and the Azores from 1878 onwards by planters who thought they might adjust more readily than their Asian counterparts to the dominant *haole*-Hawaiian culture. **Koreans** arrived during the brief period between 1902, when they were first permitted to leave their country, and 1905, when it was invaded by the **Japanese**, who themselves came in great numbers until 1907, when the Gentleman's Agreement banned further immigration. **Filipinos**, whose country had been annexed by the US in 1898, began to arrive in their stead, to find the climate, soil, and crops were all similar to their homelands.

The End of the Kingdom of Hawaii

After sugar prices dropped at the end of the Civil War, the machinations of the sugar industry to get favourable prices on the mainland moved Hawaii inexorably towards **annexation** by the US. In 1876 the Treaty of Reciprocity abolished all trade barriers and tariffs between the US and the Kingdom of Hawaii; within fifteen years sugar exports to the US had increased tenfold.

By now **King David Kalākaua**, the "Merrie Monarch", was on the throne. He is affectionately remembered for his role in reviving traditional Hawaiian pursuits such as *hula* and surfing, and for having become in 1881 the first monarch to travel all the way round the world. However, he was also the tool of the plantation owners – the direct Kamehameha line had by now died out, and he was elected King as their candidate. In 1887 an all-white (and armed) group of "concerned businessmen" forced through the "Bayonet Constitution", in which the king surrendered power to an assembly elected by property owners (of any nationality) as opposed to citizens. The US government was swiftly granted exclusive rights to what became Pearl Harbor.

When after Kalākaua's death his sister and heir **Queen Liliuokalani** proclaimed her desire for a new constitution, the businessmen called in the US warship *Boston*, then in Honolulu, and declared a provisional government. The Democrat US President Grover Cleveland responded that "Hawaii was taken possession of by the United States forces without the consent or wish of the government of the islands . . . (It) was wholly without justification . . . not merely a wrong but a disgrace." With phenomenal cheek, the provisional government rejected his demand for the restoration of the monarchy, saying the US should not "interfere in the internal affairs of their sovereign nation". They found defenders in the Republican US Congress, and declared themselves a **republic** on July 4, 1894.

A Republican president, McKinley, came to office in Washington in 1897, claiming "annexation is not a change. It is a consummation." The strategic value of Pearl Harbor was emphasized by the Spanish-American War in the Philippines; and on August 12, 1898 Hawaii was formally annexed as a territory of the United States.

The Twentieth Century

At the moment of annexation there was no question of Hawaii becoming a state; the whites were outnumbered ten to one, and had no desire to afford the rest of the islanders the protection of US labour laws, let alone to give

them the vote. (One leader, Sanford Dole, said that natives couldn't expect to vote "simply because they were grown up".) Furthermore, as the proportion of Hawaiians of Japanese descent (*nisei*) increased (to 25 percent by 1936), Congress feared the prospect of a state of people who might consider their primary allegiance to be to Japan. Consequently, Hawaii remained for the first half of this century the virtual fiefdom of the Big Five, who through their control of agriculture (they owned 96 percent of the sugar crop) dominated transport, banks, utilities, insurance and government.

Things began to change during World War II. The Japanese offensive on Pearl Harbor meant that Hawaii was the only part of the United States to be attacked in the war, and it demonstrated just how crucial the islands were to the rest of America. On the Big Island, all ports except Hilo were closed after the Pearl Harbor attack, and most of the Waimea area became a military training camp.

The main trend in Hawaiian history since the war has been the slow decline of agriculture and the rise of tourism. Strikes organized along ethnic lines in the sugar plantations had consistently failed in the past, but from 1937, labour leaders such as Jack Hill and Harry Bridges of the International Longshoremen's and Warehousemen's Union began to organize workers of all races and all crafts, in solidarity with mainland unions. In September 1946, the plantation workers won their first victory. Thanks to the campaigns that followed, in which the labourers of Hilo played a prominent role, the long-term Republican domination of state politics ended, and Hawaii's agricultural workers became the highest paid in the world. Arguably, this led to the eventual disappearance of all their jobs in the face of third-world competition. Agriculture on the Big Island had already been dealt a severe blow by the *tsunamis* of April 1, 1946, which devastated Hilo and destroyed the sugar railroad along the Hāmākua coast, and fifty years on almost all the sugar mills have closed.

Hawaii finally became the fiftieth of the United States in 1959, after a plebiscite showed a 17-to-1 majority in favour, with the only significant opposition coming from the few remaining native Hawaiians. **Statehood** triggered a boom in tourism – many visitors had had their first sight of Hawaii as GIs in the war – and also in migration from the mainland to Hawaii. On the Big

Island the most obvious effect has been the growth of the Kona coast and the decline of Hilo. Very much the seat of power on the island during the plantation years, Hilo now finds itself treated as something of a backwater by the entrepreneurs who have flooded into the sun spots of the western coast.

The major issue now facing the Big Island is the struggle to preserve its environment while creating new jobs to replace those lost by plantation closures; see the *Environment* section on p.181 for further details. The island's economy seems fated to become ever more closely tied to the tourist industry. Fifty million dollars were invested in January 1993 to extend the runway at Kona's Keāhole airport in order to accept direct flights from Asia, Europe and Midwest, but so far visitor numbers have yet to climb back to the levels reached prior to the Gulf War.

One recent very welcome boost to the island's coffers came with the filming of Kevin Costner's notoriously profligate epic *Waterworld* at Kawaihae, which was estimated to have injected $30 million into the local economy – a staggering $300 per head. On the Big Island at any rate they love the idea of a sequel. Otherwise, the island occupies a couple of specialized niches, as the United States' largest producer of both ginger and coffee – Kona coffee has a well-deserved reputation as being among the finest in the world. In more local terms, the island produces eighty percent of the state's home-grown fruit and beef, although that amounts to a small proportion of what Hawaii actually consumes.

Official figures showing the growth of the Hawaiian economy since statehood conceal a decline in living standards for many Hawaiians. Consumer prices in the state went up by 73 percent during the 1980s, while wages rose by only 13 percent. Real estate prices in particular have rocketed, so that many islanders are obliged to work at two jobs, others end up sleeping on the beaches, and young Hawaiians emigrate in droves with no prospect of being able to afford to return.

The Sovereignty Movement

In the last decade, broad-based support has mushroomed for the concept of **Hawaiian sovereignty**, meaning some form of restoration of the rights of native Hawaiians. Pride in the Polynesian past has been rekindled by such means as the voyages of the *Hōkūle'a* canoe (see p.184), and the successful campaign to claim back the island of Kahoolawe, which had been used since the war as a Navy bombing range. The author Michael Kioni Dudley (see p.190) secured five percent of the vote in the 1994 elections for state governor by focusing on sovereignty issues.

The movement has reached the point where everyone seems sure that sovereignty is coming, but no one knows what form it will take. Even the US government has formally acknowledged the illegality of the US overthrow of the Hawaiian monarchy and apologized (see opposite), while the state has set a ponderous machine in motion by organizing a plebiscite to decide whether to elect a constitutional convention to discuss the alternatives.

Of the three most commonly advanced models for sovereignty, one sees Hawaii as an independent nation once again, recognized by the international community, with full citizenship perhaps restricted either to those born in Hawaii or prepared to pledge sole allegiance to Hawaii. Another possibility would be the granting to native Hawaiians of nation-within-a-nation status, as with native American groups on the mainland, while others argue that it would be more realistic to preserve the existing political framework within the context of full economic reparations to native Hawaiians.

With dozens of different groups claiming to speak on behalf of native Hawaiians – including the self-proclaimed King Kamehameha VI, in jail in Colorado for refusing to pay US taxes – there's a real danger of the movement dissolving into factionalism. There may also turn out to be a parallel with events of a century ago, with a sympathetic Democrat President (Cleveland then, Clinton now) being replaced in office by a Republican for whom the interests of the federal government are an absolute priority.

A separate but closely related issue is the failure by both federal and state government to manage 200,000 acres set aside for the benefit of native Hawaiians in 1921. The state has now agreed to pay Hawaiians more than $100 million compensation, though disputes remain over quite where that money will come from and to whom it will go.

The Apology To Native Hawaiians

Resolved by the Senate and the House of Representatives of the United States of America in Congress assembled

SECTION 1. ACKNOWLEDGEMENT AND APOLOGY

The Congress—

(1) on the occasion of the 100th anniversary of the illegal overthrow of the Kingdom of Hawaii on January 17, 1893, acknowledges the historical significance of this event which resulted in the suppression of the inherent sovereignty of the Native Hawaiian people;

(2) recognizes and commends efforts of reconciliation initiated by the State of Hawaii and the United Church of Christ with Native Hawaiians;

(3) apologizes to Native Hawaiians on behalf of the people of the United States for the overthrow of the Kingdom of Hawaii on January 17, 1893 with the participation of agents and citizens of the United States, and the deprivation of the rights of Native Hawaiians to self-determination;

(4) expresses its commitment to acknowledge the ramifications of the overthrow of the Kingdom of Hawaii, in order to provide a proper foundation for reconciliation efforts between the United States and the Native Hawaiian people; and

(5) urges the President of the United States to also acknowledge the ramifications of the overthrow of the Kingdom of Hawaii and to support reconciliation efforts between the United States and the Native Hawaiian people.

SECTION 2. DEFINITIONS

As used in this Joint Resolution, the term "Native Hawaiian" means any individual who is a descendant of the aboriginal people who, prior to 1778, occupied and exercised sovereignty in the area that now constitutes the State of Hawaii.

SECTION 3. DISCLAIMER

Nothing in this Joint Resolution is intended to serve as a settlement of any claims against the United States.

Approved November 23, 1993

/s/ William Clinton

Ancient Culture and Society

No written record exists of the centuries between the arrival of the Polynesians and the first contact with Europeans. Sacred chants, passed down through the generations, show a history packed with feuds and forays between the islands, and the rise and fall of dynasties, but didn't concern themselves with specific dates. However, oral traditions do provide us with a detailed picture of the day-to-day life of ordinary Hawaiians.

Developing a civilization on the most isolated islands in the world, without metals and workable clays, presented the settlers with many challenges. Nevertheless, by the late eighteenth century, when the Europeans arrived, the Hawaiian islands were home to around a million people. Two hundred years later, the population has climbed back to a similar level. Now, however, virtually no pure-blooded Hawaiians remain, and the islands are no longer even close to being self-sufficient in food. The geographical distribution has changed too; it's striking how often the accounts of the early explorers describe being greeted by vast numbers of canoes in areas which are now all but uninhabited. The Big Island's population would have been far larger than the 130,000 it is today, and Oahu's population smaller, but no precise figures are known.

Daily life

In a sense, ancient Hawaii had no economy, not even barter. Although then as now most people lived close to the coast, each island was organized into wedge-shaped land divisions called **ahupua'a**, which stretched from the ocean to the mountains. The abundant fruits of the earth and sea were simply shared out among the inhabitants within each *ahupua'a*.

There's some truth in the idea of pre-contact Hawaii as a leisured paradise, but it had taken a lot of work to make it that way. Coconut palms had to be planted along the seashore to provide food, clothing and shade for coastal villages, and bananas and other food plants distributed inland. Crops such as sugar cane were cultivated with the aid of complex systems of terraces and irrigation channels. *Taro*, whose leaves were eaten as "greens" and whose roots were mashed to produce *poi* (see p.23), was grown in *lois*, which like rice paddies are kept constantly submerged, in the great valleys of Waipi'o and Pololū.

Most **fishing** took place in shallow inshore waters. At Ka Lae, you can still see holes drilled for use as **canoe moorings** – fishermen would tie their canoes to these loops by long cords, which enabled them to fish in the turbulent waters without having to fight the sea. Fish-hooks made from human bone were believed to be especially effective; the most prized hooks of all were made from the bones of chiefs who had no body hair, so those unfortunate individuals were renowned for their low life expectancy. Nets were never cast from boats, but shallow bays might be dragged by communal groups of wading men drawing in *hukilau* nets (Elvis did it in *Blue Hawaii*, and you occasionally see people doing it today). In addition, the art of **aquaculture** – fish-farming – was more highly developed in Hawaii than anywhere in Polynesia. It reached its most refined form in the extensive networks of fish-ponds that ring much of the coast; the royal fish-pond at **'Anaeho'omalu** at the Waikoloa Beach Resort, where the "protected mullet" were reserved for the sole use of high chiefs alone, is one of the best examples (see p.75).

Few people lived in the higher forested slopes, but these served as the source of vital raw materials such as the *koa* wood for canoes and weapons. The ancient people even ventured to the very summit of Mauna Kea; as the only point in the entire Pacific to be glaciated during the last Ice Age, it has the hardest basalt on the islands. Stone from the **adze quarry**, 12,400 feet up, was used for all basic tools.

The islanders lived in simple, windowless huts known as *hales*. Most of these were thatched with *pili* grass, though in the driest areas ordinary people didn't bother with roofs. Buildings of all kinds were usually raised on platforms of stone; rounded boulders were taken from river beds and hauled long distances for that purpose, as well as being used to make roads. Matting would have covered the floor, while the pounded tree bark called *kapa* (known as *tapa* elsewhere in the Pacific, and decorated with patterns) served as clothing and bedding. Lacking pottery, households made abundant use of gourds, wooden bowls and woven baskets.

The most popular pastime was **surfing**. There's a petroglyph of a surfer among the carvings at Pu'u Loa (see p.155), and there was even a surfing *heiau*, at Kahulu'u near Kailua. Ordinary people surfed on five- to seven-foot boards known as *alaia*, and also had *paipus*, the equivalent of the modern boogie board; only the *ali'i* used the thick sixteen-foot *olo* boards, made of dark oiled *wiliwili* wood. On land the *ali'i* raced narrow sleds on purpose-built, grass-covered *hōlua* slides and staged boxing tournaments.

The Ali'i

The ruling class, the **ali'i**, stood at the apex of Hawaiian society. In theory, heredity counted for everything, and great chiefs demonstrated their fitness to rule by the length of their genealogies. In fact the *ali'i* were educated as equals, and chiefs won the very highest rank largely through physical prowess and force of personality. To hang on to power, the king had to be seen to be devoutly religious and to treat his people fairly.

For most of its history, the Big Island was divided between up to six separate chiefdoms, with major potential for intrigue, faction and warfare. Canoes being the basic means of transportation, it was also feasible for chiefs to launch inter-island campaigns, and the north of the island in particular was prone to fall under the control of the kings of Maui.

Complex genealogies of the great *ali'i* still survive, but little is recorded other than their names. The first ruler to unite the entire island – **'Umi-a-Liloa**, who ruled from the *taro* fields of Waipi'o Valley – is listed as representing the sixtieth generation after the sky god Wākea. He was responsible for Hawaii's first legal code, the *kanawai*, which concerned itself with the equal sharing of water from Waipio's irrigation ditches, and was among the first to make human sacrifice an instrument of state policy.

Other names to have been preserved include the six or seven Big Island chiefs listed by Hawaiian historian David Malo as having been either banished or killed by popular revolt, and the enigmatic ruler Lono, who may have been Umi's grandson. Legends suggest that he lost his throne after quarrelling with, or even

murdering, his wife and left the Big Island in a half-crazed fit of self-loathing. Some say that he regained his sanity, returned to unite the island, and was subsequently deified as Lonoikamakahiki, patron of the annual *makahiki* festival. Others claim that the Hawaiians predicted his return for centuries, and believed these prophecies to be fulfilled by the arrival of Captain Cook (see p.64).

Religion

It's all but impossible now to grasp the subtleties of ancient Hawaiian **religion**. So much depends on how the chants and texts are translated; if the word *akua* is interpreted as meaning "god", for example, historians can draw analogies with Greek or Hindu legends by speaking of a pantheon of battling, squabbling "gods" and "goddesses" with magic powers. Some scholars however prefer to translate *akua* as "spirit consciousness", which might correspond to the soul of an ancestor, or even to the motivational force within a wristwatch, and argue that the antics of such figures are peripheral to a more fundamental set of attitudes regarding the relationship of humans to the natural world.

The **Kumulipo**, Hawaii's principal creation myth, has been preserved in full as a chant, passed down from generation to generation. It tells how after the emergence of the earth "from the source in the slime", more complicated life forms developed, from coral to pigs, until finally men, women and "gods" appeared. Not only was there no Creator god, but the gods were much of a kind with humans. It took a hundred generations for Wākea, the god of the sky, and Papa, an earth goddess, to be born; they were the divine ancestors of the Hawaiian people.

It may well be misleading to imagine that all Hawaiians shared the same beliefs; different groups sought differing ways of augmenting their *mana*, or spiritual power. Quite possibly only the elite *ali'i* paid much attention to the bloodthirsty warrior god Kū, while the primary allegiance of ordinary families, and by extension villages and regions, may have lain towards their personal *'aumākua* – a sort of clan symbol, which might be a totem animal such as a shark or an owl, or a more abstract force, such as that embodied by Pele, the volcano goddess.

Spiritual and temporal power did not necessarily lie in the same hands, let alone in the same places. Hawaiian "priests" were known as **kahunas** (literally, "men who know the secrets"), and were the masters of ceremonies at temples called **heiaus**. The design of a *heiau* was not always consistent, but as a rule it consisted of a number of separate structures standing on a rock platform (*paepae*). These might include the *hale mana* or "house of spiritual power"; the *hale pahu* or "house of the drum"; and the *anu'u*, the "oracle tower", from the top of which the *kahunas* would converse with the gods. Assorted *ki'i akua*, symbolic wooden images of different gods, would stand on all sides, and the whole enclosure was fenced or walled off. In addition to the two main types of *heiau* – the **luakinis**, which were dedicated to the war god Kū, and held *leles* or altars used for human sacrifice; and **māpeles**, peaceful temples to Lono – there were also *heiaus* to such entities as Laka, goddess of the *hula*. Devotees of Pele, on the other hand, did not give their protectress formal worship at a *heiau*. Most *heiaus* were built for some specific occasion, and did not remain in constant use; the best example on the Big Island is the great *luakini* at Pu'ukoholā, erected by Kamehameha the Great as proclamation of his plans for conquest (see p.81).

Hawaiian religion in the form encountered by Cook was brought to the Big Island, and subsequently to the rest of the archipelago, by the Tahitian warrior-priest Pa'ao, who led the last great migration to Hawaii. The war god Kū received his first human sacrifices at *luakini* temples such as those at Mo'okini (see p.94) and Waha'ula Heiau near Kīlauea, which was recently destroyed by lava flows.

Pa'ao is also credited with introducing and refining the complex system of **kapu**, which circumscribed the daily lives of all Hawaiians. *Kapu* is the Hawaiian version of the Polynesian *tabu*, often written in English as *taboo*. Like all such systems, it served many purposes. Some of its restrictions were designed to augment the power of the kings and priests, while others regulated domestic routine or attempted to conserve scarce natural resources.

Many had to do with food. Women were forbidden to prepare food, or to eat with men; each husband was obliged to cook for himself and his wife in two separate ovens, and to pound the *poi* in two distinct calabashes. The couple had to maintain separate houses, as well as a *Hale Noa*, where a husband and wife slept together. Women could not eat pork, bananas or coconuts, or several kinds of fish. Certain fish could only be caught in specified seasons; and a *koa* tree could only be cut down once two more were planted in its place.

No one could tread on the shadow of a chief; the highest chiefs were so surrounded by *kapus* that some would only go out at night. Although bloodlines defined one's place in the *kapu* hierarchy, might tended to dominate over right, so the ruling chiefs did not necessarily possess the highest spiritual status. One of Kamehameha's wives was so much his superior that he could only approach her on all fours.

The only crime in ancient Hawaii was to break a *kapu*, and the only punishment was death. It was possible for an entire *ahupua'a* to break a *kapu* and incur death, but that penalty was not always exacted. One way guilty parties could avoid execution was by hotfooting it to a *pu'uhonua*, or "place of refuge". The Big Island is thought to have had at least six of these, perhaps one per *ahupua'a*; the one in Hōnaunau remains among the best-preserved ancient sites in all Hawaii (see p.67), while other refuges are known to have stood in Waipi'o Valley and Hilo Bay. In addition, anyone who managed to get to the king himself was considered to be in a *pu'uhonua*.

The Hawaiian Environment: Past, Present And Future

Of all the places in the world, I should like to see a good flora of the Sandwich Islands.

Charles Darwin, 1850

Much of the landscape on the Big Island seems so unspoilt and pollution-free that many visitors remain unaware of how fragile the environmental balance really is. However, native life forms have still had less than two millennia to adapt to the arrival of humans, while the avalanche of species introduced in the last two centuries threatens to overwhelm the delicate ecosystems altogether.

Hawaii is a unique ecological laboratory. Not only are these the remotest islands on Earth, isolated by a "moat" at least 2000 miles wide in every direction, but having emerged from the sea as lumps of lava they were never populated by the diversity of species that spread across the rest of the planet.

Those animals which found a foothold evolved into specialized forms unknown elsewhere, some peculiar even to one small part of an island – out of more than ten thousand species of insect, for example, 98 percent are unique to Hawaii. Because of their uniqueness, these species are particularly vulnerable to external threats; half of Hawaii's indigenous plants, and three quarters of its birds, are already extinct, while 73 percent of all the species in the United States classified as threatened or endangered are unique to the islands. More than one hundred species of Hawaiian plant now have fewer than twenty remaining individuals in the wild.

The Arrival of Life

During the first seventy million years after the Hawaiian islands started to appear from the ocean, new plants and animals arrived only by sheer coincidence, via a few unlikely routes. Such were the obstacles that a new species only established itself once every 100,000 years.

Some drifted, clinging to flotsam washed up on the beaches; others were borne on the wind as seeds or spores; and the occasional migratory bird found its way, perhaps bringing insects or seeds. The larvae of shallow-water fish from Indonesia and the Philippines floated across thousands of miles of ocean to hatch in the Hawaiian coral reefs.

No birds other than the strongest fliers made it, and neither did any land-based amphibians or reptiles, let alone large land mammals. At some point a hoary bat and an intrepid monk seal must have got here, as these were the only two mammals to predate the arrival of humans.

As the Hawaiian environment was relatively free of predators, many plants prospered without-keeping up their natural defences. Thus there are nettles with no stings, and mint with no scent. Conversely, normally placid creatures turned savage; caterpillars content to munch leaves elsewhere catch and eat flies in Hawaii.

As each new island emerged, it was populated by species from its neighbours as well as stragglers from farther afield. This process can still be seen on the Big Island – the youngest and least densely populated of the islands – where Hawaii's last remaining stand of pristine rainforest still attempts to spread on the new land created by Kīlauea. Although lava flows destroy existing life, fresh lava is incredibly rich in nutrients, and water collects in its cavities, where seeds or spores soon gather. The basic building block of the rainforest is the *hāpu'u* tree fern. Patches of these grow and decay, and in the mulch the *'ōhi'a lehua* gains a foothold as a gnarled shrub; in time it grows to become a gigantic tree, forcing its roots through the rock. After several hundred years, the lava crumbles to become soil that will support a full range of rain-forest species. In addition, lava flows can create isolated "pockets" of growth that quickly develop their own specialized ecosystems – Big Island examples include the "bird park" on the Mauna Loa road (see p.158), and the lost world inside the Pu'u Huluhulu cinder cone (see p.155).

The Polynesian World

Many of the seemingly quintessential Hawaiian species, such as coconut palms, bananas, *taro* and sugar cane, were in fact brought from Tahiti by the Polynesians, who also introduced the islands' first significant mammals – goats, dogs and pigs.

The settlers set about changing the island's physical environment to suit their own needs, for example, constructing the terraces and irrigation channels of Waipi'o Valley. While their animals wrought destruction on the native flora, the settlers themselves had a significant impact on the bird population. They snared birds to use their feathers in cloaks, helmets and leis; bright red feathers came from the i'iwi bird, while yellow became the most prized colour of all, as yellow birds such as the mamo and 'ō'ō grew progressively rare. The nēnē, a mutated Canadian goose whose feet had lost their webs to make walking on lava easier, was hunted for food and the auku'u heron, the curse of the fish ponds, was driven from its native habitat.

On the whole, however, the Hawaiians lived in relative harmony with nature, with the kapu system helping to conserve resources. It was the arrival of foreigners, and the deluge of new species that they introduced, that really strained the ecological balance of Hawaii. Among the first victims were the Hawaiians themselves, decimated by the onslaught of foreign diseases.

Foreign Invaders

The ships of the European explorers carried food plants and domestic animals around the world, in order to adapt newly discovered lands to the European image. The Big Island's first cattle, for example, were presented to Kamehameha the Great by Captain George Vancouver of the Discovery in February 1793, and allowed to run wild. They ate through grasslands and forests, as well as through the Hawaiians' crops; when they were eventually rounded up and domesticated by the Parker Ranch, it formalized the change in land usage they had already effected. Horses had a similar initial impact and, to this day, wild goats remain a problem.

Wild pigs, however, have had an especially devastating effect on the forests of the Big Island. It is said that for every twenty humans in Hawaii, there lurks a feral pig, though tourists are unlikely to spot one. These pigs combine the strong characteristics of the Polynesian pigs brought by early settlers with later European arrivals. Rooting through the earth, eating tree ferns, eliminating native lobelias and greenswords and spreading the

seeds of foreign fruits, the pigs have in most places destroyed the canopy that should protect the forest floor. In addition, they have created muddy wallows and stagnant pools where mosquitoes thrive – the resultant avian malaria is thought to be the major cause of the extinction of bird species.

Eradicating the wild pig population is a priority for conservationists. In principle that goal gels with that of the amateur hunters, though so-called "Pig Wars" have arisen, because the hunters want to leave enough pigs for their sport to continue and the scientists want to eliminate the pigs altogether. In the highlands along the Hāmākua coast, men with pick-up trucks and packs of dogs fight and kill the tuskers with knives, while riders on horseback, armed with rifles, scour the valleys between Waipi'o and Pololū. Farther south in Volcanoes National Park, six full-time hunters defend the rainforest using modern technology to track down the pigs, including placing electronic tags on released "Judas pigs" to lead them to their feral brethren.

Another spectacular disaster was the importation to Hawaii of the **mongoose**. It was introduced onto the islands by sugar plantation owners, to keep down the rat population, which had arrived by stowing away on visiting ships, along with other species such as forest-choking weeds. Unfortunately, the nocturnal rats thrived while the mongooses slept, having gorged themselves on birds' eggs during the day. Only Kauai, where the mongoose never became established – myth has it that an infuriated docker threw the island's consignment into the sea after he was bitten – now retains significant populations of the many Hawaiian birds who, in the absence of predators, had decided it was safe to build their nests on the ground.

Environmentalists fear that Hawaii's next likely arrival will be the **brown tree snake**, which has been hitch-hiking its way across the Pacific since World War II, sneaking into the holds of ships and planes and colonizing new islands.

Issues and Prospects

The state of Hawaii has a short and not very impressive history of legislating to conserve its environment, and what little has been achieved so far appears to be jeopardized by Republican moves to reign in the powers of the Endangered Species Act. One positive development is that the whole state is on the point of being officially declared as a **humpback whale** sanctuary, though the Navy is dragging its heels about certain areas just offshore from its installations.

On the Big Island, a resurgence in respect for what are seen as Native Hawaiian values has dovetailed with the influx of New-Age *haoles* to create an active environmental movement, which has had plenty of issues to occupy its attention. In particular, the depressed state of the island's economy has made it vulnerable to grandiose schemes designed to attract outside funding.

One recurrent theme is the idea that the Big Island's future prosperity might rest in generating **energy** for the rest of the state; at present, Hawaii as a whole imports 92 percent of its fuel. The plan includes such components as harnessing the geothermal power of the Kīlauea region, which has already been attempted by the Puna Geothermal Venture (see p.136), and then exporting electricity via a submarine cable all the way to Oahu. That would involve crossing the deep 'Alenuihāhā Channel between the Big Island and Maui; the literal translation of 'Alenuihāhā is "great billows smashing", which suggests why it might not be a good idea.

Another ambitious project was the much-vaunted plan to build a commercial **spaceport** to launch satellites and the Space Shuttle from Pālima Point, just outside Volcanoes National Park in Ka'ū. It was never really necessary for opponents to voice their spiritual and metaphysical objections; the fact that the site is on the flanks of the world's most active volcano, prone to landslides and *tsunamis,* spoke for itself. Native Hawaiian campaigners who regard

the observatories on top of Mauna Kea as desecrations of a sacred site have on the other hand had little success in reining in the construction work up there.

There has also been much debate over what is to become of the island's system of **irrigation channels**. Developed long before European contact and adapted to meet the needs of the plantations, their infastructure is now rapidly falling into disrepair. As the ancient Hawaiians knew all too well, maintenance is extremely labour-intensive; without swift action, however, the opportunity to revive small-scale agriculture may soon pass.

The power of the **tourism** lobby has for the last few decades been great enough to override environmental objections to the growth of the Kohala resorts; the opening of the *Hapuna Beach Prince* hotel at the island's best beach in 1994, after an island-wide ballot voted narrowly to allow the project, was a blow to campaigners. There are also concerns that the Kohala resorts are damaging their immediate environment; the combination of golf courses and coral reefs may be ideal for holidaymakers, but that won't last if fertilizer and silt washed down from the greens and fairways end up choking the reef to death. However, it does now look as though the era of resort-building is drawing to a close. The huge hotel complex envisaged for Pōhue Bay, below Ocean View at the southern tip of the island, seems unlikely to come to fruition, and perhaps the Big Island is destined for a period of relative equilibrium after its recent hectic changes.

The Return of the Voyagers

Although archeological and linguistic evidence had shown that the Polynesians deliberately colonized the Pacific, how they actually did so remained a mystery until about twenty years ago. In 1973, a group of Hawaiians set out to rediscover the skills and techniques of their ancestors. Ben Finney, an anthropologist from Honolulu's Bishop Museum, Tommy Holmes, a racing canoe paddler, and the artist Herb Kane founded the **Polynesian Voyaging Society**, to build replicas of the ancient ocean-going vessels, and use them to reproduce the early voyages. In particular, they were determined to prove that it was possible to make sustained, long-distance return trips across the Pacific without modern instrumentation or charts, despite the trade winds that consistently blow from the northeast.

The great canoes, or *wa'a*, of the ancient Hawaiians were scooped from single *koa* trunks, six feet in diameter and at least fifty feet long, using stone adzes, and knives made of bone, shell or coral. Surfaces were sanded with the skin of manta rays, and the hulls waterproofed with breadfruit tree gum. Two such canoes were lashed together to create a double-hulled long-distance sailing canoe, and equipped with sails made from plaited pandanus leaves (*lau hala*).

The Polynesian Voyaging Society's first vessel was the *Hōkūle'a*, named for the "Star of Gladness" that passes over Hawaii. Though constructed of plywood and fibreglass rather than *koa*, it was designed to duplicate the performance of a traditional double-hulled canoe. Petroglyph images served as blueprints for the shape of the sails, and extensive sea trials were carried out to familiarize the crew with the craft.

Perhaps the biggest problem was finding a **navigator**. In ancient times the children of master navigators were apprenticed from the age of five to learn the secrets of their trade; for generations, no Polynesian had acquired the necessary skills. Furthermore, although information on routes across the southern Pacific was preserved in cryptic chants that survived elsewhere in Polynesia, only the barest details of the ancient migrations could be gleaned from Hawaiian lore.

When the *Hōkūle'a* embarked on its maiden long-distance voyage, in 1976, it was navigated by **Mau Piailug**, from the Central Caroline islands of Micronesia. The boat triumphantly achieved its purpose by reaching Tahiti in just thirty days, and in subsequent years sailed all over the Pacific. By using a north wind to sail east from Samoa to Tahiti it refuted Heyerdahl's statement that it was impossible for canoes from Asia to sail into the trade winds of the Pacific, while between 1985 and 1987 it went to New Zealand and back, a 12,000 mile round trip.

Meanwhile, a young Hawaiian crew member of the *Hōkūle'a*, **Nainoa Thompson**, became fascinated by the lost art of navigation. Mau Piailug had managed to chart his course to Tahiti due to years of experience on the Pacific, and the relative familiarity of the night sky. Thompson set out to rediscover the specific techniques that the ancient Hawaiians would have used.

Of the two main elements to the task of the navigator, **way-finding** is the ability to plot and keep track of a long-distance course as accurately as possible. Although way-finding involves constantly monitoring the state of the ocean, the winds and the currents – except for brief catnaps, the navigator has to remain awake for the entire voyage – it is rooted in close astronomical observation. In a fascinating partnership with modern science, Thompson managed to glean a lifetime's worth of experience of the motions of the night sky through spending long hours in the planetarium at the Bishop Museum. The precise techniques he developed, which involved finding "matching pairs" of stars that set or rise at the same time, may not be identical to those used by the original Polynesians. They have, however, conclusively demonstrated that voyages without navigational aids are possible.

The other essential component to navigation is **land-finding**, the art of detecting land when you know it must be close at hand. From the deck of a sailing canoe on the open Pacific, the horizon is just four miles away; to avoid sailing right past your objective, you have to watch for the many little signs that land is nearby. The most obvious of these is the behaviour and colour of cloud formations; as a rule the Big

Western myths and misconceptions

Western scientists, unwiling to credit Polynesian culture with any degree of sophistication, were for hundreds of years unable to account for the presence of the Hawaiians. When Captain Cook reached the Hawaiian islands, he was amazed to find a civilization that shared a culture and language with the people of the South Pacific. Europeans had only just developed the technology to make expeditions such as Cook's possible, and they found it hard to believe that the Polynesians were already able to plot and sail an accurate course across a three-thousand-mile expanse of ocean. The Hawaiians were unable to explain how they had achieved this feat; although their chants and legends were explicit about their Tahitian origin, they no longer undertook long-distance sea trips, so the specific navigational skills had been forgotten.

At first it was thought that the Hawaiians came from an as-yet undiscovered continent; when that vast landmass proved not to exist, it was suggested that they had survived its submergence. Some argued that the islanders had simply been deposited by God. The consensus came to be that the Polynesians had drifted accidentally from island to island, with successive groups of storm-tossed unfortunates making lucky landfalls on pristine unoccupied islands. One hypothesis, "demonstrated" by Thor Heyerdahl's *Kon Tiki* expedition in 1947, was that the Polynesians came originally from South America, having been swept out to sea on balsa wood rafts as they fished off the western coast.

There are strong reasons to reject the theory of accidental drift. The islands of the Pacific are so tiny and so far apart that vast quantities of drifting rafts would be required to populate every single one. Moreover, the fact that migratory groups clearly brought the plants and animals necessary for survival indicates that the process of colonization was carefully planned, and almost certainly involved return trips to the home base. Crucially, in the case of Hawaii, neither wind nor wave will carry a vessel across the Equator; travel between Hawaii and Tahiti is only possible on a craft that uses some form of power, be it oar or sail. One of the linchpins of Heyerdahl's argument was the presence in Polynesia of the sweet potato, unquestionably of South American origin. His claims that Polynesian languages showed South American roots have however been disproved by modern analysis, which shows a linguistic spread from Asia rather than America. At some point Polynesians must have drifted off course to South America, and succeeded in returning.

Island for example is "visible" from around a hundred miles away, thanks to the stationary clouds over its giant volcanoes. The nightly homeward flight of birds to their island nests is another indication, while much can also be read into the swells and currents of the sea itself.

The *Hawai'iloa*, a canoe built of wood at the Bishop Museum and launched in 1993, went another step towards reproducing the glories of the past. Unfortunately no *koa* tree large enough to construct such a canoe was found; instead the Tlingit of Alaska donated two four-hundred-year-old Sitka spruces, which were felled with appropriate ceremonies. Soon afterwards on the Big Island, the 26-foot-long single-hulled *koa*-wood canoe, *Mauloa*, was constructed at the Pu'uhonua O Honaunau, under the supervision of Mau Piailug.

According to legend, during the heyday of Polynesian voyaging, regular gatherings of canoes from throughout the Pacific took place at the *Marae Taputapuatea* (temple of Lono) at Raiatea, not far from Tahiti in what are now called the Society Islands. The last such occasion, in 1350 AD, broke up after a Maori navigator was murdered. As a result the Maori placed a *kapu* on the temple, and the era of ocean voyaging came to an end. After that date, no further expeditions sailed to or from Hawaii, although the last known long-distance voyage in all Polynesia was as recently as 1812, from the Marquesas islands.

In March 1995, the canoes finally gathered once again, for the first time in over six centuries. Both the *Hōkūle'a* and *Hawai'iloa* sailed from Hawaii to Tahiti, taking a mere three weeks for the journey, and on to Raiatea. Maori elders conducted ceremonies at the *marae* to lift the ancient *kapu*, and canoes from Tahiti, New Zealand and the Cook Islands joined their Hawaiian counterparts in proclaiming a new era of pan-Polynesian solidarity.

The canoes have become perhaps the most potent symbol of a Polynesian Renaissance. Their every movement is eagerly followed by children throughout the Pacific, and a new generation of navigators is being trained to assume the mantle of Nainoa Thompson and Mau Piailug.

Hula and Hawaiian Music

If your idea of Hawaiian music is Elvis doing the limbo in *Blue Hawaii*, you won't be disappointed by the entertainment on offer in most of the Big Island's hotels. A diet of *Little Grass Shack* and the *Hawaiian Wedding Song*, with the occasional rendition of *Please Release Me* in Hawaiian, is guaranteed. However, the island also boasts its own lively contemporary music scene, and it's still possible to see performances of its most ancient form, *hula*, which embraces elements of theatre and dance.

Hula

Although the ancient Hawaiians were devotees of the poetic chants they called **meles**, they had no specific word for "song". *Meles* were composed for various purposes, ranging from lengthy genealogies of the chiefs, put together over days of debate, through temple prayers, to lullabies and love songs. When the chanted words were accompanied by music and dance, the combined performance was known as *hula*.

Music was created using instruments including gourds, rattles, small hand or knee drums made from coconuts, and the larger *pahu* drums made by stretching shark skin over hollow logs. As a rule the tonal range was minimal and the music monotonous, though occasionally bamboo pipes may also have been played. Complexity was introduced by the fact that the

dance, the chant and the music would all be likely to follow distinct rhythmic patterns.

The telling of the story or legend was of primary importance; the music was subordinate to the chant, while the feet and lower body of the dancers kept the rhythm and their hand movements supplemented the meaning of the words. Dancers would be trained in a *hālau hula*, a cross between a school and a temple dedicated to the goddess Laka, and performances were hedged around by sacred ritual and *kapus*.

Hula was largely suppressed for the first century after the foreigners' arrival, and only returned to public performance at the coronation of the "Merrie Monarch", King David Kalākaua, in February 1883. By then the process of adapting music and dance to suit foreign tastes had started; the grass skirt, for example, was unknown in Hawaii until it was imported from the Gilbert Islands in the 1870s, as somehow looking more Polynesian.

Today *hula* persists in two forms. The first, *kahiko*, is closer to the old style, consisting of chanting to the beat of drums; the dancers wear knee-length skirts of *ti* leaves, and anklets and bracelets of ferns. *Auwana* is the modern style of *hula*, featuring bands of musicians playing western-style instruments. Both have their major showcase on the Big Island each April, at Hilo's **Merrie Monarch Festival** (see p.111). Some traditionalists, however, do not participate in the Merrie Monarch, regarding the idea of a competition as contrary to the essential nature of *hula* as a form of religious expression.

Slack-Key and Steel Guitar

The roots of contemporary Hawaiian music lie in the mixture of cultural traditions brought from all over the world by nineteenth-century immigrants. In particular, Spanish and Mexican *paniolos* introduced the guitar, while the *braginha* of the Portuguese plantation workers was adapted to become the Hawaiian *ukelele*.

The first step towards creating a distinctive Hawaiian sound came roughly a century ago, when the conventional method of tuning a guitar was abandoned in favour of **slack-key** tuning (*kī* *hō'alu* in Hawaiian), in which a simple strum of the open strings produces a harmonious chord. Next came the realization that sliding a strip of metal along the strings produced a glissando effect; an Oahu student is credited with inventing the **steel guitar**, as played by early virtuosos such as Sol Ho'opii.

English words were set to Hawaiian melodies, and the resultant *hapa-haole* music was by World War I the most popular music form in America. The craze for all things Hawaiian took several decades to die down, though it grew progressively more debased. By the time of the nationwide *tiki* craze of the 1950s, when mass tourism was just taking off, pseudo-Hawaiian music such as Martin Denny's cocktail-jazz stylings was still topping the charts.

The Modern Generation

Over the last twenty years, Hawaii's resurgence of pride in its music's Polynesian traditions has been combined with a determination to create something new yet genuinely Hawaiian. To outsiders, the sound created by the new generation of musicians is a fascinating hybrid. Drawing on the tradition of the ancient *meles*, but influenced by mainstream rock, country and even reggae music, it combines political stridency with sweet melodies and powerful drum beats with gentle *ukelele* tinklings.

The first prominent name in the movement was **Gabby Pahinui**, an exponent of classic slack-key guitar who in the final years before his death in 1980 achieved international fame through his recordings with Ry Cooder. His success encouraged others to stop tailoring their music to mainland tastes and it soon became apparent that there was a market for recordings in the Hawaiian language.

The most recent winners of the annual Hōkū awards, created to honour the best in Hawaiian music, are the group **Hapa**. Consisting of Barry Flanagan, originally from New Jersey, and Keli'i Kaneali'i, they combined slack-key guitar instrumentals with soaring harmonies on the huge-selling album *Hapa*.

Currently Hawaii's biggest star is **Israel Kamakawiwo'ole**, who sang for many years with the Makaha Sons of Ni'ihau. "Iz" weighs in at a colossal 757 pounds, and has been plagued by health problems, but the two albums he has released since he formed his own *Big Boy Records* in 1993 have set new standards. *Facing Future* ranged from pop hit *Maui Hawaiian Sup'pa Man* to the haunting *Hawai'i 78* – something of an anthem for the sovereignty movement – while *E Ala Ē* shows off his pure, wide-ranging voice to maximum advantage.

Finally, visitors may encounter the Hawaiian-reggae fusion known as **Jawaiian**, in

---

Buying Hawaiian Music

CDs and tapes can be bought **on the Big Island** at the following stores:

Byrd's, 64-974 Mamalohoa Hwy Waimea	☎ 885-5002
CD Wizard, 7940 Kilauea Ave Hilo	☎ 969-4800
Da Wreckx, Prince Kuhio Plaza Hilo	☎ 959-6258
JR's Music, Kopiko Plaza Kailua	☎ 326-7077
and Prince Kuhio Plaza Hilo	☎ 959-4599
Mele Kai Music, Kaahumanu Plaza Kailua	☎ 329-1454

The following companies sell Hawaiian music **by mail:**

Hana Ola Records, 5518 Rincon Beach Park Ventura CA 93001	
Harry's Music, 3457 Waialae Ave Honolulu HI 96816	☎ 735-2866
House of Music, Ala Moana Shopping Center Honolulu HI 96814	☎ 949-1051
Hula Records, 2290 Alahao Place Honolulu HI 96819	
Jelly's, 835 Keeaumoku Ave Honolulu HI 96814	☎ 942-7771
Mauna Kea Music, PO Box 116 Kamuela HI 96743	☎ 885-7770

which the traditional beat of the *pahu* drum is accompanied by a thunderous electrified bass. Reggae is very popular with young Hawaiians, but the home-grown groups don't tend to have the hard edge of the touring Jamaican bands who often call in. **Ho'ikane** from the Big Island are among the best, and are credited with being the first to introduce an up-to-date dancehall sound. Other performers include **Titus Kinimaka** – a pro surfer from Kauai's leading *hula* family – and **Butch Helemano**, who has at least nine albums to his name.

Books

An extraordinary quantity of books has been written about Hawaii and all matters Hawaiian, though you're only likely to come across most of them in bookstores on the islands themselves. All the publishers below are based in the US.

History

Joseph Brennan, *The Parker Ranch of Hawaii* (Harper & Row). This authorized history of the Big Island's famous cattle ranch kicks off well, with lively accounts of the rumbustious early days, but steadily grows tamer.

Gavan Daws, *Shoal of Time* (University of Hawaii Press). Definitive if dry single-volume history of the Hawaiian Islands, tracing their fate from European contact to statehood.

Michael Dougherty, *To Steal A Kingdom: Probing Hawaiian History* (Island Style Press). An eccentric and entertaining look at Hawaiian history, which focuses on the famous names of the nineteenth century and pulls no punches.

Noel J Kent, *Hawaii: Islands Under The Influence* (University of Hawaii Press). Rigorous Marxist account of Hawaiian history, concentrating on the islands' perennial "dependency" on distant economic forces.

Liliuokalani, *Hawaii's Story by Hawaii's Queen* (Mutual Publishing). Autobiographical account by the last monarch of Hawaii of how her kingdom was taken away. Written in 1897 when she still cherished hopes of a restoration.

Gananath Obeyesekere, *The Apotheosis of Captain Cook* (Princeton University Press/Bishop Museum Press). An iconoclastic Sri Lankan anthropologist reassesses Captain Cook from a refreshingly anti-imperialist perspective.

A Grenfell Price (ed), *The Explorations of Captain James Cook in the Pacific* (Dover). Selections from Cook's own journals, including his first landfall on Kauai and his ill-fated return to the Big Island.

Ronald Takaki, *Pau Hana* (University of Hawaii Press). Moving history of life on the sugar plantations, and the trials experienced by generations of immigrant labourers.

Ancient Hawaii

Nathaniel B Emerson, *Unwritten Literature of Hawaii – The Sacred Songs of the Hula* (Charles

---

Buying Books

All the bookstores on the Big Island that hold significant collections of books relating to Hawaii are listed below.

Basically Books, 46 Waianuenue Ave, Hilo ☎961-0144	*Middle Earth Bookshoppe,* 75-5719 Ali'i Drive, Kailua ☎329-2123
The Book Galleries, Prince Kuhio Plaza, 111 E Pauainiko St, Hilo ☎959-7744	*Waldenbooks,* Prince Kuhio Plaza, 111 E Pauainiko St, Hilo ☎959-6468
Keauhou Village Book Shop, Keauhou Shopping Village ☎322-8111	Lanihau Center, Kailua ☎329-0015

In addition, *The Island Bookshelf*, PO Box 91003, Portland OR 97291 (☎1-800/967-5944) is a mail-order service that claims to stock every guide book there is on Hawaii, as well as books on all aspects of the islands, from history to cookbooks, including maps.

E Tuttle Co). Slightly dated account of ancient Hawaii's most important art form. Published in 1909, its wealth of detail ensures that it remains required reading for all students of the *hula*.

E S Handy and Elizabeth Handy, *Native Planters in Old Hawaii* (Bishop Museum Press). A chronicle of the way of life of ordinary ancient Hawaiians, focusing on the Ka'ū region of the Big Island.

Dorothy M Kahananui, *Music of Ancient Hawaii* (Petroglyph Press). Brief but informative pamphlet covering development and forms of the *hula*.

Samuel M Kamakau, *The People of Old* (Bishop Museum Press, 3 vols). Anecdotal essays, originally written in Hawaiian and published as newspaper articles in the 1860s. Packed with fascinating nuggets of information, they provide a compendium of Hawaiian oral traditions. Kamakau's longer *Ruling Chiefs of Hawaii* (Bishop Museum Press) details all that is known of the deeds of the kings.

David Malo, *Hawaiian Antiquities* (Bishop Museum Press). Nineteenth-century survey of culture and society, written by a native Hawaiian brought up at the court of Kamehameha the Great. Like Kamakau, Malo's conversion to Christianity colours his account, but this is the closest we have to a contemporary view of ancient Hawaii.

Valerio Valeri, *Kingship and Sacrifice; Ritual and Society in Ancient Hawaii* (University of Chicago Press). Detailed academic analysis of the role of human sacrifice in establishing the power of the king – an aspect of Hawaiian religion many other commentators gloss over.

Contemporary Hawaii

Michael Kioni Dudley and Keoni Kealoha Agard, *A Call for Hawaiian Sovereignty* (Nā Kāne O Ka Malo, 2 vols). Two short books, indispensable for anyone interested in Hawaiian Sovereignty. The first attempts to reconstruct the world view and philosophies of the ancient Hawaiians; the second is the clearest imaginable account of their dispossession.

Randall W Roth (ed), *The Price of Paradise* (Mutual Publishing, 2 vols). Assorted experts answer questions about life and society in Hawaii, in short essays that focus on economic and governmental issues. Of most interest to local residents or prospective migrants, but a useful introduction to ongoing island debates.

Travellers' Tales

Isabella Bird, *Six Months in the Sandwich Islands* (University of Hawaii Press). The enthralling adventures of an Englishwoman in the 1870s, including escapades along the Hāmākua coast and a cold trip up Mauna Loa.

A Grove Day and Carl Stroven (eds), *A Hawaiian Reader* and *The Spell of Hawaii* (Mutual Publishing, 2 vols). Lively paperback anthologies of writings on Hawaii, including pieces by Mark Twain, Jack London, Isabella Bird and Robert Louis Stevenson.

James Macrae, *With Lord Byron at the Sandwich Islands in 1825* (Petroglyph Press). Short pamphlet of extracts from the diary of a Scottish botanist, including the first-known recorded ascent of Mauna Kea, an expedition to Kīlauea and an eyewitness account of the dismantling of the Pu'uhonua O Hōnaunau.

James Michener, *Hawaii* (Random House). Another romanticized romp, whose success was a major factor in the growth of Hawaiian tourism.

Hunter S Thompson, *The Curse of Lono* (Bantam Books). Inimitably overwrought account of a winter fishing vacation on the Kona Coast, involving such escapades as abandoning a demented Doberman in a suite at the *King Kamehameha* hotel.

Mark Twain, *Letters from Hawaii* (University of Hawaii Press). Colourful and entertaining accounts of nineteenth-century Hawaii, with extensive descriptions of the Big Island, written when Twain was a cub reporter. Much of the best material was reworked for inclusion in *Roughing It* (Penguin UK and US).

Navigation

Ben Finney, *Hōkūle'a: The Way to Tahiti* (Dodd, Mead & Co). Gripping story of the sailing canoe's first eventful voyage to Tahiti, by a founder of the Polynesian Voyaging Society.

Will Kyselka, *An Ocean In Mind* (University of Hawaii Press). Detailed account of the re-discovery of traditional Polynesian navigational techniques and the voyages of the *Hōkūle'a*, by a Bishop Planetarium lecturer.

Natural Sciences

Peter S Adler, *Beyond Paradise* (Ox Bow Press). Personal essays about life in Hawaii, occasionally self-indulgent but illuminating, with an interesting account of the "Wounded Island" of Kahoolawe.

John R K Clark, *Beaches of the Big Island* (University of Hawaii Press). Clark is a former lifeguard who has visited every beach in the state and researched its history and traditions. An invaluable resource for safety issues and a fascinating read, though, having been published in 1985, its practicalities are slightly out of date.

Pamela Frierson, *The Burning Island* (Sierra Club Books). The most exciting and original volume written about the Big Island; a history and cultural anthropology of the region around Mauna Loa and Kilauea, combined with a personal account of living with the volcanoes.

Frank Stewart (ed), *A World Between Waves* (Island Press). Stimulating collection of essays by authors such as Peter Matthiessen and Maxine Hong Kingston, covering all aspects of Hawaiian natural history.

A Hawaiian Glossary

The Hawaiian language is an offshoot of languages spoken elsewhere in Polynesia, with slight variations that arose during the centuries when the islands had no contact with the rest of Polynesia. Although it remains a living language, and has experienced a revival in recent years, you are unlikely to hear it spoken during a visit to the Big Island, and there should be no need to speak any other language than English. However, everyday conversations in Hawaii tend to be sprinkled with some of the more common Hawaiian words below.

The Hawaiian alphabet

Hawaiian only became a written language when the missionaries gave it an alphabet, which is the shortest in the world. It consists of just twelve letters – *a, e, h, i, k, l, m, n, o, p, u,* and *w* – plus two punctuation marks.

The letters *h, l, m,* and *n* are pronounced exactly as in English; *k* and *p* are pronounced approximately as in English but with less aspiration; *w* is like the English *v* after an *i* or an *e*, and the English *w* after a *u* or an *o*. At the start of a word, or after an *a, w* may be pronounced like a *v* or a *w*.

The glottal stop (') has the effect of creating the audible pause heard in the English "oh-oh". Words without macrons (¯), to indicate stress, are in theory pronounced by stressing alternate syllables working back from the penultimate syllable. Thanks to the frequent repetition of syllables it's usually easier than that may sound. "Kamehameha" for example breaks down into the repeated pattern *Ka–meha–meha,* pronounced *Ka–mayha–mayha.*

a	*a as in above*
e	*e as in bet*
i	*y as in pity*
o	*o as in hole*
u	*u as in full*
ā	*a as in car*
ē	*ay as in day*
ī	*ee as in bee*
ō	*o as in hole*
ū	*oo as in moon*

Glossary

'Ā'Ā rough lava

AHUPUA'A basic land division, a "slice of cake" from ocean to mountain

AIKĀNE friend, friendly

AKUA god, goddess, spirit, idol

ALI'I chief, chiefess, noble

ALOHA love; greeting

'AUMĀKUA personal god or spirit; totem animal

'ELEPAIO bird

HALA tree (pandanus, screw pine)

HALE house, building

HAOLE (white) non-native Hawaiian, whether foreign or American resident

HĀPU'U tree fern

HEIAU pre-Christian place of worship

HONUA land, earth

HULA dance/music form (*hula 'auana* is modern form, *hula kahiko* is traditional)

IMU pit oven

KAHUNA priest(ess) or someone particularly skilled in any field; *kahuna nui* chief priest

KAI sea

KAMA'ĀINA Hawaiian from another island; state resident

KĀNE man

KAPA the "cloth" made from pounded bark, known elsewhere as *tapa*

KAPU forbidden, taboo, sacred

KAPU MOE prostration

KAUKAU food

KIAWE thorny tree

KOA dark, hardwood tree

KŌKUA help

LĀNAI balcony, terrace, patio

LEHUA or **'Ō'HIA LEHUA** native red-blossomed shrub/tree

LEI garland of flowers, feathers, shells or other material

LOMI LOMI massage or raw salmon dish

LUAKINI temple of human sacrifice, used by ruling chiefs

LU'AU Traditional Hawaiian feast

MAHALO thank you

MAHI-MAHI dolphin; white fish

MAKAI direction: away from the mountain, towards the sea

MALIHINI newcomer, visitor

MANA spiritual power

MAUKA direction: away from the sea, towards the mountain

MELE ancient chant

MENEHUNE in legend, the most ancient Hawaiian people; supposedly dwarfs

MU'UMU'U long loose dress

NEI this here, as in *Hawaii nei*, this [beloved] Hawai'i

NĒNĒ Hawaiian goose – the state bird

NUI big, important

O of, or

'ŌHELO sacred red berry

'ŌHI'A LEHUA see *lehua*

'ONO delicious

'Ō'Ō yellow-feathered bird

PĀHOEHOE smooth lava

PALI sheer-sided cliff

PANIOLO Hawaiian cowboy

PAU finished

POI staple food made of *taro* leaves

POKE raw fish dish

PUA flower, garden

PŪPŪ snack

PU'U hill, lump

TARO Hawaiian food plant

TSUNAMI "tidal wave"

WA'A sailing canoe

WAHINE woman

WAI water

Index

HOTELS

RESTAURANTS

Continued overleaf

Help Us Update

We've gone to a lot of trouble to ensure that this first edition of the *Rough Guide to The Big Island of Hawaii* is up-to-date and accurate. However, things do change: new bars appear and disappear, opening hours alter, restaurants and hotels change prices and standards. All suggestions, comments or corrections are much appreciated and we'll send a copy of the next edition (or any other Rough Guide if you prefer) for the best letters.

Please mark letters "Rough Guide Big Island Update" and send to:

The Rough Guides, 1 Mercer Street, London WC2H 9QJ, or

The Rough Guides, 375 Hudson Street, 3rd Floor, New York NY 10014.

DIRECT ORDERS IN THE UK

Title	ISBN	Price
Amsterdam	1858280869	£7.99
Andalucia	185828094X	£8.99
Australia	1858280354	£12.99
Barcelona & Catalunya	1858281067	£8.99
Berlin	1858280338	£8.99
Brazil	1858281024	£9.99
Brittany & Normandy	1858281261	£8.99
Bulgaria	1858280478	£8.99
California	1858280907	£9.99
Canada	185828130X	£10.99
Classical Music on CD	185828113X	£12.99
Corsica	1858280893	£8.99
Crete	1858281326	£8.99
Cyprus	185828032X	£8.99
Czech & Slovak Republics	185828029X	£8.99
Egypt	1858280753	£10.99
England	1858280788	£9.99
Europe	185828077X	£14.99
Florida	1858280109	£8.99
France	1858280508	£9.99
Germany	1858281288	£11.99
Greece	1858281318	£9.99
Greek Islands	1858281636	£8.99
Guatemala & Belize	1858280451	£9.99
Holland, Belgium & Luxembourg	1858280877	£9.99
Hong Kong & Macau	1858280664	£8.99
Hungary	1858281237	£8.99
India	1858281040	£13.99
Ireland	1858280958	£9.99
Italy	1858280311	£12.99
Kenya	1858280435	£9.99
London	1858291172	£8.99
Mediterranean Wildlife	0747100993	£7.95
Malaysia, Singapore & Brunei	1858281032	£9.99
Morocco	1858280400	£9.99
Nepal	185828046X	£8.99
New York	1858280583	£8.99
Nothing Ventured	0747102082	£7.99
Pacific Northwest	1858280923	£9.99
Paris	1858281253	£7.99
Poland	1858280346	£9.99
Portugal	1858280842	£9.99
Prague	185828015X	£7.99
Provence & the Côte d'Azur	1858280230	£8.99
Pyrenees	1858280931	£8.99
St Petersburg	1858281334	£8.99
San Francisco	1858280826	£8.99
Scandinavia	1858280397	£10.99
Scotland	1858280834	£8.99
Sicily	1858280370	£8.99
Spain	1858280818	£9.99
Thailand	1858280168	£8.99
Tunisia	1858280656	£8.99
Turkey	1858280885	£9.99
Tuscany & Umbria	1858280915	£8.99
USA	185828080X	£12.99
Venice	1858280362	£8.99
Wales	1858280966	£8.99
West Africa	1858280141	£12.99
More Women Travel	1858280982	£9.99
World Music	1858280176	£14.99
Zimbabwe & Botswana	1858280419	£10.99

Rough Guide Phrasebooks

Title	ISBN	Price
Czech	1858281482	£3.50
French	185828144X	£3.50
German	1858281466	£3.50
Greek	1858281458	£3.50
Italian	1858281431	£3.50
Spanish	1858281474	£3.50

Rough Guides are available from all good bookstores, but can be obtained directly in the UK* from Penguin by contacting:

Penguin Direct, Penguin Books Ltd, Bath Road, Harmondsworth, West Drayton, Middlesex UB7 0DA; or telephone our credit line on 0181-899 4036 (9am–5pm) and ask for Penguin Direct. Visa, Access and Amex accepted. Delivery will normally be within 14 working days. Penguin Direct ordering facilities are only available in the UK.

The availability and published prices quoted are correct at the time of going to press but are subject to alteration without prior notice.

* For USA and international orders, see separate price list

DIRECT ORDERS IN THE USA

Title	ISBN	Price
Amsterdam	1858280869	$13.59
Andalucia	185828094X	$14.95
Australia	1858280354	$18.95
Barcelona & Catalunya	1858281067	$17.99
Berlin	1858280338	$13.99
Brazil	1858281024	$15.95
Brittany & Normandy	1858281261	$14.95
Bulgaria	1858280478	$14.99
California	1858280907	$14.95
Canada	185828130X	$14.95
Classical Music on CD	185828113X	$19.95
Corsica	1858280893	$14.95
Crete	1858281326	$14.95
Cyprus	185828032X	$13.99
Czech & Slovak Republics	185828029X	$14.95
Egypt	1858280753	$17.95
England	1858280788	$16.95
Europe	185828077X	$18.95
Florida	1858280109	$14.95
France	1858281245	$16.95
Germany	1858281288	$17.95
Greece	1858281318	$16.95
Greek Islands	1858281636	$14.95
Guatemala & Belize	1858280451	$14.95
Holland, Belgium & Luxembourg	1858280877	$15.95
Hong Kong & Macau	1858280664	$13.95
Hungary	1858281237	$14.95
India	1858281040	$22.95
Ireland	1858280958	$16.95
Italy	1858280311	$17.95
Kenya	1858280435	$15.95
London	1858291172	$12.95
Mediterranean Wildlife	0747100993	$15.95
Malaysia, Singapore & Brunei	1858281032	$16.95
Morocco	1858280400	$16.95
Nepal	185828046X	$13.95
New York	1858280583	$13.95
Nothing Ventured	0747102082	$19.95
Pacific Northwest	1858280923	$14.95
Paris	1858281253	$12.95
Poland	1858280346	$16.95
Portugal	1858280842	$15.95
Prague	1858281229	$14.95
Provence & the Côte d'Azur	1858280230	$14.95
Pyrenees	1858280931	$15.95
St Petersburg	1858281334	$14.95
San Francisco	1858280826	$13.95
Scandinavia	1858280397	$16.99
Scotland	1858280834	$14.95
Sicily	1858280370	$14.99
Spain	1858280818	$16.95
Thailand	1858280168	$15.95
Tunisia	1858280656	$15.95
Turkey	1858280885	$16.95
Tuscany & Umbria	1858280915	$15.95
USA	185828080X	$18.95
Venice	1858280362	$13.99
Wales	1858280966	$14.95
West Africa	1858280141	$24.95
More Women Travel	1858280982	$14.95
World Music	1858280176	$19.95
Zimbabwe & Botswana	1858280419	$16.95

Rough Guide Phrasebooks

Title	ISBN	Price
Czech	1858281482	$5.00
French	185828144X	$5.00
German	1858281466	$5.00
Greek	1858281458	$5.00
Italian	1858281431	$5.00
Spanish	1858281474	$5.00

Rough Guides are available from all good bookstores, but can be obtained directly in the USA and Worldwide (except the UK*) from Penguin:

Charge your order by Master Card or Visa (US$15.00 minimum order): call 1-800-253-6476; or send orders, with complete name, address and zip code, and list price, plus $2.00 shipping and handling per order to: Consumer Sales, Penguin USA, PO Box 999 – Dept #17109, Bergenfield, NJ 07621. No COD. Prepay foreign orders by international money order, a cheque drawn on a US bank, or US currency. No postage stamps are accepted. All orders are subject to stock availability at the time they are processed. Refunds will be made for books not available at that time. Please allow a minimum of four weeks for delivery.

The availability and published prices quoted are correct at the time of going to press but are subject to alteration without prior notice. Titles currently not available outside the UK will be available by July 1995. Call to check.

* For UK orders, see separate price list

¿Qué pasa?

WHAT'S HAPPENING?
A NEW ROUGH GUIDES SERIES –
ROUGH GUIDE PHRASEBOOKS

Rough Guide Phrasebooks represent a complete shakeup of the phrasebook format. Handy and pocket sized, they work like a dictionary to get you straight to the point. With clear guidelines on pronunciation, dialogues for typical situations, and tips on cultural issues, they'll have you speaking the language quicker than any other phrasebook.

~ Now Available ~
Czech, French, German, Greek,
Italian, Spanish

~ Coming Soon ~
Mexican Spanish, Polish, Portuguese,
Thai, Turkish, Vietnamese

NORTH SOUTH TRAVEL

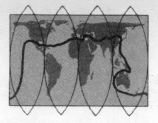

DISCOUNT FARES

PROFITS TO CHARITIES

- North South Travel is a friendly, competitive travel agency, offering discount fares world-wide.
- North South Travel's profits contribute to community projects in the developing world.
- We have special experience of booking destinations in Africa, Asia and Latin America.
- Clients who book through North South Travel include exchange groups, students and independent travellers, as well as charities, church organisations and small businesses.

To discuss your booking requirements: contact Brenda Skinner between 9am and 5pm, Monday to Friday, on (01245) 492 882: Fax (01245) 356 612, any time. Or write to: North South Travel Limited, Moulsham Mill Centre, Parkway, Chelmsford, Essex CM2 7PX, UK

Help us to help others – Your travel can make a difference

NEW *for* OLD

- *Trade in your old guides for new.*
- *Notice board for travel ads.*
- *Maps and phrase books.*
- *Extensive range of travel guides and literature.*
- *Baedeker and specialist antiquarian department.*

25 Cecil Court, London WC2N 4EZ. Tel. 0171 836 9132

BERNARD *j* SHAPERO

The TRAVELLERS' BOOKSHOP

THE LOWEST PRE-BOOKED CAR RENTAL OR YOUR MONEY BACK.

ROUGH GUIDES RECOMMENDED BY AS RECOMMENDED BY AS

Holiday Autos is the only company to actually guarantee the lowest prices or your money back at over 4000 worldwide rental locations in Europe, USA, Canada, and Australasia.

All our rates are truly fully inclusive and FREE of any nasty hidden extras. Also available in the USA and Canada are our range of luxury motorhomes and campervans. Don't waste money - book with Holiday Autos - guaranteed always to be the lowest on the market.

Holiday Autos

Holiday Autos.
NOBODY BEATS OUR PRICES.
0171- 491 1111

'A traveller without knowledge is like a bird without wings.'

Mushariff-Ud-Din (1184-1291)

STANFORDS

The World's Largest Map and Travel Book Shop

AT 12-14 LONG ACRE LONDON WC2E 9LP
MAIL ORDER SERVICE TEL 0171 836 1321 FAX 0171 836 0189

AND STANFORDS AT BRITISH AIRWAYS
156 REGENT STREET LONDON W1R 5TA

Our Holidays Their Homes

Exploring New Destinations?
Ever wondered what that means to the locals?
Ever seen things you're uncomfortable with?
Ever thought of joining Tourism Concern?

Tourism Concern is the only independent British organisation seeking ways to make tourism just, participatory and sustainable - world-wide.

For a membership fee of only £15 (£8 unwaged) UK, £25 overseas, you will support us in our work, receive our quarterly magazine, and learn about what is happening in tourism around the world.

We'll help find answers to the questions.

Tourism Concern, Southlands College, Wimbledon Parkside, London SW19 5NN UK Tel: 0181-944 0464 Fax: 0181-944 6583.

SLEEP EASY
BOOK AHEAD

AUSTRALIA
02 261 1111

CANADA
FREEPHONE 0800 663 5777

DUBLIN
01 301766

LONDON
0171 836 1036

BELFAST
01232 324733

GLASGOW
0141 332 3004

WASHINGTON
0202 783 6161

NEW ZEALAND
09 379 4224

IBN INTERNATIONAL
BOOKING
NETWORK

Call any of these
numbers and your
credit card secures a
good nights sleep ...

in more than 26 countries

up to six months ahead

with immediate confirmation

HOSTELLING
INTERNATIONAL

*Budget accommodation you can **Trust***

You are
A STUDENT

You travel
THE WORLD

You want
TO SAVE MONEY

Here's how

The International
Student Identity Card

Available at Student Travel Offices Worldwide.

Entitles you to discounts and special services worldwide.